BEYOND GIFT·OLOGY

BEYOND
GIFT·OLOGY

Earn Endless Word of Mouth with a System That Turns Relationships Into Referral Partners

JOHN RUHLIN

INTERNATIONAL BESTSELLING AUTHOR

LIONCREST
PUBLISHING

BEYOND GIFTOLOGY
Earn Endless Word of Mouth with a System That
Turns Relationships Into Referral Partners

FIRST EDITION

ISBN 978-1-5445-4812-8 *Hardcover*
      978-1-5445-4810-4 *Paperback*
      978-1-5445-4811-1 *Ebook*
      978-1-5445-4809-8 *Audiobook*

GIFT·OLOGY

CONTENTS

*"In everything I did, I showed you
that by this kind of hard work
we must help the weak, remembering the words
the Lord Jesus himself said:
'It is more blessed to give than to receive.'"*

—ACTS 20:35

A SPECIAL THANK-YOU FROM LINDSAY RUHLIN

As John's wife of fifteen years, I was gifted with the opportunity to come alongside him in his calling of "Loving on People." I'm in awe to look back at his journey in creating the GIFT·OLOGY Group and those who supported John along the way. He certainly would have never taken full credit for what this has become since its inception, but on his behalf, I'll credit his vision, wisdom, and tenacity for the daily discipline, commitment, and grit he put into it.

He would be incredibly grateful for his family and friends who cheered him on, and especially the team at GIFT·OLOGY Group for doing so much heavy lifting to carry it forward in his absence.

TO THE GIFT·OLOGY TEAM,

Thank you for the incredible way you have shown up for myself, the girls, and the company in the recent months after John's passing. Your love and support showed the principles of GIFT·OLOGY in every single way. You have selflessly pushed forward to continue John's mission of twenty-plus years to believe in and breathe life into every aspect of what it means to serve others from a standpoint of establishing a connection and R.I.C.H. relationships. These concepts, of course, go far beyond business, and you have exemplified that in every way.

From the bottom of my heart, thank you.

TO ROD NEUENSCHWANDER,

I know that picking a business partner is quite possibly second next as risky and, shall I say, rewarding as picking a spouse...complete discernment, alignment, and trust must be established. I watched you take on John as a business partner in a time when it wasn't easy to believe his vision, or to imagine that his big ideas could come to fruition. There were significant hurdles to overcome and grow the business to the sizable impact it has today.

I've witnessed you and John work tirelessly, side by side, to grow and expand the concept and reach of the company, weather turbulent times, build families in the midst, and continue to dream about what could be on the horizon. I know for certain that John's passing is not the end. His way of thinking and dreaming is interwoven into every aspect of the business, and you have been instrumental in allowing that to happen.

Thank you for taking the leap of faith so many years ago to see the beauty in John's vision and to sacrifice and contribute so much to call it forward.

TO THE READER,

The concepts in this book are not necessarily new or profound but offer simple, yet powerful, strategies, reminders, and nudges to make meaningful connections and work together in community.

Quite simply, the way God designed mankind to live: lift one another up, think beyond yourself, serve your fellow brother, and grow together.

TO GOD BE ALL THE GLORY AND PRAISE

With Gratitude and Grit,
—Lindsay Ruhlin
In honor of how John would always close his messages.

BY CAMERON HEROLD

I first met John Ruhlin on the twentieth anniversary of the Entrepreneurs' Organization in Las Vegas in 2007, just after I finished my role as the COO of 1-800-GOT-JUNK? John saw me speak, where I discussed growing the company from $2 million to $106 million in 6.5 years. We quickly became good friends. Then, the teacher became the student, and I learned in depth from John about the power of referral-based sales, generating referrals, and using gifting strategically with clients, prospects, suppliers, and team members. Despite speaking for pay almost eight hundred times, in twenty-nine countries, I can point you to the exact spot, within ten feet, where John introduced himself seventeen years ago.

From 2007 until John died in 2024, we spent time together at countless events for entrepreneurs.

The way we became friends after that first meeting in Las Vegas has become the story of legends. He talks about it in Chapter 1 of his book *GIFT·OLOGY* and probably told the story one hundred–plus times from stages. Even his eldest daughter said, "OMG, you're the Brooks Brothers guy." I no longer wear their clothes. Lululemon is my jam now, but when he filled my hotel room in 2007 with $7,000 of

Brooks Brothers clothing as a gift, he launched our relationship and my learning about gifting and referrals.

Over the years, more and more gifts arrived at my homes in Vancouver and Scottsdale. He sent two-foot-tall piggy-bank-shaped animals for my kids in 2010, engraved chef knives in 2011, and full blocks for each home in Canada and the USA. In 2014, a huge lockbox filled with cash arrived at my home as a thank-you for referring him to be a speaker at a large event. In 2010, John paid $25,000 to sponsor me by putting a Cutco sticker on the back of my iPhone for twelve months. We even got press coverage about it. John is also partially responsible for almost cutting off my thumb. (My ADD likely contributed to the chaos, as I attempted to talk on the phone while chopping onions for a beef short rib recipe. But I phoned him on the way to the hospital, and it was his knife.)

John was forever the better part of our friendship. He frequently stopped on the side of the road to FaceTime me out of the blue, and he always finished our calls by saying, "Who can we love on in your network?" or "What clients of yours can I heart bomb for you?" or "What CEOs or COOs from the COO Alliance can we send gifts to for you?"

John's infectious gifting and heart bombing became part of my marketing mix. I didn't have to track the ROI. I didn't even *care* about the ROI; I just liked sending out gifts. In fact, often the energy I got from gifting using the services of the GIFT·OLOGY team translated into days of a positive energy buzz for me, which resulted in more momentum and sales in other areas too. Hundreds of COOs who joined the COO Alliance received engraved Cutco chef knives with their names on them—typically something like "Culinary Creations, from Zach Morrison's Kitchen." Every guest on my *Second in Command* podcast received an engraved knife too. Long-term COO Alliance members got $2,000 of custom-made coffee mugs, in a luxury wood box, with a video about the mug automatically playing when they opened it.

My kids and wife would always comment about John's gifts. My clients often shared photos of them on social media. And they always knew they were from me—even though they never had my logo. I even became self-conscious of ever giving out anything with a logo on it.

John's gifts led to some core connections for us. Because of his gifts to me, I always felt some level of reciprocity for him. I wanted to help him, so I did—often referring him to clients and for spots on countless stages as a speaker. Few know this, but the first three or four stages John ever spoke on were products of referrals from me...referrals I felt compelled to make, due to his gifting and heart bombing of me over the prior months and years. I often introduced him and got him on stage. I pushed to get EO and YPO chapters to hire him as a speaker well before he had his first book published. I pushed MMT (MastermindTalks) to get him to speak and bring him in as a member before almost anyone had him on a stage. This elite group of CEOs became a core part of his tribe and our mutual friends. For years, I pushed him to join Baby Bathwater and Genius Network. I even introduced him to Scribe Media to get his first book, *GIFT·OLOGY*, published, and the $2,000 referral fee they gave me found its way back into John's pocket, as referrals to him continued.

As a now mutual friend of ours, Joe Polish, says, "Life gives to the giver, and takes from the taker." John was a giver. The last photo I have of me with him was at an event earlier this year, run by Joe Polish.

Word-of-mouth from gifting is powerful. Word-of-mouth from caring is powerful. Six hundred people flying in from all over North America to attend John's celebration of life was proof that a farm boy from Ohio constantly thinking of others—and referring them—demonstrates value and gets you invited and pulled into the right rooms and meetings. This is especially true when you do it without an ask or reciprocation required. Heart bombing works.

John never even swore (or, as he said, "cussed"), and I tried for years to get him to lay down *one* f-bomb, even five days before he died, with a $1,000 bribe to swear once for me and I'd donate the money for him. He just gave it his massive laugh and grin.

John lived core values. That also made him *so* easy to refer. He was polite, he was present, and he appreciated others deeply. In fact, I think

John knew that referring others made me look good. His introductions were always caring. And even though over the years he often asked for introductions or referrals from me, I readily made them and often excitedly because he'd made so many deposits into my life.

I'm grateful to have known John and loved him as a close friend for seventeen years. His legacy has created a butterfly effect of heart bombing people in the business worlds and beyond. I am gutted at his loss; he was too young, with far too much still to live for. And wow, did he ever love his wife and four girls.

John's legacy will live on. His life was a gift, and through this book and what it teaches us all, he continues to give.

Cameron Herold
Founder, COO Alliance
Author of *Vivid Vision* and *The Second in Command*

PICK YOUR PATH

I couldn't believe I'd made it...

As I sit in a Genius Network meeting, surrounded by a circle of luminaries, I'm overwhelmed in the best way. This is a room like no other.

Across from me is my new friend, Chris Voss, former FBI lead international kidnapping negotiator and bestselling author who's sold over four million books. Near him, Evan Carmichael, YouTube powerhouse with over 3.7 million subscribers who sold his first company at just nineteen.

J. J. Virgin, TLC's *Freaky Eaters* co-host and founder of Mindshare Summit, brings her fierce health industry influence. My dear friend, Tommy Mello, the unstoppable CEO of A1 Garage Door Service, whose $200 million empire—valued at over a billion dollars—has profoundly shaped my journey. Whitney Jones, three-time Ms. Fitness Olympia, creator of the FEARless brand, is strength personified. Nearby, Peter H. Thomas, the visionary who built Century 21 Canada into a $9 billion empire, is ready to share insights on how he redefined an industry.

And at the end of the table, Mark Tarbell, *Iron Chef America* winner and culinary master, representing a unique mix of artistry and business acumen. He's launching a winery. And I'm already thinking of people I can introduce him to.

I'm amid multimillionaires, industry gods and goddesses, legends who've changed entire fields. Some have paid over a hundred thousand dollars just to be here.

Why Joe Polish would welcome me—a goat-milking farm boy from Ohio—humbles me beyond words. It helped that I met Joe through his close friend, Cameron Herold—my dear friend of seventeen years and the source of countless referrals.

I close my eyes and thank my creator.

I am truly blessed.

It wasn't always this way...

Rewind just a few years, and you'd find a very different John. I vividly remember sitting across from my business partner, Rod Neuenschwander. A series of bad business decisions had left me financially drained, with bankruptcy looming on the horizon. The stress was almost unbearable.

To make matters worse, we had been victims of theft. I can still picture the scene: hauling our remaining possessions out of the thief's home, box by box, while being monitored suspiciously. It was a humiliating and terrifying experience—one that seemed to mark the end of all my entrepreneurial dreams.

Rod and I could laugh about those days later, but it felt like my world was collapsing. I was a far cry from the successful businessman mingling at high-profile events. The contrast between that low point and where I stand today is stark—a testament to the power of relationships.

This dramatic swing in fortune wasn't the result of a lucky break or a sudden windfall. It was the product of a deliberate strategy, one I stumbled upon out of necessity but have since refined into a powerful approach to business and life. It became my secret weapon, propelling me from the brink of failure to heights I never imagined possible.

- What they do: As the co-founder of Ruhlin Partners, Rod partners with underperforming founders and leads them to a wealth-creating event.
- Who they serve: Service and knowledge-based industries. Founders who are self-aware enough to recognize partnerships are necessary for their success.
- What they *don't* do: Rod is not a consultant—it's partners or nothing.
- Who is *not* a fit: Startups and capital-intensive industries.

By the way, you're going to see a lot of business leader "Big 4s." I want you immersed in this concept—the full explanation will come in Chapter 5. But back to the purpose of the book.

In the following pages, I will share exactly how I did it and how you can do it too regardless of where you're starting from. Whether you're at rock bottom like I was, or you're already successful but looking to reach new heights, the principles I'm about to share can transform your business and your life.

Get ready to discover how relationships can take you places marketing can't.™

HOW TO READ THIS BOOK

This book serves as a complete guide to building and harnessing strategic business relationships, and turning them into a powerful word-of-mouth growth engine. However, I understand that different readers may have different needs and time constraints. With that in mind, here are my recommendations for how to approach this book.

Must read: Parts One and Two (Chapters 1–6). These chapters lay the foundation for understanding R.I.C.H. relationships and the Referral Partner Transformation (RPT) System. They are essential for everyone.

After that, you have two main options:

Option A: Read the next four parts (Chapters 7–18). This will give you an in-depth understanding of how everything works together and fill in any gaps you currently have.

Everybody has gaps, including and especially me and our team, and we teach this stuff!

The "read it all" method is great for operators who want to be thorough and have details. It's especially useful for team members who have been handed this book and told, "We need to do this. Read this and let's implement whatever is inside."

Remember, relationships are art, not science. As with art, there's no one way to do things. If you're already getting referrals and snowballing up, you're likely doing a lot right!

Option B: Read the most actionable part (Part Three, Four, Five, or Six) based on where you are in your business, and implement immediate changes to your systems and behaviors.

If this is you, let's look at how to select your go-to section:

- Want your first partner, first referral, and powerful momentum in a new industry? Read Part Three (Chapters 7–9).
- Want to become an industry A-lister and go from peers to partners without chasing, wasting, or waiting? Read Part Four (Chapters 10–12).
- Want to inspire your current partners and get even more referrals with stronger conviction and better results? Read Part Five (Chapters 13–15).
- Want to build a referral machine beyond you by engaging different people with different protocols? Read Part Six (Chapters 16–18).

Whichever you choose, keep your eyes peeled along the way for "R.I.C.H. RESOURCES" to add value and help you on your journey. These are not cheesy white papers. These are tools that our team, even some of our agency clients, use in their operations and SOPs.

They will increase the value of your book purchase exponentially.

Finally, Part Seven will answer specific questions you might have. It's like the troubleshooting section of your TV instructional manual. But like the manual, there's going to be a lot of nuance. And like the manual, you can't interact with it in a back-and-forth.

Good thing we have a solution for that.

THE R.I.C.H. RELATIONSHIP SOCIETY

Some people write books solely to sell their "thing." I promise I won't do that. That said, if one book could solve every problem, we wouldn't need anything else. That's why we've built a membership for people who are committed to overhauling their marketing plan. It contains four elements:

- **Course.** All the digital manuals, spreadsheets, and SOPs for you or your team. Everything in this book, everything we use, and more.
- **Community.** A place full of curated givers and relationship builders, ready to share insights, wins, and answer your questions.
- **Coaching.** Live monthly coaching with the finest conversation coaches I've ever met. So much of relationships comes down to "Say *this*, not *that*, in XYZ situation."
- **Catalog.** A curated collection of a hundred-plus favorite GIFT·OL-OGY gifts, organized by price, occasion, and impact—ideal for any industry, regulated or not.

I'll mention the R.I.C.H. RELATIONSHIP SOCIETY a couple more times as we move forward. But again, this book is not a bait and switch. I promise these pages will over-deliver.

Final note: This book does not focus at all on your offerings. The standard guidance, "Be remarkable, be awesome, and be the best," still applies. It is assumed that if you are reading this, you are highly competent and desirable.

If not—go fix that first.

And if you don't know? Join the R.I.C.H. RELATIONSHIP SOCIETY. They will tell you.

Our systems are *also* not about "right and wrong, only one way to do things." If you're currently getting referrals, you're likely doing a lot of things correctly. But there are always areas of opportunity.

As we embark on this journey together, remember this: **Relationships can take you places marketing can't.**™ Whether you're starting from scratch or looking to elevate your already-successful business, the principles in this book can transform your approach to business and life.

Are you ready to get started? Let's dive in.

PART ONE

STRATEGIC RELATIONSHIPS

CHAPTER 1

THE RELATIONSHIP SNOWBALL

For most businesses, founders, service professionals, and sales leaders doing under $10 million in revenue, the Relationship Snowball is the world's greatest marketing plan. But what exactly is this strategy that I credit with my success?

The Relationship Snowball is a simple yet powerful concept: "Start where you are, exceed expectations, make friendships, and get wonderfully introduced to new networks of previously inaccessible individuals."

When I was a young professional in my twenties, I had no relationships, no handouts, no connections. I wasn't from the area and had no local network to lean on. But I gave where I could. I started by mentoring a kid who had relationship capital but no understanding of what to do with it. This led to success with Cutco, which opened doors at Advisors Excel. Before I knew it, I had gone from begging, to speaking for free, to charging $50,000 for keynotes.

As my career progressed, I ran an international agency that worked with twenty-five pro sports teams, and I spoke on large stages. All of this was built on referrals—a testament to the power of the Relationship Snowball.

But let me be clear: I didn't invent this concept. It's a biblical principle known as the Matthew Effect, which refers to the Parable of the Talents. In this parable, servants who had been good stewards of what they had been given were given more. In other words, the rich get richer—financially, spiritually, and relationally.

The Relationship Snowball is how David beats Goliath. And if your goal is to become Goliath, it's how you build a team of Davids. While a competitor can copy your marketing, your messaging, or your website, they cannot copy your relationships. When you have a network of people willing to introduce you to *new* networks of people who know, like, and trust *you* more than they trust your competitors, you've built an unassailable moat around your business.

THE FAILURE OF TRADITIONAL MARKETING

Traditional marketing puts you on a hamster wheel. You're playing somebody else's game, rather than your own:

- You post on social media, but you don't control who sees it.
- You write a blog post, but you don't control if it shows up in search results.
- You place digital ads, which are auctions for eyeballs that you also don't control.

Traditional marketing has constraints. It has bottlenecks. It's limited by budgets, algorithms, and most of all, by customer skepticism. People can manipulate Google search results. There are whole industries built on favorably manipulating algorithms. This is not a game of "Who has the most talent?" or "Who has the best offering for the consumer?"

As the amount of information has quintupled, algorithms dictate the haves and have-nots. And it's not just social media and search engines. Traditional marketing has become a bloody, red ocean. It's a mosh pit for the megaphone, a royal rumble for the spotlight, with disproportionate spoils to the winners—most of whom aren't moving societal zeitgeist to some kind of gold standard. Instead, they punch, posture, and polarize to stay within the good graces of algorithms that reward "eyes on ads."

Modern marketing is essentially digital sharecropping. If you participate, you're building your wealth on somebody else's property. You can build your platform for years and have it taken away from you in an instant. And as with sharecropping, there's nothing you can do about it. Tech companies have the necessary legal protections in place.

We've all heard stories of major cell phone carriers not delivering text messages from, say, Little League coaches to their players, citing reasons like "It looked like spam" or "Your privacy is safe with us." Some of you may have even experienced it personally:

1. A new platform hits (often a copycat of something else).
2. First movers create fear ("Get with it or get left behind").
3. You invest resources into building your brand platform.
4. It may go well for a while (or it may not).

And then, the inevitable happens:

5. You lose first-mover advantage as others copycat.
6. The algorithm changes. Your exposure gets crushed.
7. More people = more noise = suddenly you've got to pay to play.

Remember when Mark Cuban called out Mark Zuckerberg? To paraphrase: "The Dallas Mavericks were Facebook pioneers. Now the only people who can find us are people who click our ads. What a scam!"

This happens on every platform, every time. Or worse—how many prominent YouTubers had their income go up in smoke because their account was banned, locked, or downright deleted?

The internet, while a noble idea, has been corrupted by human nature. As Evan Williams, co-founder of Twitter, aptly put it: "The trouble with the internet is that it rewards extremes. Say you're driving down the road and see a car crash. Of course you look. Everyone looks. The internet interprets behavior like this to mean everyone is asking for car crashes, so it tries to supply them."[1]

It gets worse. In the next section, we'll explore why the people you most want to reach are often immune to traditional marketing tactics, and how the Relationship Snowball can help you break through those barriers.

THE PEOPLE YOU MOST WANT TO MEET DON'T CONSUME TRADITIONAL MARKETING

Here's a hard truth many marketers don't want to admit: The people you most want to meet aren't consuming traditional marketing. There's no amount of money you could spend to reach them and get them to know, like, and trust you the way an introduction from their inner circle would.

Consider this: In a survey by InsideView, an online provider of sales-relevant content, over 90 percent of C-level executives said they "never" respond to cold calls or email blasts. Let that sink in for a moment. Most top-level decision-makers lack the time or desire to scroll social media, click digital ads, answer unknown calls, dissect online reviews, or open their own mail.

Why is this? These high-value individuals are part of an exclusive club, and when they need something, they ask their inner circle. Isn't that what *you* do? Don't you bring your biggest questions to your trusted network?

These individuals are used to getting what they want. They understand the power of shortcuts and that network is net worth. Their logic goes: If they don't know about you, you must not be worth knowing.

---

1   David Streitfeld, "'The Internet Is Broken': @ev Is Trying to Salvage It," *New York Times*, May 20, 2017, https://www.nytimes.com/2017/05/20/technology/evan-williams-medium-twitter-internet.html.

But if their inner circle introduces you? It's a gift. A joy. They trust their inner circle, and now they trust you. You come prepackaged, presold, pre-branded.

This is why I want you around intelligent, high-powered, connected, relational people whose word weighs one thousand pounds to everybody in their circles. And here's a secret: It doesn't matter what your personality is! Most people don't know this, but I am an introvert. The hardest thing in the world for me is to be in crowds of people, after a speech, listening to people thank me. But it's 100 percent worth those uncomfortable moments if it means I get to spend time with people a thousand miles above my pay grade.

Traditional marketing can make you a living. But building a business on strategic relationships *can make you a fortune*. It's not what you know, it's who you know, *and who likes you*. It's who is willing to advocate for you when you're not around.

THE ENGINE: THE POWER OF WORD-OF-MOUTH

At the heart of the Relationship Snowball strategy lies an incredibly potent force: word-of-mouth. It's the most powerful form of advertising, bar none. Why? Because while advertising weighs ounces, trust weighs tons.

People trust their inner circle more than they trust companies or even the most intelligent marketing campaigns. What *you* say about yourself means nothing compared to what *others* say about you. Trust is the horsepower of marketing, and an un-incentivized referral partner (more on why incentives are bad in Chapter 2) obliterates any and every other marketing channel.

The data backs this up. According to Salesmate, 73 percent of buyers prefer to work with sales professionals referred by someone they know. Nielsen's research shows that 92 percent of consumers trust brand advocates over other forms of advertising. Up to 50 percent of all purchasing decisions are influenced by the opinions and input of others.

What makes word-of-mouth so powerful is that it's unignorable. When two friends are talking, there are no barriers to get through. It costs nothing. And most importantly, it accumulates and compounds. One person can have dozens of conversations. Ten people can have hundreds. Build a system to energize those relationships and over ten years, those ten people can have thousands of conversations.

That is credibility money can't buy.

I learned the power of word-of-mouth firsthand during my time with Vector Marketing and Cutco cutlery. This experience taught me you can sell billions of dollars and accumulate tens of millions of customers exclusively through word-of-mouth advertising.

Word-of-mouth isn't just the most powerful form of advertising—it's also the oldest. People talked long before they could read. And in today's digital age, offline conversations remain a force that even the most sophisticated algorithms can't control or replace.

By harnessing the power of word-of-mouth through the Relationship Snowball strategy, you're not just marketing—you're building a network of advocates who will take you places that traditional marketing never could. In the next section, we'll dive into the specific method that makes this possible: the art of the 3-way introduction.

THE METHOD: 3-WAY INTRODUCTIONS

At the heart of the Relationship Snowball strategy lies a powerful tool: the 3-way introduction. Think of it as cutting the line to the front of the club, walking straight into the VIP room, or enlisting the cooperation of the gatekeeper instead of trying to combat them.

A 3-way introduction isn't just about connecting two people. It's about the power of edification. We're not merely looking for a "John, meet Mary. Mary, meet John" exchange. We're aiming for kind words and emotional impact that create a strong foundation for a new relationship.

I've become addicted to making introductions. If I can create opportunities or fill needs by sending a simple text message, it would be selfish not to do so. But not every introduction is a good one. Have you ever received an intro that felt obligatory or burdensome? Like someone else was piling onto your to-do list? That's not demonstrating value—it's destroying it.

Having made thousands of intros over the years, mostly via text (because it's easy and it shares cell numbers) and often with a video (because it's more friendly and personable), I've gotten pretty good at them. Here's a real example:

> Steve, meet Mike. Mike, meet Steve. Steve owns PRIME and is one of the most thoughtful, creative, over-the-top givers. He's built his entire business on relationships, has a book coming out called *Winning through Giving*, and has built his entire business with partnerships. He's really incredible with integrating companies and making everybody feel like they're winning. He's cut from a similar cloth as us.
>
> Steve, I've already told you about Mike. He's one of the smartest humans I've ever met. He's a funnier, smarter version of me. His brain just works at a whole other level. And so he'll have insight on what a partnership could look like...who to start with, maybe who to pilot with, but I think there's a lot of good things that can come from you guys just talking and building a relationship.
>
> Hope you guys can connect in the next seven days and can't wait to hear what results from it. Much love, gents. Bye-bye.

Remember, it's not just what you know. It's not even who you know. It's who you know, who likes you, and who trusts you. The 3-way introduction is your tool for expanding that circle of influence.

THE VISION: A BETTER WAY TO DO BUSINESS

Many business leaders live in a rutted comfort zone of how many clients and customers they can serve, manage, or succeed with. This creates a lack of urgency to fill their cup to overflowing. Because having more high-powered, high-quality introductions than you have time for creates problems. And subconsciously, many leaders operate in a way to avoid these problems. However, if you're ready to think beyond your own self-imposed glass ceiling and embrace problems of abundance, what exists on the other side is a life you may not even recognize.

The snowball creates incredible long-term opportunities and really cool choices that other people on the hamster wheel never get to make:

1. Grow and expand | Deeper, wider, or both
2. Build a waiting list | Work at your own pace
3. Choose your customers | Only work with friends
4. Raise your prices | Redesign your offerings
5. Or all of the above

Take Steven Birkland, who owns Trimwerks LLC, a two-man home renovation company with his brother. They work purely on referrals. They put people on a waiting list of *unknown* length, sometimes years, and customers *love* getting that call because he's *that* highly recommended by his partners.

Imagine *your* business having a waitlist three years long to work with you. Or being able to add a *zero* to all your prices, because that's what people were willing and wanted to pay. How about the year-long waiting list? The 10x price increase? New opportunities? New verticals for your business? Hyper-selectivity? Whatever your next desired season of business (which will remodel your day-to-day life)—an endless demand of presold, high-quality referrals is what makes it possible.

HIRING WITH THE POWER OF RELATIONSHIPS

This same concept applies to building your team. The best people you'll meet aren't going to come from an Indeed ad. That's because the best people are rarely actively job hunting. If any of you are on the cusp of hiring somebody (or somebodies), I've been in the place of business where I'm thinking, *What if I hire them, and they're sitting around with nothing to do?* Then, I take on the work myself, and everybody I care about suffers because I'm trying to play superman.

But when you have a dozen referral partners introducing you to high-quality humans, they find *you*. The question pivots from "How can I hire someone and pay them as little as possible?" to "How many times over is this new hire going to pay for themselves?"

Here's the bumper-sticker version of this: Your million-dollar partners...the best people on the right side of your snowball...you must operate as if you HAVEN'T. EVEN. MET THEM YET. The people you're connecting with in year one should look very different from the ones you're hanging out with in year three, four, five, and beyond. Play the long game and develop those atomic relationship habits that will attract nines and tens into your orbit and make you a one-of-a-kind in your marketplace.

I mean, if a goat-milking farm boy can do it, you can too.

FISHING FOR REFERRALS VS. BUILDING A FISHING FLEET

Throughout this book, we're going to explore a fundamental shift in how you approach word-of-mouth. It's the difference between "go chase referrals" and "go chase referral partners." This distinction is crucial, and it's at the heart of the Referral Partner Transformation (RPT) System.

Think of it this way: Chasing individual referrals is like spending your days trying to catch fish one at a time. Sure, you might land a few, but it's exhausting, time-consuming, and ultimately limiting. Cultivating referral partners is like building relationships with other fishers who own entire fleets. They can bring you more fish than you could ever catch on your own.

You've heard the adage: "Give a man a fish, and you feed him for a day. Teach a man to fish, and you feed him for a lifetime." Well, we're taking that concept one step further. We're not just teaching you to fish for referrals; we're showing you how to build relationships with the owners of fishing fleets.

When you focus on chasing individual referrals, you're constantly starting from scratch. Each referral is a onetime event, and you're always on the hunt for the next one. But when you cultivate referral partners, you're creating a sustainable system. These partners become ongoing sources of high-quality referrals, often presold on your value before they even reach out to you.

This approach is more than just a tactic; it's a complete shift in strategy. It's about playing the long game, investing in relationships that will yield dividends for years to come. By the end of this book, you'll understand why chasing referral partners is not just more effective, but also more fulfilling and aligned with the principles of R.I.C.H. relationships we'll explore.

Remember, we're not just looking to catch a few fish. We're aiming to build a thriving ecosystem of mutual benefit and success. That's the power of the Referral Partner Transformation (RPT) System, and that's what sets it apart from traditional referral strategies.

CHAPTER 2

ROR, NOT ROI

My friend, Phil M. Jones, professional speaker and author of *Exactly What to Say*, knows very well the compounding effect of genuine relationships—including how one authentic connection can lead to multiple opportunities and elevated status in your industry. Phil had the opportunity to do significant work with Volkswagen, which led to a quarter-million dollars' worth of business...including creating a custom edition of *Exactly What to Say for the Auto Industry*. Where that success started, though, was with—you guessed it—a relationship. That's the real story here.

Phil says it all started with Scott McKain, a seasoned professional speaker who first held the relationship with Volkswagen. Their connection began with a shared love of bourbon and the speaking profession. Despite a twenty-year (-ish, who's counting?) age difference, Phil and Scott developed a meaningful friendship by taking time to get to know one another outside scheduled moments.

Using his expertise in messaging, Phil spent some time providing Scott insights on reinventing his speaking business. Based on that exceptional gesture, Scott then put his reputation on the line to recommend Phil, customer experience expert Shep Hyken, and me for a speaking tour all the way in Brisbane. It was an incredible experience. During this tour, we traveled together and delivered multiple presentations. Instead of just showing up and leaving, though, we actively sat in each other's presentations and dedicated time afterward to discuss improvements, asking ourselves, "How do we make good, better?"

This shared experience, particularly while we were away from our families, created a deep level of camaraderie. The relationship capital we built during this time made cross-pollinating referrals easy and natural because we had real stories to share about each other.

The story came full circle when Scott later inducted Phil into the National Speakers Association Hall of Fame.

This perfectly illustrates how one genuine relationship can create appreciating value. When you pour into relationships with people who can speak well of you, your word-of-mouth multiplies. Your reputation and marketplace position change—which is the opposite of being transactional, a nag, or any of the other "don'ts" we're going to cover in this chapter.

PHIL'S BIG 4

- What they do: Phil helps people elevate their confidence and competence in all of life's critical conversations.
- Who they serve: Everyone from parents to politicians, from the medical industry to the military industry.
- What they *don't* do: Phil doesn't write scripts for people.
- Who is *not* a fit: People who are looking for the easy button, the fast pass, or for someone to do all the work for them.

THE MOST NAGGY-REFERRAL-ASKER EVER...

Let me paint you a picture of what not to do: Imagine a well-meaning but misguided professional who's been told the key to success is to "just ask for referrals." They take this advice to heart, perhaps a bit too enthusiastically.

This person becomes the embodiment of the "naggy-referral-asker."

They're at every networking event, business card in hand, ready to pounce on any unsuspecting victim. Their conversations always seem to steer toward the same destination: "So...do you know anyone who might need my services?"

They pursue relentlessly, sending email after email, making call after call. "Just checking in to see if you've thought of anyone who might need what I'm offering!" Their LinkedIn messages are a constant stream of thinly veiled requests for introductions.

The result? People avoid them. Their phone calls go to voicemail. Their emails languish unread in inboxes. They've become the business equivalent of that friend who's always trying to sell you something from their latest multilevel marketing venture.

This approach is not only ineffective—it's counterproductive. It damages relationships instead of building them. It turns potential allies into reluctant acquaintances. And worst of all, it misses the point of what true relationship building is all about.

I've seen countless professionals fall into this trap, thinking persistence alone will win the day. But here's the truth: Nagging for referrals is like trying to force a plant to grow by pulling on it. You might think you're helping, but you're just uprooting the very thing you're trying to nurture.

The irony is, these "naggy-referral-askers" often come from a place of genuine need and desire to succeed. People have told them referrals are the lifeblood of business (which is true), but they have been given the wrong tools to obtain them.

As we dive deeper into this chapter, we'll examine why these common referral methods are ineffective and discuss how we can replace them with strategies that truly work. We'll learn how to build relationships that lead to referrals, without ever asking for them directly.

Remember, the goal isn't to become the person everyone avoids at networking events. It's to become the person everyone wants to introduce to their most valued contacts. And that, my friends, requires a completely different approach.

COMMON REFERRAL METHODS ARE BROKEN

Let's face it: Most referral strategies people have taught you are about as effective as a chocolate teapot. They're not just ineffective; they're *actively harmful* to your relationships and your business. Let's break down why these common methods are so fundamentally flawed.

ASKING

You've probably been told the key to getting referrals is simply to ask. "You don't ask, you don't get," right?

Wrong.

Here's the harsh truth: People don't enjoy asking for referrals. In fact, according to research from Sales Insights Lab, 58 percent of salespeople ask for fewer than one referral per month, while 40 percent rarely ask at all.[2]

Why? Because it feels desperate. It feels like you're admitting you can't generate business on your own. Your demon brain hisses, "If you were so successful, why do you need the charity of others?" This discomfort leads to inconsistent asks, poorly executed scripts, and a failure to reach the best potential referrals.

NAGGING

Have you ever experienced a professional who just *will not* leave you alone? They wear you down until you agree to help them, but you resent them afterward. Is that how you want to be remembered?

When you nag, you reek of desperation. And desperation is kryptonite for the high-value contacts you want to meet. The movers and shakers of the world want to be around other successful people. They're already surrounded by yes-men and wannabes. Nagging tells them, consciously or subconsciously, "We are *not* on the same level."

---

2   Marc Wayshak, "23 Surprising New Sales Statistics for 2023 from Our Groundbreaking Studies!" Sales Insights Labs, January 2, 2022, https://salesinsightslab.com/sales-research/.

PLANTING SEEDS

I'm all for telling prospects and customers that you work primarily on referrals. It shows confidence and implies satisfaction. But some "gurus" take this way too far, teaching strategies like, "I won't even do business with someone if they don't make a verbal agreement to refer me once the job is complete."

Sure, this method might get you more referrals. But not the ones you want. Confident desperation is still desperation. You're not building relationships; you're creating contractual obligations—a surefire way to turn long-term advocates into reluctant, short-term participants.

NETWORKING EVENTS

Picture this: a bunch of overly caffeinated, overly smiley, mediocre extroverts handing out business cards at 7:00 a.m., crossing their fingers the phone will ring that afternoon. Instant gratification would be nice, wouldn't it?

Sorry, Charlie. It doesn't work that way. The magic bullet is there's *no* magic bullet.

Most networking events are just takers trying to take. Who wants to go to an event where you're the most impressive person in the room? The one who everybody else wants and needs advice from? (Educated guess: none of you.)

The most impressive people—the ones you want to meet—do not need and do not attend these events.

DOING NOTHING: REFERRALS BY ACCIDENT

Now, let's consider the other side of the coin—the "do nothing" approach. This is where many good businesses find themselves, dependent on organic word-of-mouth.

It's easy to fall into this trap. After all, if you're providing a quality product or service, people will naturally talk about you, right? Yes, *but* this creates a belief that making happy customers is the *only* lever for word-of-mouth.

When you anchor referrals to your performance, you think there's nothing you can do to impact them. You become reactive, thinking, *Keep doing good work and word-of-mouth will happen naturally.* That's like paddling a boat into the middle of the ocean and saying, "Well, wherever the wind takes me, I guess that's where I'm going to go."

Many people hide behind "just do good work" as an excuse, because:

- They're scared to appear needy, greedy, or desperate.
- They don't feel sincere or authentic when following a script.
- They lack urgency, thinking: "I have enough in the pipeline. There's no need for more."
- They're entitled. They don't think they should *have* to ask.
- They'd rather work on what they're *good at* and *comfortable with*, versus the relational stuff (which they're decent at but don't have time for because it's not a system or a habit).

For these reasons (and others we'll get to, trust me), the RPT System is proactive, not reactive. The focus is on energizing relationships to work on your behalf and keeping them energized so the snowball builds.

You're not going to just sit back and wait for referrals-by-accident. "Once-in-a-while, lucky" referrals. "I know a guy" referrals. MSP whisperer, Robin Robins, calls that vulture marketing, which is "when you wait for a simple piece of 'dead' business to fall on your lap. Waiting for something to die requires no skill, no ambition, and offers you no control over your own fate."[3]

The RPT System is the exact opposite. It's a hunter strategy, not a scavenger strategy.

---

3   Robin Robins, "What Is Marketing Supposed to Do for Your MSP?," Technology Marketing Toolkit, April 28, 2022, https://www.technologymarketingtoolkit.com/blog/what-is-marketing-supposed-to-do-for-your-msp.

Blessed professionals don't sit around waiting for favor.

I abhor referral-by-accident. And I abhor entitlement. In the next section, we'll dive deeper into why the "I earned it" mentality holds you back and how to shift your mindset for true referral success.

"WHEN I GET A REFERRAL, IT'S BECAUSE I EARNED IT."

Many people think this way. They're not bad people, but their operating system has a bug in it.

If this is how you think about referrals, here are six ways it'll infect your behavior and damage your true referral potential:

1. You won't ask who referred you, and you won't know if they don't volunteer it.
2. You won't clarify who the referrer is if you can't/don't identify them at first.
3. You won't speak well of the person who referred (so nothing positive gets back to them and you're missing an *easy* positive feedback loop—"Oh, John thinks well of me! We're buddies! I will send him more referrals!").
4. You won't contact the person who referred you and thank them (people who don't say thank you a lot are, by definition, completely entitled).
5. You won't report positive progress (which is the easiest way, often as simple as a text message, to report, "Hey! I'm taking care of the person you referred to me!" and making them think, "I should send that person more!").
6. You definitely won't pay homage to the relationship when the referral closes (like with an awesome gift, a handwritten note, or at the very least a video thank-you).

All these *won'ts* lead to one thing: You get fewer and fewer referrals because you're giving the referral giver a two-out-of-five-star experience.

This is why entitled people live on the hamster wheel. They're replacing referral sources instead of accumulating referral sources. But here's the thing: These previous referral givers are *still* giving referrals...just not to you. Well-connected, influential nines and tens give referrals to *many* people, for *many* things, in *many* industries.

That means you, as the recipient, aren't being compared to the other plumbers or the other graphic designers or other agents or other consultants or other health coaches or other speakers...

You're being compared to *all* of them.

REFERRAL GIVERS ARE NOT AGNOSTIC

Let me share a story that illustrates this point perfectly.

A friend's wife once built a vibrant house-cleaning business. But not her own. Somebody else's house-cleaning business.

Purely through referrals. Over one dozen closed customers.

Backstory: This family is...umm...very particular...about their "deep cleans." They had already kicked tires on two dozen cleaners and were left disappointed. Until they found "the one!" A true cleaning warlord. Months passed. Flawless cleans, each and every time. And as a reward? Wonder Woman's business was recommended to everyone in the neighborhood. Every friend. Every local family member, some of whom employed her services three times per week.

Which...whoa. That's a lot.

At first, the house cleaner megastar behaved graciously.

Rates went up during the pandemic. Buddy's family, however, was grandfathered into the old rate. They sampled free products. Tips and pleasantries were exchanged in abundance. But then something bad happened. The Queen-of-Clean started taking Buddy's wife for granted.

It wasn't just sloppy service—which happened.

Or more frequent rate increases—which also happened.

Or even the lack of thank-yous after yet another affluent referral.

It was the bickering. In person. Over the phone. Even in text, at weird times. Maybe it was the rush of success. The overwhelm of growth. Self-sabotage. Who knows.

Result: The pair broke up. Partnership be gone.

My buddy's family found a new superstar. And the ex's business slowly crumbled as more and more of her old referrals noticed the same pattern and jumped ship to their friend's new cleaner.

Business is not easy, especially the business of cleaning toilets. But what *should* be easy: Dance with the one who brought you.

Every business is a relationship business. Therefore, every decision, action, and behavior should support relationships, which is clearly *not* how our busy house cleaner saw things. The moral of the story is simple: Don't live in a world of entitlement. Operationalize thanking somebody after every referral, big or small, deal or no deal.

In the next section, we'll explore why traditional "Do This, Get That" referral programs are fool's gold, and why they often do more harm than good to your business relationships.

FOOL'S GOLD: "DO THIS, GET THAT" PROGRAMS

A "Do This, Get That" loyalty program is a formalized incentive for referrals. "If you send me a referral, I'll give you a _____." The more you do, the more you get.

They can be product based. Discount based. Cash based. But the real truth of the matter is that whatever the setup, whatever the reward, they're still carrot based.

Now, I think relationships can evolve into this, but I am vehemently against:

1. Designing a program.
2. Telling everybody about it.
3. Promoting it to people like you're running some kind of sweepstakes.
4. Thinking your system is complete and you've done all you can do.

You haven't. There's a lot of Band-Aid advice on the internet regarding asking. Most of it is lotus advice: enamoring in its simplicity, but far from optimized for what you're trying to accomplish.

When communicated up front, such programs are, in essence, bribery. They share your enthusiasm for making money and your lack of care for your customers and partners. How do you think new customers will feel when they realize the person referring them was trying to capture an incentive? Or win a contest? Or score a bounty? They reduce relationships to transactions, some version of "you scratch my back, and I'll scratch yours."

Systematically, they possess other problems.

"Do This, Get That" incentivizes quantity, not quality. It's like rolling your snowball over dirt and ice chunks. This sort of bribery usually attracts the least loyal and least valuable relationships—those interested in claiming the reward, not in helping the recipients. Don't just take my word for it; a 2013 study from "The Role of Metaperception on the Effectiveness of Referral Reward Programs" by Wirtz, Orsingher, Chew, and Tambyah proves such programs do more harm than good, professing that when there's a reward at stake, referrers worry about how it'll make them look to others.[4] This worry can make them less likely to recommend something, especially if the reward is big.

It's also true that for the altruistic, a "Do This, Get That" program feels incredibly tone-deaf and troubling. Not to mention, "Do This, Get That" programs are inherently vulnerable to a better offer! Someone else can come along and offer bigger, better incentives. Now you spend more money, and it becomes a race to the bottom.

I agree with Seth Godin, who said, "The problem with race-to-the-bottom is you might win."[5]

And as Ana Andjelic posits in *From Loyalty to Membership*, "The irony of most of today's loyalty programs is that they aren't about loy-

---

4 Jochen Wirtz et al., "The Role of Metaperception on the Effectiveness of Referral Reward Programs," *Journal of Service Research* 16, no. 1 (2013): 82–98, https://doi.org/10.1177/1094670512462138.

5 Seth Godin, "The Race to the Bottom," *Seth's Blog*, August 20, 2012, https://seths.blog/2012/08/the-race-to-the-bottom.

alty at all. They have more to do with economic calculation and gain management than with the true affinity for a brand."[6]

Translation: Real loyalty is built on long-term stuff: trust, affection, relationship.

ROR BEATS ROI—WHAT IS ROR?

ROR stands for "Return on Relationship" and stands in stark contrast to ROI ("Return On Investment"). Not only in how to earn it, but also in its potential.

Because ROI is a transactional term. A 2x term. A marketing system, used by pragmatists: Put in one dollar, get back two. It's a safe play (sometimes!) and is subject to diminishing returns. On the other hand, ROR is a possibilities term. A 10x term. A priority system, used by leaders, who view relationships as assets that appreciate with every investment. With compounding (and extraordinary) benefits.

It's the difference between shopping at a supermarket and nurturing a garden. It's easy to drive to the store and buy groceries, but it takes faith to buy seeds, dig holes, and water dirt. Maybe a little luck, too, for the environment to be right. Like a garden, ROR spending can be uncertain, unknown, and the timing unpredictable. *If* the investment bears fruit at all.

But a good garden can feed your family for decades.

R.I.C.H. RESOURCE #1

"Is this an ROI problem or an ROR problem?" The best business leaders command both. Visit **RPTsystem.com** to discover a simple ROR/R.I.C.H. framework.

---

6   Ana Andjelic, "From Loyalty to Membership," *The Sociology of Business*, Substack, February 11, 2020, https://andjelicaaa.substack.com/p/from-loyalty-to-membership.

The currency of ROR is loyalty, not dollars. But loyalty leads to dollars. Because loyalty inspires people to do things that salary and contracts can't. Fear, threats, and pressure can't. Incentives, bonuses, and promises can't. Persuasion, ultimatums, authority, and expertise can't.

Money is extremely poor relationship control. As the axiom goes, "People don't care how much you know until they know how much you care." What this really means is people who like your behaviors and trust your motivations will align their interests with yours.

Your competitors can copy a lot of things, but not your relationships, which means ROR is the ultimate competitive advantage in any marketplace.

But don't believe me. Believe the science...

ADAM GRANT AND THE WRONG-GIVER MINDSET

In his characteristic well-researched style, Adam Grant identifies three types of reciprocity profiles in his book *Give and Take*: givers, takers, and matchers.[7]

- Givers are the selfless, focusing on the interests of others, even at their own personal expense.
- Takers are the selfish, using people for their own gain, and thinking only of their own needs.
- Matchers are the scorekeepers, focusing on "squaring up" anytime a relationship does something for them.

The science is clear. One of these groups is more successful than the others. And it may not be what you were hoping.

Spoiler alert: The givers came in last.

---

7   Adam Grant, *Give and Take: Why Helping Others Drives Our Success* (Penguin Books, 2013); and Adam Grant, "In the Company of Givers and Takers," *Harvard Business Review*, April 2013, https://hbr.org/2013/04/in-the-company-of-givers-and-takers.

- A study of engineers in California: The least successful engineers were those who gave more in collaborations than they received. Ouch.
- A study of medical students in Belgium: The lowest grades belonged to those with a "giving" academic style. Dang.
- A study of salespeople worldwide: A "giving" sales approach generated two and a half times less in annual sales than the norm. *Game over.*

Adam's research, summarized: "On average, givers earn 14 percent less money, have twice the risk of becoming victims of crimes, and are judged as 22 percent less powerful and dominant."

But wait. There's more.

Givers also came in first!

Thirty years ago, the sociologist Fred Goldner wrote about what it means to experience the opposite of paranoia: pronoia. According to the distinguished psychologist Brian Little, pronoia is "the delusional belief that other people are plotting your well-being or saying nice things about you behind your back."[8]

"If you're a giver," Adam concludes, "this belief may be reality, not a delusion."

Take the study of Belgium medical students.[9] It was only at the start of medical school when givers underperformed. Their grades increased each year, and by year six, the givers earned substantially higher marks than their peers. When the givers became doctors, they climbed higher still. And what's more? This pattern holds true across all occupations.

As Adam's research concludes: "The top performers were givers, and they averaged 50 percent more annual revenue than the takers and matchers."[10]

That's more like it! Conclusion: Be a giver (but *not* a sucker).

---

8   Grant, *Give and Take.*

9   Grant, *Give and Take.*

10 Grant, *Give and Take*; and "To Give or Take? The Surprising Science Behind Success," Farnam Street Media, accessed December 17, 2024, https://fs.blog/adam-grant-give-and-take/.

WHAT ARE R.I.C.H. RELATIONSHIPS?

Transactional relationships keep you on the hamster wheel along with everyone else, but R.I.C.H. relationships, as part of the RPT System, can take you places marketing can't by offering:

- Access to revenue, opportunities, and deal flow.
- The best efforts of powerful referral partners, on your behalf.
- Loyalty of clients, partners, and employees who money can't buy.

R.I.C.H. relationships are all that and more. Not just because they make you *feel* rich (they do). Not only because they'll *make you* rich (they do that too). They are your core inner circle, a source of joy and enthusiasm, your best business friends, and maybe even your best nonbusiness friends as well.

They are:

- *R*eciprocal. Both parties feel like they're winning. Like they're getting more out of it than the other person—a dynamic that perpetuates appreciation and affection and eliminates scorekeeping.
- *I*nfluential. These individuals hear your best ideas first. You love to brainstorm with, get advice from, and reciprocate with them in kind. Such respect is a non-romantic version of intimacy.
- *C*onnected. You enjoy shared values, not just shared interests. A willingness for shoulder-to-shoulder adventure and investing time in both good times and bad. *your* people.
- *H*umble. They ask more questions and do more listening than preaching, bragging, or complaining. Vulnerability is not a weakness. It's a conduit for deeper trust.

I'll never forget pouring my heart out to a "friend" who, as I was spilling my beans, kept looking at his phone. Contrast that with my business partner, Rod, who would sit, listen, and ask questions. And, in a few words (as Rod often does) would communicate a bottomless well of empathy and understanding. I want you around intelligent, high-powered, connected, empathetic people whose word weighs 1,000 pounds to everybody in their circles. I want you around people like Rod. And trust me, you want to be around people like Rod.

Think about your relationships with your referral partners on a spectrum:

- Person A refers you to others by saying—"I know someone."
- Person B refers you to others by suggesting—"You should meet this person."
- Person C refers you to others by insisting—"You *must* do business with this person! Here, let me make a 3-way introduction."

Person C is the R.I.C.H. relationship. Which of those conviction levels are *you* creating currently? What do you *want* to be creating?

Read on.

CHAPTER 3

SO MUCH MORE

My friend, John Hall, strategic advisor at Relevance, co-founder of Calendar, and keynote speaker—has seen firsthand how meaningful gestures can transform relationships from transactional to deeply personal. In the days following the passing of a close friend, John struggled to maintain his normal routine and find his footing. During this difficult time, he received an unexpected gesture of support from Brant Bukowski, the co-founder of Veterans United. Brant is very well connected and runs a five-thousand-person company, but what Brant is clearly *not* is too busy to prioritize relationships.

John said:

> Brant took the time to write me a heartfelt letter expressing how my friend's life had made an impact, acknowledging our years of friendship. He offered words of support and understanding during my grieving process. Along with the letter, he gave me a special bottle of tequila, suggesting that at some point, I might want to raise a glass in celebration of my friend's life. What truly touched me was the third element of his gesture—a unicorn float for use at the lake where we host people. Brant understood that when I'm sad, I tend to stop doing things for others, which is contrary

to my natural inclination of enhancing people's lives when I'm happy. The float was his way of encouraging me to return to that positive space of hosting and bringing joy to others.

For John, the impact of Brant's thoughtfulness was immediate and lasting. It helped pull him out of his rut—something that could have lasted much longer without his intervention. The very next day, John began to rebound, getting back to performing well at work, and rediscovering his excitement for life. More importantly, this gesture created what John called a "cement moment," moving from short-term to long-term memory and creating a permanent imprint of support during a difficult time.

This experience has had a lasting effect on John and Brant's relationship. Now, if John ever encounters a veteran needing a loan or someone requiring their services, Brant and Veterans United immediately come to mind.

And it's worth noting in all the months since this gesture, Brant has never asked for anything in return.

This just goes to show how relationships with real bonds can be game changers both personally and professionally. In this chapter, we will get you thinking bigger about the latter.

JOHN'S BIG 4

- What they do: At Relevance, John helps companies become content and industry leaders through digital, organic strategies.
- Who they serve: Any company looking to increase their influence, trust, and credibility in a specific industry.
- What they *don't* do: John doesn't do print advertising.
- Who is *not* a fit: People who are in it to elevate themselves purely for ego and not to add value to their customers and employees.

VICTIMS OF OUR OWN SUCCESS

Success is a double-edged sword, my friends. While it's what we're all striving for, it can create a nasty case of relational poverty. Here's how it goes down:

Success creates busyness. Busyness crowds out relationships. And suddenly, the important (relationships) gives way to the urgent (everything else). I've seen it happen time and time again. Success turns likable, charismatic, relationship-oriented leaders into tunnel-visioned ambulance chasers. It turns superstar quarterbacks into game managers.

You know what I'm talking about. The squeaky wheel gets the grease. You find yourself working in the urgent, ignoring the important. Haven't you gone to sleep feeling like you worked ten hours and got nothing done, other than a long day of whack-a-mole?

The result? As you're making new relationships, you're not accumulating. You're replacing. Even worse? You aren't aware of the accumulation-versus-replacement problem because you're likely still getting referrals as a result of the velocity of your business.

Here's a telltale sign your system is broken: Your best referral givers are your most recent relationships. These referrals are being driven by recency, not by relationship. A good system creates a scenario where you're getting more and better referrals from a partner in year five compared to year one. Think about it: What does it say about your relationship system if you're experiencing a consistent "year one and done"?

This is where we default to referrals-by-accident. It's the easy solution to the important, but not urgent, challenge of "I know this is important, but my attention is on the urgent."

But here's the thing—it doesn't have to be this way.

SOLUTION: REFERRALS BY DESIGN

Let's get one thing straight: Your referrals should be process-driven, not product-driven.

What does that mean? It means systemizing your relationship plan. Here's how you do it:

1. **Strategy:** Categorize your relationships. This isn't about being cold or calculating; it's about being smart. Not everyone can (or should) be a top-tier referral partner. Know who's who so you're not being the sucker.
2. **DoVing:** (More on this in Chapter 4.) Decide what methods you'll use to communicate. Play to your strengths. Are you great on the phone? A wizard with handwritten notes? Figure out what works for you and lean into it.
3. **Timing:** Formalize the online/offline communication stack with referral partners. Don't leave it to chance or "when you remember." Make it a system.

Now, if you're running a "Do This, Get That" program, you might need to change your timing, messaging, and onboarding. Or heck, maybe even eliminate it altogether.

I can hear some of you saying, "But John, I'm already getting good referrals without a designed process."

Let me handle this one last time. Consider the possibility:

- You're not maximizing your ROR potential.
- Not all referrals are created equal.
- You're getting the also-rans, not the gold.

Let's say you're a realtor (or looking for a realtor to sell your home).

If I'm recommending you to somebody, there's a tremendous difference between me saying "I know a gal" and "I have *the* answer for you. She's an absolute master at creating demand-at-the-deadline. In fact, I recommended my neighbor James to her. And she sold the house for $80,000 over asking. And the weekend she did her open house, I came home to a line of parked cars up and down the street."

See the difference? Conviction sells. Or in a referral situation, conviction presells.

Furthermore, a partner will do much more for you than a recency-driven, "I know a guy" customer.

The bottom line? Don't leave your referrals to chance. Design a system that works for you and your business. Your future self will thank you.

WHAT IS A REFERRAL PARTNER?

Now that we've talked about systemizing your referrals, let's get clear on what (or who) exactly we're talking about when we say "referral partner."

A referral partner is:

1. A client/customer or somebody with connections to your ideal client/customers. And here's the kicker: Referral partners do *not* need to have given you any money. (We'll get into that later.)
2. A person who understands your business and your needs (and you, theirs).
3. A person who regularly introduces you to amazing prospects (often presold).
4. The recipient of frequent relationship-building gestures, often in the form of gifts, to remind them of their importance to you and your family.

Referral partners snowball introductions out of their loyalty and love for both parties. Not because of a transaction. But here's the thing: Not everybody you meet is a potential partner.

Now, listen up because this is important: Nothing is too good for these people. Referral partners are the most valuable relationships I have. Therefore, no amount of praise, thanking, gifting, or appreciation is too good for them.

This isn't just about how you care for them directly. It's about how you care for each person they introduce you to. Every introduction they make costs relational capital and deserves to be treated as such—even (and I'd argue, especially) if they introduce you to someone who isn't helpful at the moment.

Let's say I'm a home builder and I get a referral from my buddy Scott who wants to do an indoor remodel. It's a $15,000 job at most, and I'm more of a $1.5 million or $150,000 renovation kinda guy.

What would a blessed giver do in that situation?

- Treat the person referred to me with curiosity, *not* as if I were annoyed.
- Recommend somebody who does smaller jobs.
- Make the introduction to somebody smaller than me.
- Follow up with a thank-you to the original referrer and report positive progress.

And as I report the progress, I work in a clarifier. I say: "We've actually grown to the point where we are focusing exclusively on six-figure jobs. But anybody you send me, I'll make sure I connect them with the right person who can help! So keep it coming."

So now, I'm the home builder, and I have a hot lead, who's got $15,000 burning a hole in his pocket.

What do you think I'm going to do with that? You think I'm just going to hang up and say good luck? No way! I'm going to introduce him to one of *my* referral partners, somebody smaller than me, another blessed giver who loves doing $15,000 renovations (and who knows I'm looking for $150,000 renovations, which is something he doesn't do).

This is why there's no such thing as a bad referral. I'm either getting new business or getting currency for my partners to get new business—who, in the future, will send *me* business. The easiest way to get referrals is to give them.

Remember, building a network of referral partners isn't just about expanding your business. It's about creating a web of mutually beneficial relationships that lift everyone involved. That's the power of the RPT System.

25 REFERRALS: 5X5 BEATS 25X1

For referrals, let me tell you something that might surprise you: Deep is better than wide. Five referrals from each of five champions is better than one referral from twenty-five champions. Twenty-five total in both cases, but with very different outcomes.

Why? Because *who* a referral comes from changes:

- What they were told.
- Whether they were presold.
- And how they show up.

A frequent giver is going to have more:

- **Conviction.** Whose movie recommendation is more trustworthy: The guy who saw it once? Or the one who saw it five times? Conviction sells.
- **Clarity.** The more someone talks about you, the better they get at it. They speak in specifics. And specificity is persuasive.
- **Credibility.** "I've recommended John to five other people. He answered questions. Helped give direction. And four of the five hired him." What's more credible than social proof? (After all, you are updating referral givers with positive progress of their referrals, aren't you?)
- **Consistency.** Someone who referred you five times already is...well, five times more likely to refer you again versus a once-giver.

The final reason five multi-givers are better than twenty-five one-and-doners is you, the referral recipient, have more...

- **Control.** It's easy to love on, energize, and build relationships with five people. But creating impactful, consistent recency for twenty-five lukewarms isn't cheap. (And if it IS cheap, it's likely crappy and not helping you win.)

This is why we have a gifting agency—because dripping gratitude on relationships is 1000 percent necessary. And for busy professionals who have the resources, we can provide this service at a very high level ($50,000–$500,000+).

But what if you *don't* have the resources? Because the majority of leaders don't, and I wouldn't have been able to hire us during my first decade in business. So, plan B: You need to qualify and prioritize your referral relationships. Because if you pour into people who can't (or won't) be serious partners, you're wasting time, money, or both.

For example, take my friend Mike. He tells a story about a realtor who lavished him with gifts. He lives in a nice area, and she wanted referrals to his neighbors. The problem was he could never refer her. Why? (A) Because his best friend is also in real estate. And (B) he didn't need her ten-dollar coffee mug because he already owns a two-thousand-dollar mug (from me).

He eventually had to politely ask her to stop. Which...was probably awkward.

If only she had qualified before investing into the relationship.

(This book includes two more stories like this—each just as painful for the well-meaning but misguided giver.)

Because isn't the ideal scenario to have twenty-five champions who are 5x multi-givers?

Think bigger about your relationships.

REFERRAL CHAINS A.K.A. REFERRAL FAMILY TREES

A snowball occurs when people introduce you to people, who introduce you to *more* people, while they continue to refer.

One of my team members calls them "referral family trees." This concept works because, for trees and families to grow healthily, you *must* take incredible care of the roots.

Person A introduces you to person B, who introduces you to person C, who...

For our purposes, a referral chain looks like this:

Person A → Person B → Person C → Person D → Person E, etc.

You know you have R.I.C.H. relationships and excellent referral systems when person A introduces you to *a lot* of person Bs. Most leaders act like there's only three wishes in the bottle. What if I told you there were actually *twenty-seven* referrals in person A's bottle? (And counting?)

Most referral getters are only "getting" because of recency bias from their newer relationships—those who are most fresh in their memory. But if you're building R.I.C.H. relationships, the people most recommending you should be the people you've known the longest, not the shortest!

You want to be like a squirrel, accumulating resources—not like a monkey, swinging from branch to branch. At the end of the day, getting to person C is lucky, but getting to person M is skill. When something happens over and over, habits and behaviors drive the system. It is your choice to be conscious or unconscious of those habits, to engineer them or to cross your fingers and hope.

Systemizing consciously doesn't have to feel like work when you do it right. Doing outreach and building relationships takes courage, but—as several R.I.C.H. RELATIONSHIP SOCIETY members have pointed out in our online forums—"it feels like fun." Before you know it, by the time you're on person F or G, you're meeting people you never thought possible.

I'm living proof this works. But let me share a story of somebody other than John Ruhlin.

Brian McRae's story. One introduction → $50 million in production.

In my early days as a loan officer, I received a call from a man who desperately needed to refinance his home. He was in a tough spot. And the more we talked, the more my heart bled for the guy. I wanted to go above and beyond to help. In fact, I even went to his house to close the loan. (One sales leader in my office would brag about never doing this. "Clients come to *me*." Whatever.)

Little did I know this would be the start of a game-changing relationship. As it turned out, this man was an estate planning attorney. And, in his gratitude, he referred me to his clients and contacts.

Through him, I was introduced to a man named Kevin, who was a forward-thinking financial advisor. He got what I was doing right away. And, as they say in Hollywood, the rest is history. Kevin's network would create over $50 million in production value for my business. Thank you, Mr. Attorney, for changing my family's life.

That's the power of referral chains. One introduction can lead to a cascade of opportunities you never saw coming. But it all starts with nurturing those initial relationships and treating every introduction as the valuable gift it is.

UNEXPRESSED GRATITUDE

The great enemy of our time is unexpressed—or under expressed—gratitude. Gratitude deficits create unfinished business in relationships. And worse, the unappreciated can't even bring it up because they don't want to look like a child, in need of coddling.

As Pastor Andy Stanley so eloquently puts it, "Few things sting more than ingratitude. Ingratitude communicates: 'I don't even see you. I don't recognize what you've done. I don't recognize your effort. I don't recognize your sacrifice.' Ingratitude communicates: 'You owed me that so why would I thank you for that?'"[11] Unfortunately, many referral getters operate this way.

---

11   Andy Stanley, "Give Thanks: An Attitude of Gratitude," Andy Stanley, November 23, 2020, YouTube video, 28:53, https://www.youtube.com/watch?v=U7aneTHx2iw&feature=youtu.be.

"Ingratitude hurts," Stanley continues. "Which is odd, because the other person really didn't do anything *to us*. They just didn't do anything *at all*. You thought they would hit the tennis ball back, but they just stood there and let it bounce against the fence behind them. And that's the odd thing about ingratitude: The recipient is always aware. But the culprit is rarely aware."

Have you ever felt underappreciated? Unrecognized? Unseen? Don't let unexpressed gratitude be the silent killer of your relationships. Make it a habit to acknowledge and appreciate those who contribute to your success, no matter how small their role might seem. What really matters is who we care for and who has cared for us. Unfortunately, most of us busybodies default to being 3S givers.

3S GIVER VERSUS 3P GIVER

We all get to choose what type of giver we are: a 3S giver or a 3P giver. Let's take a look at what those terms mean in this conversation and in the bigger picture.

3S GIVERS

- Spontaneously: give when they have the time or when they think of it.
- Sporadically: give rarely, if ever.
- Sparingly: ask "What's the *least* I can do?" (for this relationship, to check a box).

Side note: I could also add a fourth S, which would be "scarcity." I hope that's a dirty word for you because it certainly is for me. I have enough years under my belt to see that it's really easy to gradually get into a place of scarcity in my thinking: your lifestyle, your schedule, what you've accumulated and now you want to preserve...and you don't even know it's happening. If your margins are too thin to invest 10 percent into your relationships, you need to either raise your prices, lower your lifestyle, or a little bit of both. Either way, this would be a sign that you need greater relationships. Because nothing is going to get you further faster than meeting the right person or people.

3P GIVERS

- Priority: give as often as possible, every opportunity you have.
- Percentage: ask "What's the *most* I can do?"
- Progressive: see generosity build over time (another reason why givers experience the snowball and takers get the hamster wheel).

If you've been running your business a long time as a 3S giver, then becoming a 3P giver can seem like a really overwhelming and daunting task—which is why I'll end with something uplifting, some brilliant thinking by the team over at Category Pirates.

Almost every decision made in business is very incremental. It's safe for the company. It's safe for investors. And it's safe for employees.

People are wired to think, "If you beat your past performance by a penny or two, you're winning."

But that's not how you become the market leader. It's not how you build wealth. And it's not how you go from working fifty hours per week to playing golf on a Tuesday morning (or whatever your thing is that you'd rather be doing).

To be exponential, you have to take risks.

In the words of business leader Peter Drucker: "People who don't take risks generally make about two big mistakes a year. People who do take risks generally make about two big mistakes a year."[12] Same number. Hmm.

---

12 Widely attributed to Peter Drucker, cited in Jeff Shore and Dan Bova, "These 10 Peter Drucker Quotes May Change Your World," *Entrepreneur*, September 16, 2014, https://www.entrepreneur.com/living/these-10-peter-drucker-quotes-may-change-your-world/299936.

Will Smith once said that what separates him from others is that he's willing to die on a treadmill. Are you willing to die on the treadmill of relationships?

You can give without loving. But you can't love without giving.

PART TWO

REFERRAL FOUNDATIONS

CHAPTER 4

BUT FIRST, DOV

This tale comes from Jesse Flocken—founder and CEO of Clearly Relevant, a growth marketing agency based in beautiful Gilbert, Arizona.

It's about a guy named Paul—Tall Paul, to be exact. And trust me, it's not just his height that makes him stand out.

Now, Tall Paul (he's 6′9″) used to be a worship pastor. These days, he works as a development manager for Gilbert Christian Schools, raising money for classroom and campus improvements. Quite the career change, right?

Early on, Tall Paul made a rule for himself when discussing finances: "I won't ask for anything until I've had three meetings with someone." If you're in sales, fundraising, or trying to get money to change hands, you know that's not a best practice.

(He quickly came to a realization—more on that in a second.)

Picture this: Paul's at coffee with a previous partner. The man across the table owned several successful businesses, and flexed a net worth into multimillions with little time for meetings.

And there's poor, inexperienced Paul, trying to "create a culture of generosity." Somehow.

Now, I wasn't there. But we've all had these meetings, right?

I imagine an exchange of the usual pleasantries. Paul paying the bill. Maybe some genuine connection and relational conversation as the two got to know each other. Ending with: "Well, I've gotta run to my next meeting. Let's wrap this up. It was a pleasure meeting you, Paul."

"So glad we got to sit down and talk! I hope you have a wonderful Tuesday!"

They shake hands. Paul turns to leave.

"Wait...that's it? Aren't you gonna ask me for money?"

"Nope! See ya!"

(Jesse declared those last three words an exact quote.)

Tall Paul went to his next meeting. And then the next. And the next—likely executing what the RPT System calls a "Connection Day." Smart man! When he returned to the office the next day, there was an envelope on his desk. Inside was a check for $28,000 and a note from his new coffee friend that said, "It's a start. Let me know how else I can help."

Gulp.

Tall Paul grew partnerships from $90,000 the year prior to over $7 million in three years. The school expanded from three campuses to four and is currently fundraising for a high school addition. His "culture of generosity" captured a long tail of partners that may never have considered donating.

What's his secret? Well, if you were to ask Tall Paul about his one rule, he would say, "I don't ask for anything until I've had three meetings with someone..."

And his realization?

"Weirdly enough, I never have to ask for anything."

The lesson here? Sometimes, the most powerful ask is no ask at all. When you focus on building genuine relationships without expectation, amazing things can happen.

- What they do: Jesse's agency specializes in consulting, messaging, SEO, digital ads, coaching, and Sprint workshops that turn big ideas into reality.
- Who they serve: Leaders that want growth *or else*.
- What they *don't* do: No shortcuts or one-size-fits-all solutions.
- Who is *not* a fit: Anyone looking for low-cost, short-term, or surface-level marketing efforts that lack the drive to win.

ZERO EXPECTATIONS

I am a Christian. And foundational to the Christian religion is the idea of unmerited favor. God's love for us is endless, so we can love generously, without holding back.

What a blessing.

Of course I, and every other Christian, fail miserably at this. Many of us hoard our love, treating it like currency—a method of transaction. Sometimes we praise others, hoping it will make them like us more. Sometimes we lend a hand, but deep down, we have our own agendas. True love can't be given freely if we're secretly expecting something in return.

My friend, Steve Sims, in his book *Go for Stupid*, talks about planning a barbeque. When he speaks, he'll ask his audience, "What questions would you ask the host?"[13] Most men ask seven questions before they ask the crucial one: "What can *I* bring?" (Interesting sidenote: Most women ask this question first.)

The sad fact is most people ask what they can get, not what they can give. A lot of truly wonderful people have tried (and are trying as you read this) to help their fellow humans get better at this. Joe Polish, author of *What's in It for Them?* (and founder of world-famous

---

13 Steve Sims, *Go for Stupid: The Art of Achieving Ridiculous Goals* (House of Nomad SOC, 2022); and Steve Sims, "Go for Stupid with Steve Sims," February 7, 2023, in *Win the Day*, podcast, 14:30, https://jameswhitt.com/go-for-stupid-with-steve-sims/.

Genius Network), has a personal tagline: "Make your give greater than your want."[14] John Hall, author of *Top of Mind* (and founder/seller of numerous companies), says, "Be somebody who is deeply and consistently meaningful in another person's life."[15] Jonathan Keyser, author of *You Don't Have to Be Ruthless to Win* (and a commercial real estate magnate) says, "The universe cannot handle imbalance. The more you give, the more you get."[16]

Your takeaway—other than Ruhlin has a lot of author friends whose first names begin with the letter J—should be this: If dozens of smart and successful people are all saying the same thing, it must be important.

The best business leaders have an attitude of "Nobody owes me anything." Don't expect warmth if you're not willing to throw a log in the fireplace. In fact, just be cool to people all the time, just because. Zero expectations. Expecting (and asking for) *nothing* in return. And no, this isn't just about being nice; it's about rewiring your brain to approach relationships differently. When you give without expectation, you create a positive energy that people can't help but respond to. And that is how you build a network that will move mountains for you.

What are your hidden motivations? What are *you* bringing to the barbeque?

EVERYBODY (ALWAYS) NEEDS SOMETHING

Our lives are not perfect. The goal of the add-value give is simple: See a need, fill a need.

More Joe Polish wisdom:

---

14 Joe Polish, *What's in It for Them? 9 Genius Networking Principles to Get What You Want by Helping Others Get What They Want* (Hay House, 2022); and Joe Polish, "Change One Question to Change Your Life with Joe Polish," April 19, 2023, in *Achieve Your Goals with Hal Elrod*, podcast, 57:00, https://miraclemorning.com/joe-polish/.

15 John Hall, text message to Michael Monroe, summer 2024.

16 Jonathan Keyser, text message to Michael Monroe, summer 2024.

There's a lot to be said about suffering. The bottom line is to focus on how you can help other people. Focus on what you can give to them first. Don't expect the world to give you anything without creating value first. So, when I ask someone, like a famous person to do an interview with me, I either will buy something from them, or I'm already a client, or I will send them a really nice letter. I will have an introduction from somebody that knows them, that can make the introduction for me. I will do the interview, not in a self-servicing way, but I intend on distributing it and sharing their message with lots of people. People always ask me how did I develop the relationship with Richard Branson? Most people don't know I invested 250,000 dollars up front, into his foundation, which I wanted to do and I'm fully okay with supporting. Before I even know if anything would come out of it, I wanted to do that. So, I paid.[17]

Polish's (and Tall Paul's) methods are supported by data. Only 2 percent of sales happen during the first point of contact.[18]

Even if your industry is regulated to the max, there is always one thing you can do: appreciate people. It's something everybody needs, and you can't overdo it. There's no such thing as an "appreciation stomachache."

Unfortunately, far too many people are generic with their appreciation. Too many shortcuts ("TY"), too much cliché ("Thanks for being you!"), and too much unexpressed gratitude (remember Chapter 3?).

Specificity is persuasive. Specificity has impact. Specificity proves you were paying attention.

Which leads us perfectly into our next topic: how to spot these opportunities to add value.

---

17   Joe Polish, "The One About the Magic Rapport Formula," August 1, 2011, in *I Love Marketing*, podcast, 1:23:48, https://ilovemarketing.com/episode-029-the-one-about-the-magic-rapport-formula/.

18   Brendan Connaughton, "14 Sales Follow-Up Statistics for Pipeline Success in 2024," Qwilr, last modified February 25, 2024, https://qwilr.com/blog/sales-follow-up-statistics/.

SURVEILLANCE

Harvey Mackay wrote the book I *wish* I had written on networking and demonstrating value: *Dig Your Well Before You're Thirsty*.[19]

The idea of adding value is you will develop the habit of surveillance: having your radar up, always looking for ways you can help your key relationships. Now, this does not mean everybody. You are not a giver sucker. You are a strategic giver. This also does not mean you have to act on every opportunity. That would get overwhelming quickly.

Surveillance in this context means being attentive and curious in all interactions, both online and offline. If you live in a state of curiosity in every conversation you have, and you pick up on these little things, chances are you can identify opportunities to add value in your relationships.

My friend Jeffrey Gitomer calls it "antennas up." It's not a sales tactic—it's a way of living and a way of relating to people. All business is H2H (human-to-human), and getting it right means developing a practice of noticing:

- Casual Listening: Note that people always mention wants and needs without realizing it.
- Hobbies/Interests: Ask a dozen questions and take notes.
- Social Media: Scan for likes and interests—especially what they comment on.
- Ask Siblings: Ask "What do you think of *this* idea?" (good) versus "What do I buy my wife?" (bad).
- Past Conversations: What big discussions can you remember from the last year?
- Record Any and All Frustrations: In the giving world? Their bad news is your good news.
- Observe Them While Shopping: Notice the "too expensive" stuff that catches their eye.
- Favorite Brands or Stores: Just don't buy gift cards. Please.

---

19   Harvey Mackay, *Dig Your Well Before You're Thirsty* (Currency Doubleday, 1997).

- The Unexpected Practical Luxury: Upgrade their everyday life.

Relying on memory results in lazy, uninspired giving. Our memories always fail. Instead, build systems and habits. For instance, a mobile note-taking app might be the answer. More on this in future chapters. If a nugget appears unexpectedly, excuse yourself to record thoughts from the moment, so you don't lose them.

Speaking of the moment: What do you do when you spot an opportunity? You guessed it! See a need, fill a need.

This practice of surveillance isn't about being creepy or stalker-ish. It's about being genuinely interested in the people around you. When you pay attention, you'll be amazed at how many opportunities you find to add value. That is how you start building those R.I.C.H. relationships we've been talking about.

DOVING AND THE ART OF THE INTRODUCTION

I was reminded of the "five-minute favor" terminology by my friend (and executive trainer) Sulemaan Ahmed. Five-minute favors are low-cost investments that yield massive returns.

The "five-minute favor" is a simple practice of being in the mindset of carving out just five minutes of your day to do something that will benefit the lives of others in your network, without expecting anything in return. And it works! Adam Grant has said that the five-minute favor is his single favorite habit that he learned while writing his best-selling book, *Give and Take*.

I love the concept of the five-minute favor because it captures the big idea that we can add massive value to people without being suckers. However, I don't want people to get fixated on the thought that anything over five minutes is too much, nor do I like the transaction or neediness of the word "favor." That's why we call it something a little more scientific—plus, I really like acronyms.

The term is **DoVing: demonstrations of value.** Doing something impactful for others at a low personal cost.

The idea of "**demonstrations**" is we have to prove our worth in business. We have to earn the right to snowball up. The concept of "**value**" is that we need to be increasing that of the other party—by their standards, not ours. See a need, fill a need.

DoVing isn't just about us helping someone. It's about showing that, despite our many inadequacies, we are worthy of a seat at the adult table. DoVing raises our status in the herd.

Let me give you an example.

I mentioned in Chapter 1 how there were few things I enjoyed more than making great introductions. It is the ultimate five-minute favor. (Bonus: If you turn it into a five-minute favor instead of an eight-second favor, you will change the way people feel about you overnight.)

DoVs have nuance, introductions included. But having made thousands of intros over the years, I've gotten pretty good at them. **Here are my three best tips on being a better introducer, with real-life examples.**

1. **EDIFY.** Say lots of nice things about each person. You want people psyched to meet each other, so pump tires. This can be professional and factual, but personal and emotional is even better.

    Example: "Sara, meet Michael. He is the CEO of XYZ Corporation, leading a company that's tripled in size the past five years. But you'd never know it, because he's the most humble guy you'll ever meet. Michael, Sara is an accomplished entrepreneur who founded three successful startups and was recognized as a Forbes' 30 Under 30. I'm in awe of her achievements as a leader and the impact she's making through her charitable giving."

    Two minutes of research before an introduction will blow people's minds. Notice, too, the power of professional and personal edification.

2. **NEEDS.** Share any known problems or challenges. Provide as much information as possible around any gaps. If only one party has a need, communicate how the other can solve it.

Example: "Brad is looking to have his outdoor patio remodeled before his in-laws visit at the end of the summer. He's willing to pay for quality, but doesn't want to deal with 'maybes' and 'mights.' Brad, just so you know, Stephen is a deadline master. He and his brother finished our kitchen remodel five days earlier than he promised, much to the delight of my wife!"

By being specific about Brad's problem and Stephen's solution, I created buy-in for each party. So simple.

3. **SEEDS.** Speak into a possible future. You want their first interaction to be memorable and meaningful, so plant seeds around what a future interaction could look like.

Example: "Julia, let me introduce you to Mark. He's a decade-long real estate investor who has an exceptional track record of identifying lucrative properties. Mark, Julia is a twenty-year agent with a deep understanding of the market and a huge network of clients. Your expertise in investments and Julia's eye for value could be an insane combination. How about we organize a lunch where you can exchange insights and explore potential collaborations? I'll be glad to take care of the reservations and make it a memorable experience for both of you."

Making a reservation is quite the DoV. Another option: Tease an idea for a collaboration, and go from there.

Your referral partners do not need to be this skilled with introductions when connecting prospects to you, but if you model this for them, they will absolutely notice. And get better.

Not all referrals are equal. Wrapped in edification and praise, introductions can feel more like a red-carpet, celebrity moment than a casual, "Here's a mechanic I know." Imagine how people feel when you introduce them this way.

The key here is to make every introduction count. Don't just connect people...create opportunities. When you master this art, you become the person everyone wants to know because you're not just a contact—you're a catalyst.

TEN ADDITIONAL DOVING METHODS

Let's dive into ten other methods of DoVing. And no, you don't have to use all of them; pick the ones that resonate with you and your style.

1. **Share broadly.** I read a lot and consume a lot of content. When I come across something awesome, I ask, "Who can I share this with?" This could be a book, a YouTube video, an article, an email newsletter...you name it. (And no, it doesn't have to be a business newsletter. The one I've shared the most is a *Daily Dad* newsletter.)

2. **Amplify those you care about.** I hate posting on social media, but I love hitting "share" on somebody else's post (one of my VIPs) and then writing a little caption about the original poster—especially if it's something cool, like a promotion, a milestone, or even a birthday.

3. **Remember the ABCs.** I consider the ABCs to encompass anniversaries, birthdays, Christmas, and other holidays. I put everybody's events into one calendar, and then I send them a one-on-one (not public, not on Facebook) message—usually an audio or a quick video—the day before the event. This is so key! I want to be the first person wishing them a happy fill-in-the-blank, and I don't want to get lost in the shuffle.

4. **Send *your* content in a meaningful way.** Say I wrote something, filmed something, or did something I'm proud of. Say also I posted about it publicly. The next question I have is (and you might be noticing a pattern): "Who would like this?" If someone rises top of mind, I share it with them one-on-one.

5. **Embrace CCC.** CCC stands for compliments, congratulations, and condolences. Compliments are the big ones and fairly easy to spread, but with congrats and condolences, we sometimes tend to hold back. Remember, there's no such thing as going too far when somebody is experiencing a high or low. Don't be afraid to go there.

6. **Reminisce out loud.** Relational leaders reminisce out loud. My friends, do *not* hog nostalgia! Every day, if you picked one connection from your playbook and sent them a voice or video message

that started with "Remember the time when...," you'd double your business in two years. An atomic habit.

7. **Send handwritten notes.** This is pretty self-explanatory, and if you're not doing it by now, you're insane. In our digital world, it's the easiest way to stick out. Don't worry—you don't need to have great handwriting or sound like a Hallmark card. Stay with me, and I'll share the hacks you need to write the best notes for anybody you know.

8. **Try hobby shout-outs.** I have a colleague and friend, Dave, who always congratulates me when my favorite sports teams win big games. He does this for everybody. How he remembers, I have no idea—but I love it, and I love him. Not surprisingly, so does everyone else. It's not hard to see why.

9. **Share a meal.** *Never Eat Alone* is a fantastic book by Keith Ferrazzi. Think about this: You're going to be eating anyway, use it as an opportunity to connect. My favorite quote from the book, by the way, is, "Real networking is about finding ways to make other people more successful," which is exactly what we're doing here.[20]

10. **Invite, invite, invite.** Send personal invites to join you at webinars, get-togethers, games, business events...anything you were going to be going to anyway. We all know a ton of business is done on the golf course. If you were already planning to head out, why not make it a foursome?

You can see there are many different methods, and you won't use every single one. Different personalities gravitate to different strategies, so choose the one(s) that work for you.

You can build an incredible Relationship Snowball without being on a single social media channel. If, unlike me, you're a raving extrovert, then be a chronic inviter. The key is to find what works for you and make it a habit. Consistency is king when it comes to building relationships.

---

20 Keith Ferrazzi, *Never Eat Alone* (Crown Business, 2014).

MY FAVORITE: GIFTING (AND WHY)

Choose your own adventure from the list above, but there's one DoV method that you *must* incorporate—even if you think you're bad at it (I was too): **gifting**. It's nonnegotiable because nothing will allow you to fast-forward relationships in a leveraged way like gifting will.

You can always make more money, but you can never get your time back—and time is what gifting gives, truly. It allows you to love on people without martyring yourself or without killing your family life by spending every open evening, weekend, and morning at another professional commitment or another airport. Think about it: Your VIPs have families too that they'd rather be spending time with. Have you ever attended a business get-together because you felt like you had to? Have you ever had to:

- "Sell" the event to your spouse (who didn't want to go)?
- Act like you were really excited about it (even though you weren't)?
- Inconvenience your family, your schedule, or your plans to appease someone?

If so, it's worth asking: Did these resource-intensive get-togethers achieve their desired outcome? Or was the real outcome bad acting (or great acting) covering up hidden eye rolls?

This is the problem with time-based relationship building: It isn't guaranteed to succeed, it's limited in whom you can give it to, and its opportunity cost is infinitely expensive.

I would contend the greatest gift you can give people you truly care about is their time back. No getting in the car. No acting. No small talk. No hangover. A good gift gives everyone their time back and creates a surge of relational butterflies, all in a matter of minutes. Not hours. Not days.

Even better, the right gift is used every day—a practical tool for the whole family. It's doing the relational work for you, even when you're not there.

Remember, gifting isn't just about the object you're giving. It's about the thought, the intention, and the message behind it. When done right, it's the most powerful way to show someone you value them and their time. And that, my friends, is how you build relationships that last.

GIFTING AS A SYSTEM

DoVs and the RPT System are all about operationalizing relationship building with strategic gifts, savvy communication, and a giver's mindset, which is a very different method than most referral trainings.

One of my favorite parts of my job is reading our tribe's relational wins. A "relational win" is what we call a gift-inspired thank-you message. Not all clients share them with me, and that's totally okay. But when they do? Man, they're fun to read.

Sometimes it's a video. A screenshot of a text message. Or an email. I love them all. And I *really* loved this email. A LOT.

* * *

SUBJECT: WTF?!?

Buddy,

Finally got back home after way too long and got your incredible gift. Im almost at a loss for words. But in short, I'm in awe! This is one of the most thoughtful, beautiful, and creative gifts I have ever received.

I talk about how hospitality is making people feel seen- I FEEL SEEN!

Sincerely, I'm overwhelmed- and so unreasonably appreciative.

You're the best. Thank you!!!

Sent from my iPhone

* * *

"Buddy"—that's when you know you're doing it right.

This particular gift was a world-class practical luxury—an Artifact Mug. Go to ArtifactMug.com for more info. It is a gift that is cherished, used every day, with a handwritten note, and no—you don't need to write the note yourself.

Jeff Bezos doesn't write his own notes. And you are cooler than Bezos.

"Why would I give gifts like this?"

The answer to this question is simple and so incredibly important: because gifting fast-forwards relationships, and relationships can take you places marketing can't.™ Gifting gets you introductions that no amount of money spent on marketing could buy—introductions to people who would never find you through traditional channels. This looks like talent *not* looking for work where your job postings are, clients who need your help and trust their friend's recommendation more than Google results, and more. Which, according to every study I've read is...everybody.

Beyond introductions, gifting is also a cornerstone of referral-partner maintenance. Attention from leadership often falls under the adage, "The squeaky wheel gets the grease," meaning the people who are *most* with you are usually the last ones thanked. Make them feel seen. Make them feel WTF?!

"How do I give gifts like this?"

You won't find them on Google. One way to give gifts like this is to hire our agency for tens of thousands of dollars to do it for you. The other way is to invest the time, energy, and money to learn how to do it yourself.

The fastest way to do that? Join the R.I.C.H. RELATIONSHIP SOCIETY. Our team keeps an up-to-date catalog of our favorite gifts, with prices ranging from two-dollar stationery to two-thousand-dollar houseware products. Currently we have over one hundred gifts organized by price, occasion, and impact.

And while I'm blatantly self-promoting, maybe pick up a copy of *GIFT·OLOGY*. Wink wink...

"Isn't this bribery?"

Again, I want to call attention to a common method that is not on the DoV list: a loyalty and incentive program, like Starbucks points or airline miles. It's not a "do this for me, and you'll get that as a reward" kind of dynamic.

People who bust out their formal incentive programs within the first two or three conversations? Ick. *That* is bribery. *That* screams "taker." *That* says, "I don't care about what you need. I'm interested in what you can do for me."

One of the most common gifting objections I hear is: "I don't want to come across as bribing people." Well, duh! The way to avoid bribery is purely in your communication. This is especially important if you're in a regulated industry that has limitations or restrictions.

Here are three good communication guidelines for any items on the DoV list, regardless of whether you're spending money or not:

1. NO expectation of anything in return. If you're not okay with the money or effort required to execute a DoV *unless* you get something in return, don't do it. Period.
2. NO mention of previous behavior. Don't ever say anything like,

"I wanted to thank you for introducing me to Vicki Reid." Don't say anything that could be interpreted as transactional. Not even, "Hey, I owed you one because you bought coffee last time we were out." Scorekeeping kills romance, and romance is the essence of intimate relationships.

3. NO discussion of current deals, transactions, or decisions. Bribery is interpreted by the receiver, not the giver. It's best to be short, clear, and even a little silly, which I'll teach you about soon.

The only way to build a Relationship Snowball is with lots of little pushes until you have a snowman. And you don't get a snowman if you aren't pushing consistently. What does this mean? When you commit to being a giver and commit to a marketing plan centered around relationships, your day-to-day, week-to-week behaviors reveal themselves. Giving can't be a "when I remember" or "once in a while" thing for it to work well. As the saying goes, "Motivation keeps us going and discipline keeps us growing."

ARE YOU LEAVING PEOPLE IN AWE?

"We all know the story," says PR pro Michael Smart. "A traveler is mind-blown by a hotel concierge who didn't just recommend a show but scored impossible-to-get tickets, backstage passes, and five-star dinner reservations."

Are you DoVing at that level? Are your key relationships getting that type of treatment?

When you do the least for others, they do the least for you.

Remember, the goal here isn't just to give gifts or do favors. It's to create experiences that leave people in awe. When you consistently go above and beyond, you become unforgettable. And in business, being unforgettable is priceless.

As we wrap up this chapter, I want you to ask yourself: How can I take my relationship building to the next level? How can I start seeing needs and filling them in ways that truly wow people? Because when you master this art of generosity, you'll find that doors open in ways you never imagined possible.

CHAPTER 5

UNDERSTAND EACH OTHER

Ellen Long—co-founder and consultant at Build Prove Sell—was recently diagnosed with Hashimoto's, an autoimmune disease. When she went on a podcast discussing the news, the host assumed it had taken *years* to get the diagnosis. Why? Because it usually does. This condition is often missed at first, as the symptoms present in a complex way.

Ellen replied, "Actually, I got lucky. I had my labs tested and immediately texted three doctors in my network. They all confirmed I had it."

Was Ellen lucky? Or had she just built meaningful relationships? Had she delivered so much value, and been *so* clear both in the delivery of that value and in who she is as a person and a professional that it came back around?

I know it's option B for two reasons. One, I know Ellen to be a wonderful human being who breadcrumbs value everywhere she goes. And two, I know clarity pays off. I've seen it. We're going to talk about it a lot in this chapter.

Ellen knows that, too, now—but getting it was hard-won knowledge. She said when she first started Build Prove Sell, they weren't sure how to explain themselves. Prospective clients would get on the phone and say things like, "I have no idea why I'm here. Someone just said you were amazing."

Finally, after a lot of those meandering (but well-intentioned) calls, Ellen worked with an agency to develop a clear brand message. The impact was swift and massive. They started getting speaking gigs and higher-quality clients. Most tellingly, a client who had been in Ellen's orbit for nine months visited the revamped website and said, "Oh wow! I knew you were awesome and I needed to work with you. I just read your website, and I finally understand exactly what you do."

That's the power of clarity, friends.

ELLEN'S BIG 4

- What they do: Ellen helps entrepreneurs build, prove, and sell their businesses, about two to three years before they want to get to the sale.
- Who they serve: Entrepreneurs with businesses worth $10 million to $100 million.
- What they *don't* do: Ellen and her company are not brokers.
- Who is *not* a fit: People who have a fixed mindset or who don't have a bigger mission than money.

CLARITY CONVERSATIONS: WHAT ARE THEY?

Are you curious what this Big 4 business is all about? Well, we're about to go there.

I recommend premarital counseling to every young couple. That's because most people plan a honeymoon, but they fail to plan a marriage. Don't be most people! You want your partnerships to last forever. But that can happen only if you huddle up and get clear on the near future. If your partner loves pets, but you're allergic to fur, you need to know ahead of time. The same goes for business relationships. That means having a Clarity Conversation, which is a structured discussion where each party discusses their Big 4:

1. What we do.
2. Who we serve.
3. What we *don't* do.
4. Who is *not* a fit.

A Clarity Conversation isn't just an information swap. It's a rapport-building dialogue—twenty to thirty minutes of memorable connection, whether over coffee, lunch, or an unhurried, agenda-free Zoom chat.

The best Clarity Conversations end with a contact card exchange (have yours at the ready), perhaps a selfie (for the profile photo), and the preferred method of making new introductions (text or email).

Let's take a look at a few obvious examples:

- Financial planner and realtor: The financial planner refers clients who are ready to buy homes, while the realtor sends new homeowners needing financial planning for mortgages and investments.
- Personal trainer and nutritionist: The trainer sends clients in need of dietary plans, and the nutritionist refers clients looking to elevate their health with physical training.
- IT consultant and business coach: The IT consultant refers business owners needing to scale, while the coach sends clients looking to upgrade their tech systems.
- Event planner and florist: The planner refers clients needing floral services, and the florist sends clients requiring full-event planning for weddings or corporate events.
- Graphic designer and PR specialist: The PR specialist refers clients needing rebranding to the designer, while the designer sends clients needing media exposure to the PR specialist.
- Chiropractor and yoga instructor: The chiropractor refers clients needing physical therapy to the yoga instructor, and the yoga instructor sends students with chronic pain to the chiropractor.

Let me guess your next question…

"DO I *HAVE TO* SEND THE OTHER PARTY REFERRALS?"

No. Your job is to DoV (demonstrate value—see Chapter 4 for a refresher). And sure, sending referrals might be an easy way to do just that. It's also true many of your best referral partners will be asymmetrical, depending on your industry. This might include customers referring a home professional service to their friends or other "downstream business relationships," such as a realtor referring to their preferred lender. In both examples, referrals rarely flow in the other direction. And this doesn't mean you have to resort to nagging with these individuals. As you learned in Chapter 3, it's better to get five from five than one from twenty-five. Partnering always beats pleading.

Clarity Conversations uncover how to best value the other person—whether through quick five-minute favors (before referrals) or thoughtful "peak moment" gestures (after referrals). Like premarital counseling, it's two people learning how to love each other.

That's why Clarity Conversations are personal exchanges, not an email.

Let me give you an example of mutual value, where only one party is receiving referrals: A web designer and a content creator have a Clarity Conversation. The web designer agrees to refer clients who need content for their new websites. And while the content creator might meet individuals who need a website, they likely already have one. To add value, the content creator provides search engine optimization (SEO) guidelines and Google My Business (GMB) review tips for all the web designer's clients. They might also share templates, frameworks, or even offer a pro bono coaching session. This enriches the web designer's offering at no additional cost, and the creator becomes that much easier to refer. No money exchanging hands. Mutual DoVs. Both parties win.

Givers are magical, which is why you don't date givers. You marry them. And in this case, you aren't limited to just one partner.

Remember, the goal isn't to create a tit-for-tat exchange of referrals. It's about finding ways to add value to each other's businesses.

When you approach partnerships with this mindset, you'll find that the referrals often take care of themselves.

DELIVERING RADICAL CLARITY

People give referrals to look good and to be helpful, not just to be nice. That's why, by positioning yourself honestly, you present more exclusively—and your referral partner can puff their chest out by referring an expert (not just another guy on Google).

This level of clarity isn't just about being specific; it's about painting a vivid picture of who you are, what you do, and who you serve. When you can articulate this clearly, you make it easy for others to see exactly who in their network would be a perfect fit for you.

Observe these two examples of two different professionals, one of which is trained in the RPT System and one who is not:

[Untrained]: "I'm looking for copywriting clients."

[Trained]: "I write email newsletters for software companies. Most of them don't have professional writers on their team, so they give the job to anyone with a pulse. The result is poorly written promotions that your customers hate reading. My tried-and-true solution is not to sell, but to educate. Basically, I make sales by being a fun email teacher."

[Untrained]: "If they're looking for emails, I'd love to talk to them."

[Trained]: "While I'd love to serve everyone, I don't write help-desk manuals. And I don't work with companies that churn out content just to check a box. It's usually not a fit because those types of emails frustrate customers and can actually hurt a brand's reputation."

Do you notice the specificity? The fifth-grade language?

If you're already a client, the above will cement your understanding.

If you're not a client but exist in the industry, the above will demonstrate expertise and raise your status as a worthy referral to give.

In the next section, we'll explore how this clarity creates confidence in your referral partners, leading to more and better referrals. **Remember, if you're easy to explain, you're easy to refer.**

CLARITY CREATES CONFIDENCE

When people have clarity about who you are and what you offer, you become easy to talk about. And (I can't say this enough) when you're easy to talk about, you're easy to refer.

Being easy to talk about means knowing your Big 4. Here they are again:

1. What we do.
2. Who we serve.
3. What we *don't* do.
4. Who is *not* a fit.

If you're wondering how to communicate your Big 4, try out the following templates:

- "What I do is [boring, easy-to-remember, description] for [target market]. The problem most of those people face is... My tried-and-true solution is... Basically I [big, helpful-sounding idea]."
- "While I'd love to serve everyone, I don't [service you avoid] and I don't typically work with [customer group that's not a match]. It's usually not a fit because..."

I recommend you practice this—out loud. To yourself. To others. To everyone. On podcasts. In the mirror. In the car. Daily, until you have it memorized.

The clearer and more specific you are, the easier it is for others to communicate your value with confidence and accuracy. Over time, as they talk about you more and more, they're only going to get better at it, which perpetuates more referrals.

This is so important because, let's face it, nobody wants to look stupid. Clarity gives partners the courage to speak up on your behalf. Think about it: If you've ever received a referral that was completely off target, and you didn't follow up with a correction or positive progress (like I mentioned in Chapter 2), it's likely because the person who referred you didn't fully grasp your business. That's a big issue, and if you can't help the people they send your way, they don't apologize. They just stop referring to you.

Now they've left your snowball. And you're back on the hamster wheel with everyone else.

Remember, your goal is to make your referral partners feel like experts when they talk about you. The more confident they feel, the more likely they are to make those introductions. It's not just about what you say, but how easy you make it for others to say it too.

THE RIGHT ENVIRONMENT

Where should you have a Clarity Conversation? The truth is that it's less about the physical location and more about creating an atmosphere that encourages candor and banter. That said, let's look at a few best practices.

In-Person Is Best: Whenever possible, aim to have Clarity Conversations in person. As the blooming partnership deepens, so should the environment. If your first meeting was over a phone call, try to make the next one a coffee meetup, lunch, or a hangout before or after a live event.

Elevate the interaction as the relationship grows. You want to go to a place where "everybody knows your name." (Status points if you can introduce them to a barista, waitress, or owner.)

Bonus tip for these in-person conversations: Don't be shy about going to *them*. Sometimes, it's best to meet in their space, especially if their environment provides context to their needs or operations. For instance, visiting their office might give you insights into their business you wouldn't get elsewhere. Plus, it can show respect for their time and responsibilities.

Virtual Conversations: If in-person isn't an option (and if you work remotely, like we do, it's not) then a video call is the next best thing. But remember, a video call should still feel personal. Choose a quiet, well-lit space, and make sure you won't be interrupted. Even though it's virtual, the setting should reflect the importance of the conversation.

Avoid Distractions: Wherever you meet, ensure it's a place free from distractions. The last thing you want is to be interrupted during a crucial part of a Clarity Conversation. When I do calls like these, I'm usually walking the trails behind my house—a place where children cannot interrupt.

The environment you choose sets the tone for your conversation. It's not just about finding a quiet place to talk; it's about creating a space where both parties feel comfortable, valued, and ready to engage in meaningful dialogue. Remember, the goal is to build a relationship, not just exchange information.

HOW TO STRUCTURE A CLARITY CONVERSATION

What's a marriage without a little romance and rapport?

You have the environment. You both showed up. Now what?

You're not on your own here; there's a system. Let's look at the best way to structure this important interaction.

Step 1: Build rapport. Put away your phone when they show up. Lots of smiles and eye contact. Lots of energy. Lots of curiosity about their day and/or whatever was happening before they showed up. My favorite rapport question (ask anyone I've ever called) is, "What am I interrupting?"

Step 2: Share your intent. Remind your prospect why you wanted to meet. Set the expectation of what it is you want to talk about. That might be, "I'd like to learn more about your business [or 'your world' if this is a conversation with a consumer] and share more about my business, where we're at, and where we're going." These people should feel like they're about to become insiders.

Step 3: Understand each other. Asking great questions and active listening are incredibly attractive qualities. If you do surveillance well, you'll uncover areas where you can demonstrate value, and you'll have the opportunity to share your Big 4.

(Do you have that memorized yet? Keep pushing!)

Step 4: Propose next steps. Review any promises you've made to one another before shaking hands (or hugging, or waving goodbye) and leaving. Good conversations will leave you with a to-do list that might say something like, "Okay, I need to introduce him to this person, text him the name of the author we were talking about, and email him about XYZ." You want to move from conversation to action, which is why the next step is so important.

Step 5: 24-Hour Follow-Up Now. Don't rely on memory alone. After your Clarity Conversation, take the time to document what you discussed. This is not a contract and doesn't need to be formal—a simple email or text message will do. But you want it documented. More on this in Chapter 12.

ASKING QUALITY QUESTIONS

God gave us two ears and one mouth, which means talk as often, as much, and as loudly as possible...according to some people's logic. Let's all use that power wisely. With that in mind, here are some examples of exceptional questions that naturally uncover the Big 4, both yours and theirs.

EXCITEMENT QUESTIONS

These are designed to get to the heart of what matters most, right now. They can get deep in a hurry:

- "What's the most exciting thing you're working on right now?"
- "What's something in your business you're particularly proud of at the moment?"

OBSTACLES AND CHALLENGE QUESTIONS

Here, you are positioning yourself as somebody who can help. Remember, their bad news can be your good news if you can figure out how to help:

- "What's the biggest challenge you're facing as it pertains to your business?"
- "What's a problem you've had more than once in the last year?"
- "What type of expert are you looking to hire right now?"
- "Are you having difficulty hiring for any positions right now?"

FUTURE-TALK QUESTIONS

To align your efforts with their long-term goals, ask future-focused questions:

- "If we were having this conversation three years from now, what would have to happen for you personally and professionally for you to feel happy with your progress?"
- "If we were having this conversation a year from now, what new initiative would you have in place at your company?"
- "If we were having this conversation next quarter, what new position would you have hired someone for?"

PROBLEM-SOLVING QUESTIONS

The following surveillance questions can be a gateway to immediate action:

- "If I could make an introduction for you—who would you want to meet and why?"
- "What would be the most important book or resource you could read right now?"

BEYOND THE PROMPTS

You are not a robot. There's a lot more to having meaningful Clarity Conversation than asking the right questions with the right words, though that part is certainly important. Keep these tips in mind as you think about how to structure your interaction:

- **Master the art of taking turns.** If you're on the clock, split the time evenly—fifteen minutes for their needs, fifteen minutes for yours. You can even set the expectation up front: "I know we only have thirty minutes, so let's make sure we each get to share what's most important."
- **Share your needs.** When they discuss their challenges, naturally segue into your own. "I've been focused on [your challenge or goal], and I'd love to hear your thoughts on it." You're not just asking for help—you're creating a mutual exchange. Balance is key.
- **Visioneer the partnership.** Ask, "What could it look like for us to work together?" This question is about creating a clear path forward. It's an opportunity to outline the terms of your collaboration, set expectations, and ensure that both parties are on the same page.
- **Keep building your Clarity Conversation muscle.** Remember that vague questions lead to vague answers. The more precise your questions, the more actionable the information you'll receive. Many of my referral partners, myself included, can get into tangents about a vacation they took seven years ago. It's okay to interrupt and redirect: "Wait, go back to what you were saying before!"

Start putting your Clarity Conversation into practice. Test it out with a few referrals and see how it goes. If something isn't working, revisit the conversation and adjust as needed. The goal is to create a living, and an evolving, partnership that benefits both of you over the long term. And, if you get to the end of your time and haven't discussed the Big 4, well...I've been there. Lesson learned. Do better next time (more tips on this in Chapter 19).

The great thing about a Clarity Conversation is that it's impossible to fail—unless you were yawning and looking at your watch, time with potential partners always moves the relationship forward.

THE REFERRAL RUNWAY

Say you've had a Clarity Conversation—you've talked about how you can help each other, you've agreed to help each other, all before they've actually referred a paying customer.

Congratulations! They are on the runway, and the airplane has speed. But until they've actually referred you business (that has closed), that plane is most definitely still taxiing to takeoff.

If they've made it to the runway with you, they're probably a giver—at least a matcher. But you're not going to invest significantly into this relationship yet until they clear the first referral hurdle. This is critical because our relationships are prioritized by what people do, not what they say they're going to do.

The way to get them into the air is to stay in meaningful touch with these people (keyword: meaningful). We don't want to be the way-too-eager boyfriend or girlfriend. We want to demonstrate value but do it at a low personal cost. Why? Because it would be unwise to overinvest in taker relationships...even though they're saying all the right things to present as givers.

Here's Joe Polish again, describing takers:

> You know the type—the only time you hear from them is when they need to borrow something, or they need a favor, or they need a connection. But they don't call you up, volunteering to help you and to be useful. Then when they call, you don't really want to answer because they're not calling to give; they're not calling to share; they're not calling to be vulnerable, connect, or to invite you somewhere.

Joe is so right.

What this means to us is that after your Clarity Conversation, if they have never referred you business, you will put them on the runway. And you will execute the runway protocol (more on that in Chapter 12). After they've referred you a closed sale, you can put them into the Referral Partner Transformation (RPT) System (more on that in Chapter 13).

Starting to see how you can operationalize referrals? Good. Let's talk about how to get the entire team on board.

CHAPTER 6

WE, NOT ME

In his excellent book, *Anyone Not Everyone*, my friend Corey Quinn accurately details the challenge of founder-led sales—and boy, are there many.

Corey knows this firsthand. As the former CMO at Scorpion, he helped take the company from $20 million to $150 million in six years.

Once upon a time, Corey had a client who wanted to break into the multilocation chain restaurant industry. His team identified one key influencer that all chain restaurant CEOs listened to: Danny Klein, the editor of *Quick Serve Restaurant* magazine.

Danny wasn't just any industry figure. He had built a comprehensive platform including the magazine, a podcast, and a strong LinkedIn presence. He was what Malcolm Gladwell would call a "maven"—someone with disproportionate influence over an entire industry.

Corey and his team developed a strategic plan to get on Danny's radar. They attended the same conferences he did, leveraged mutual contacts to make direct connections, engaged with his social media content, and invited him to appear on their podcast.

These consistent DoV efforts paid off when the CEO of Corey's company was invited to appear on Danny's podcast. Danny consistently promoted Corey's clients' restaurant software to his audience—unsolicited, unpaid, yet unexpectedly enthusiastic.

The endorsements were game-changing. Through this single relationship with a key industry maven, Corey's firm, Scorpion, gained tremendous visibility and secured numerous new clients in the restaurant industry.

This is a perfect example of focusing on the "goose that lays the golden eggs" rather than chasing the immediate opportunities in front of you—a common pitfall in founder-led sales.

COREY'S BIG 4

- What they do: Corey helps digital marketing founders escape founder-led sales.
- Who they serve: Visionary founders.
- What they *don't* do: Corey doesn't focus on short-term fixes or transactional relationships.
- Who is *not* a fit: People who only have their own best interests in mind.

THE ART OF THE S(C)ALE

The RPT System scales across teams. You might not have a team yet. Heck, you might not even have a dollar of revenue. And while it's possible to make an incredible income and live a happy life as a solopreneur—like Paul Jarvis describes in his book *Company of One*—the reality is most of us won't do business alone forever.

The moment we add even a part-timer to the team—be it our fifteen-year-old daughter or a virtual assistant in the Philippines—we add complexity. This is normal. And navigable. The sooner you: (1) embrace the system, and (2) define key elements, the sooner everyone in your orbit will contribute to your Relationship Snowball.

No more finicky algorithms, ad spend, or pushing uphill—this is about working with your relational momentum, not against it.

CHALLENGE: FOUNDER-LED SALES

Founder-led sales can sink you. You know what I'm talking about. Unfortunately, I do too. Founder-led sales refer to the process where the leader of the organization is directly responsible for driving sales efforts, securing clients, and closing deals, leveraging their personal networks, expertise, and passion for the business.

If you're the leader of a small business, you've probably experienced the following:

1. Dependence on your network: Your business relies on your direct involvement in sales. You are the cog in the machine. So, you are the clog in the machine.
2. Difficulty in diversifying sales efforts: Sales teams and outreach efforts are not as successful as you—chief referral generator and face of the company.
3. Pressure to say *yes* to any and all revenue: You're highly capable, and the business needs revenue. Of course, just because we *can* do something doesn't mean we should.
4. The market is *tough*: Your direct involvement can be the difference. Competitors can outmaneuver you without your insight and experience.
5. Struggles with the necessity of personal insight and relatability: Your personal involvement builds trust. Clients relate to you because you speak their language, which tethers you to all the things.
6. Feeling intoxicated by opportunities: Your visionary mind and authority presence attracts more interesting possibilities than you could ever take advantage of. At best, it's a distraction. At worst, you're dreaming of a way out.

The goal is not to run a business on autopilot. To go sit on a beach somewhere and drink mai tais all day—every person I know who's done this (and there's been more than one) has been grossly disappointed. The goal is to raise a team that's a better, smarter, more effective version of you. That way you're on the bow, not in the engine room. Conducting the orchestra, not playing the oboe.

This is what it's going to look like...

THREE SYSTEMS

The great Brian McRae—speaker, coach, and world-class mortgage alumni—uses an acronym for "S.Y.S.T.E.M.": "Save Yourself Stress, Time, Energy, and Money."

Remember our talk about referral chains? Person A → Person B → Person C → Person D, etc.? There's lot of room for error. The RPT System was built to cover up *all my mistakes*:

- I chose a lot of the wrong people (takers).
- As the chain got longer, I lost focus on the As and Bs. That was me being a taker. Ugh.
- And as the chains got too long, I tried to do all the work myself.

To ensure you're on the right path, here are the three systems of a world-class referral partner operations plan. Implement these systems if you wish to be a strategic giver and not a sucker.

(Note: For R.I.C.H. RELATIONSHIP SOCIETY members, we break these down into weekly checklists. But our way isn't the only way. Any process should address each of these relational buckets with step-by-step execution.)

SYSTEM ONE: PROSPECTING PARTNERS

System One, discussed in detail in Chapters 7, 8, and 9, is necessary to identify potential partners. I've already mentioned that not everybody is qualified. And if you're worried about keeping the lights on, going into a season of expansion, and need cash, or simply know a lot of great people but haven't "tapped into them" as referral givers yet, this is your system.

A partnership-prospecting system takes potential A+ givers (multiple deals closed each and every year) through a process. The people who come out the other side are then moved to System Two. The ones who don't make it—great as they are—aren't ready yet.

Congratulations. You just saved resources!

This system avoids the awkwardness of asking, instead relying on simple discovery questions, escalating into a Clarity Conversation. The most important part of this system is the communication stack, which acts as a subtle interview (they won't feel like they're being interviewed) and reveals their willingness to refer you—plus, it escalates their intent if they're qualified to be a partner and comes with no relational penalty if they're not ready, capable, or willing.

(And by the way—we know how to qualify with a single Greenlight Question. Easy.)

SYSTEM TWO: CLEARING RUNWAY

System One ends with a Clarity Conversation. System Two—mentioned in Chapter 5 and discussed in detail in Chapters 10, 11, and 12—occurs directly after the Clarity Conversation. Like a busy, international airport, your goal is to get as many people "into the air" as possible.

"Into the air" means them referring you business that closes, which is different from simply referring you business. And while there is no such thing as a bad referral, we don't want people to get discouraged by referring you business that isn't a good fit.

If your Clarity Conversation is well designed and well executed, many of these runways will be taking off. And soon, often on their first attempt! The ones who don't make it, or never make any attempt to do anything—great as they are—aren't ready yet.

Congratulations, again! You just saved resources. (Starting to see how this works?)

A+ players ghost C– players. Desperation kills referrals. This system avoids nagging, bragging, or following up incessantly.

The top-of-memory lever, instead, is laid out in Chapter 4, DoVs (demonstrations of value). You will run a simple, stay-in-touch protocol that excites people when hearing from you. This protocol scales with relationships and will fit into your weekly schedule, without annihilating your workflow. And it will be fun! Think about the things you're doing anyway, but stretched out to bless your network (more on this in Chapters 19 and 20). Note that gifting can be useful here, but only in proportion to your resources and industry allowances.

SYSTEM THREE: PERPETUATING GIVERS

This system, discussed in detail in Part Five (Chapters 13, 14, and 15), is what we're all here for. Unfortunately, it's where most business leaders have the most holes—a.k.a., no system at all.

The goal here is to appreciate, inspire, and energize your best referral givers—the people whose referrals result in a transaction—to not only give more, but to increasingly move toward the highest level of professional relationship you are comfortable with. I recommend "friendship" or "like family," though I understand that's not for everyone. You want as many people in this category as possible!

Let me repeat that: You want as many people in this category as possible.

This system should love on those people who have elected to become your personal sales force. They're "one-man marketing channels," as someone on my team once referred to Cameron Herold, the founder of COO Alliance and one of my closest partners.

These people deliver introductions—albeit maybe not perfectly, in the beginning. This is why a Clarity Conversation is necessary; so they're not introducing you to pretenders, tire-kickers, or "almosts!" Even with a perfect Clarity Conversation, not everybody will "get you" right away, and that's okay. This system includes methods for expressing profound gratitude without looking transactional and recalibrating "bad referrals" in a way that causes partners to give even more referrals in the future versus them shutting down.

(This is easy to do with the right communication. For example, this happened with one of our note-writing vendors. He handled it perfectly, and we had bigger and better referrals waiting for him the following week. It was awesome.)

To act on System Three proactively, you must be willing to install a GIFT·OLOGY-style gratitude system that fits your business, budget, and schedule. This ensures partners accumulate over time, and your relationships snowball to the top of the market.

Think Bud Fox meeting Gordon Gekko...but not illegal (ha!).

Even if you have minimal margin or can't buy gifts because you're in a regulated industry, this system includes something so simple and so powerful that every time I write about it, it consistently delivers the highest click-throughs and open rates.

Yes, friends. I'm talking about the handwritten note.

To illustrate this power, think of the story of Indra Nooyi, former chairman and CEO of PepsiCo. The job kept her pretty busy. I mean, she was making a cool $30 million a year, leading the planet's second-largest food and beverage company, and was named as one of the top ten most powerful women in the world by Fortune and Forbes.

I don't know Indra and have never met her, but she is a GIFT·OL-OGIST for her most important relationships. She once wrote a letter to the parents of all her direct reports and told them what a great job they were doing, completely personalized and handwritten, each with a specific, meaningful anecdote.

Awesome, right? In Indra's own words:

"It opened up emotions of the kind I've never seen."

Parents wrote back to her and poured their hearts out. So much so they even started their own relationship with her. (Aww!) One time a PepsiCo executive VP made an offhanded comment to his mom: "My boss [Indra, the CEO] is really giving me a tough time." The VP's mom replied with something to the tune of, "Nuh-uh! Don't say that! She's my friend! Work harder!"

This is the power of a handwritten note.

If worded correctly (big *if*) the note can be heartfelt. Endearing. And can create a watershed moment for up-and-coming friendships.

Handwritten notes demonstrate effort and thoughtfulness. Nobody's day was ever made from an Amazon gift message, printed on the receipt. But I have some notes I've saved for years.

(Pro tip: Always include a handwritten note with a gift, but you do not need to be giving a gift to write a handwritten note.)

Here are simple rules on how to be better than Hallmark:

1. **Keep it short.** Notes should fit on a postcard. To do this, seek out gifting companies that write notes in-house (like our partners do). Also, notes must be included in the drop-shipped gifts. Otherwise, you'll need to write one yourself.

2. **Keep it lighthearted and fun.** Avoid sounding dramatic or insincere. A gift lands more when people think you're doing it because you want to, not because you have to or you're supposed to. So sound fun!

3. **Tie in the gift.** For example, when gifting a charcuterie board, say something like, "Best wishes in the new year! And never getting 'board' along the way." See? Simple. Playful. Clever. And, most importantly, memorable.

4. **Express gratitude for the relationship.** Not the business. Mentioning business makes the relationship transactional, and transactional relationships are vulnerable to a better offer.

5. **Handwrite it, handwrite it, handwrite it.** Sounds obvious, but too often people print them in some sort of handwritten-looking font to save time. Don't do that. I don't care how messy your handwriting is. Handwrite the notes, or get someone to do it for you. Real pen to paper means so much more.

6. **Get some standout stationery.** I'm confident the words you write will be too clever or thoughtful for anyone to ever think about throwing the card away. But if not, some nice stationery might get them to hang on to it. We have a few personalized stationery

options in our GIFT-LOG (which I'll tell you about in the next section). Or you can get creative with *what* you are writing the note on. Can you get your hands on a vintage postcard from a place they live? Whatever it may be, the card itself matters!

7. **Do *not* include a transactional ask.** The note should spew gratitude and give off the vibe that you are giving and not expecting anything in return. Now I'm not saying don't ever end your card with, "I'd love to chat soon" and sign your phone number, but I am saying don't ever write, "Do you mind taking five minutes to leave us a Google review?" Please, please don't do that.

8. **Write how you talk.** Last but not least, be relational. If appropriate, use humor and witty language to let your personality shine through. And if not, write as though you are speaking to them from a place of real emotion or empathy. For those of you with writer's block, I recommend pretending you're talking to the person out loud and then writing down what you hear yourself say that you like best!

Several of our team members have favorite personal stationeries. I'm a metal business stationery guy myself (who throws away metal stationery?). My team loves No-Attitude Gratitude cards (Google them or search on Amazon). Little things like this matter. The value of these personal touches increases as the relationship deepens, and they can be scaled by using systems that allow for effective information sharing among team members.

Guess what? I never write my own notes. If someone else is writing the handwritten note, still sending it on your own personal stationery brings your personal touch into it. And it's true that even though tasks like writing notes can be delegated, maintaining a personal touch in those communications is crucial.

Including specific information about the recipient that was mentioned in a conversation proves attentiveness, for example, and adds massive value.

It would be fun if relationships could be a full-time job. Unfortunately, they can't. You can't make money on "just be friendly"; you need to utilize leverage.

There are three areas of leverage to consider as your volume of relationships increase and you want to maximize efficiency, staying in your "zone of genius:" teams, technology, and triggers. This looks like delegating tasks to teams that fall outside your core strengths, using technology to automate and track your relationship management efforts, and setting up triggers to ensure timely follow-ups. All three are essential strategies.

This approach allows you to focus on the most impactful activities, while still maintaining a high level of engagement with your relationships. It also helps in maintaining consistency in communication, ensuring no relationship falls through the cracks due to neglect.

TEAM: EVERYONE PLAYS A PART

One of my entrepreneurial gifts is that I'm not a control freak, but many business leaders are. They insist on doing everything themselves, and they miss out on the wonderful aspect of a team.

A team is a luxury once you begin making money. But even if you're not at the level of a team yet, appreciate and recognize the things you do not need to do. There are many. In fact, we have an expression commonly used at our meetings: "JNN" which means "John Not Needed."

(Not quite as inspiring as WWJD. Ha! But being told, even barricaded, not to do things outside your zone-of-genius is quite literally a gift.)

Let me repeat: You *do not need* to write all the handwritten notes. You *do not need* to add all the details into the CRM. You *do not need* to schedule every follow-up meeting. You *do not need* to take all the notes and track all the outcomes. You *do not need* to handle every communication. You *do not need* to manage every social media connection. You *do not need* to research every referral partner's business. You *do not need* to handle logistics for GIFT·OLOGY-style thank-yous. You *do not need* to set up reminders for anniversaries or key dates. You *do not need* to update and maintain contact lists. You *do not need* to draft follow-up emails or send books yourself. You *do not need* to manage referral partner onboarding. You *do not need* to generate or update referral reports. You *do not need* to collect feedback or testimonials from referral partners. You *do not need* to draft content for referral-related communication or newsletters.

My team would not be happy if I did many of these things, partially because of my lack of detail and aversion to some technologies. But also because that's *their* superpower. And if I don't need to be doing all those things, neither do you.

What *do* you need to be doing?

Having Clarity Conversations, which is your number one job. Let the team help with everything else, particularly the things you don't love.

TECH: YOUR IRA (NOT CRM)

The great Brian McRae says: "Every business leader on planet earth needs an IRA." In this case, IRA stands for Inventory of Relational Assets, which is oftentimes called a CRM or a database. CRM can be a dirty word for a lot of organizations, so Brian calls it this to reframe the thinking around it. Why? Because a great IRA is *not* about the software. Brian reframes it so you're thinking about your relationships as a long-term investment, like the traditional meaning of IRA—one that will grow over time and accumulates and compounds into an exquisite season of business.

The IRA is the bank account (in this case a Google spreadsheet) and functions the same way you would make financial deposits. It is a catchall, the place where you put everybody you meet or interact with.

You probably have an IRA right now. Two popular versions:

1. Cloud-based spreadsheets (Google Sheets or Teams). These are limited in features and extremely useful for linear processes.
2. CRM software (usually with a mobile app). These are anywhere from $50 to $500 per month and can get extremely feature rich—oftentimes *too* feature rich. One common criticism is people make software, and the only people who know how to fully use said software are the people who make it.

I've used a multitude of CRMs. And if you're wondering which one is my favorite, I do not have one. Many industries/teams mandate a particular brand, but there's one that's always the best database for business owners. Ready for this? The best database is the ONE. YOU. USE. The one you commit to mastering so you can get the most out of it.

An iPhone (no app, just contacts) is a rudimentary database, but it's more valuable than the software you pay for and never log into. If you don't have an IRA outside of your cell phone, or a social media platform, or business cards stuffed in your desk somewhere, you're not alone. Data says only 40 percent of business leaders actually have and use databases (which makes you scratch your head, but that's beside the point).

THE REFERRAL PARTNER PLAYBOOK (RPP)

There are four types of relationships you'll have in your partnership IRA. It helps to think of this in terms of a grading system, so you can say a grade and everyone will know where an individual is at.

People Who Have Referred You

- A+ = referred more than one in the last twelve months
- A = referred one person in the last twelve months
- System Three these people

People Who Should Refer You

- B+ = someone who has agreed to refer you (but hasn't yet)
- B = could refer you, if they wanted to (must be properly energized)
- System One and Two these people

People Who Could Refer You

- C+ = paying customers (all customers can give referrals but *not* all customers will be partners)
- C = friends and family (people you know, people who know you well)
- Engage and elevate some of these people

People Who You Want to Keep Top of Memory

- D = distribution only (one person to many people)
- Stay in front of these people by putting them on your email list, holiday card list, etc.

The goal of this book isn't to make you some kind of wizard with your IRA. Instead, I hope to give you a process of how you turn Cs, Bs, and As into A+s—and to *keep them* there, year-in and year-out.

That is why you need to have a separate place, outside your IRA, to build a **Referral Partner Playbook** (**RPP**)—a separate list of your As and Bs that communicates:

- Tracking. Have we engaged with this person on the topic of referrals?
- Response. How have we added value to this person?
- Results. What are the next steps in the relationship with this person?

The only way you'll accumulate and snowball partners is if you have a committed "next step" mentality. That's the win of the three systems—there are no questions about what to do next, only a question of whether or not you will do it.

I know what you might be thinking: *Can't I just do this in my CRM?* And the answer is yes...that is, *if* you and/or your team keep the proper CRM hygiene and have the understanding on how to use the various features to "pull" your partner list perfectly. (Candidly, we do not.)

Your goal is to have regular meetings to look at the progress of these relationships. Those meetings might be every other day (if you're just getting started), weekly, or monthly once you get into the groove. More on what this meeting will look like in Chapter 17.

We—and many members of the R.I.C.H. RELATIONSHIP SOCI-ETY—use something separate from our CRM. It's the highest pinnacle of technology to track our most important relationships: a Google spreadsheet. Ha! Let's examine a few reasons why you might choose to have a similar spreadsheet approach:

- Low barrier-to-entry. Learning new software is a frustrating lift and can be exponentially more so with every new team member participating.
- Simplicity. There's no need to pay for extra software seats for horse-power that team members aren't going to use.
- Frugality. Anybody can make an RPP. No financial investment required.

So, when I say it doesn't have to be fancy, I mean it. The only reason pen and paper won't work is because multiple people can't see it—although, for the record, you already know I'm a fan of pen and paper for other things.

RELATIONAL TRIGGERS

A team exists so nothing falls through the cracks. They should help you with surveillance. For instance, does somebody in your organization love social media? They should be scrolling regularly through the feeds of the people in your RPP (or curating a feed that has those people in it).

Your team needs to be ready to answer the question: "What should trigger a DoV in a VIP professional relationship?" In other words, what should trigger an effort on you or your team's part? Let's take a look at a few staples.

Calendar Triggers

- A-B-C-E = Anniversaries, Birthdays, Christmas, Events. Remember, send these ahead of time so you don't get lost in the noise.
- Thinking-of-you or fun "holidays." For this one, think Taco Tuesday. You can find an entire list of ideas at https://nationaldaycalendar.com/.
- Other meaningful milestones. Think about personal moments for your VIPs and/or their inner circle, and see those as opportunities for further connection. For example, is there an event, holiday, or celebration next month where you can send a gift proactively? Is there someone in your network celebrating a milestone soon who deserves celebration?

Life Triggers

- Celebrations.
- Congratulations.
- Condolences. Remember, you want to be there when life happens to your contacts. You don't want to be the person who says, "I'm so sorry! I had no idea!"

Milestone Triggers

- Someone signs. If someone signs a contract or you close a deal, send a celebratory thank-you. Don't forget to thank the person who gave the referral, if that's the case—with no strings attached.
- Someone shows interest in your company. Make a second impression with a savvy follow-up gesture.

A note as you consider triggers: As my friend, the great Brian McRae, says, "every referral gets acknowledged." Now, this doesn't mean you gift for every referral, but if you're not thanking people, even for the nonqualified, you're not going to get any more referrals (more on this in Chapter 13).

Our gifting agency was born out of necessity. *We* didn't want to have to do this ourselves, so we built the systems and the partnerships with vendors, then we made sure those systems and partners were all talking with each other in a way that made this process efficient and repeatable. Eventually, we figured out what to call ourselves, and GIFT·OLOGY was born. I'm telling you this because if you don't want to do the systems and vendor partners lifting, that is why our agency exists. I'm also telling you how to do it on your own in this book, for those of you who do have the time. I'm looking for a way for us all to win.

In Part Three, we'll look at the ways symbiotic winning can happen and give you the tools to make it so. For free. For real.

Let's get after it.

CHOOSE YOUR OWN ADVENTURE

- **Part Three**—Industry Break-In: First partner, first referral, lasting momentum.
- **Part Four**—Industry A-Lister: Turn peers into partners without chasing.
- **Part Five**—Referral Overflow: Givers give more with stronger conviction.
- **Part Six**—Grow Beyond You: Different protocols, different people, all at once.

PART THREE

OUTCOME #1

INDUSTRY BREAK-IN

1. SYSTEM

PROSPECTING PARTNERS
Earn your first partner, first referral.

IDENTIFY | Who to approach
(CH.7)

PACIFY | Harmless starter
(CH.8)

CLARIFY | The BIG 4
(CH.5 & 9)

CHAPTER 7

START WITH WHO

You read my story at the beginning of this book. But allow me to punctuate my career in one sentence.

Who I know has taken me, my family, GIFT·OLOGY, and the Ruhlin Group so much further than *what I know* or *what I've done.*

So if you're just starting out, like I once was, I want you to join me in being supernaturally, undeservedly, abundantly blessed.

If you have no revenue, no money, and are breaking into a new industry with no connections, you're about to learn the fastest method to relevancy: word-of-mouth. It isn't just the best form of advertising; it's also the cheapest. The right relationships with the right partners can invent your business overnight.

BUT THERE'S A CATCH

Let's start with the major **obstacle:** Many leaders limit their search for referral partners to existing customers or familiar industry sectors. This approach is a dead end if you're an introvert (like me) with no customers (like younger me).

It also pits industry professionals against each other as everyone chases the same power players. It's David versus Goliath, and the unknown guy can't compete.

What you want, instead, are unique, high-quality connections that others overlook. That's how you win—not by nagging clients or sucking up to the people everyone else is sucking up to.

The **solution** involves reaching out to people in your network, without being awkward, and having one productive conversation after another. This is how David beats Goliath. With small pebbles.

"BUT I DON'T KNOW THE RIGHT PEOPLE!"

Think again. That excuse didn't work for me as a goat-milking, Ohio farm boy. And I won't let it work for you.

In this chapter, I will show you how to get access to everyone you need. You might be surprised how connected you already are—just as I was when an attorney at a Cutco presentation changed my family's future with a single, providential comment. *Thank you, Paul.*

Remember, your next big break isn't hiding in some fancy marketing strategy or expensive ad campaign. It's in the relationships you already have—or are just one introduction away from making.

By the end of Part Three, you will:

Earn your first partner, first referral, and lasting momentum.

Here's the three-step process for how to get there from where you're at currently:

1. **Identify.** Answer the question: Who do I start with? (Chapter 7)
2. **Pacify.** Reach out and begin a conversation in a harmless way. (Chapter 8)
3. **Clarify.** Talk about yourself in a way that empowers others to talk about you. (Chapter 9)

After doing this successfully one time, you will want to do it again and again.

So commit to the solution and leave this season of business as quickly as possible.

THE RIGHT WHO

You are going to contact people who know who you are (no cold pitching to strangers), whom you have direct access to (it wouldn't be weird to reach out to them), and who have direct contact with your target market (ding!). That is what a referral partner is—someone who regularly interfaces with the people you want to meet. Someone who is already known, liked, and trusted.

Picture a stylist or a barber talking with their client while in their chair. Or a dentist or a chiropractor talking to their client on the table. You're an easy mention in a conversation that is already taking place. You're not an extra to-do item. You're a bullet point, not a burden.

This is why, even though I may not know you, I feel confident in making the following statement:

You have access to everyone you need.

I ask this question frequently: Can you think of a time where *who* you knew was more important than *what* you knew? Another question: Who introduced you to your spouse, your industry, your business partner, your big idea, your coach, mentor, best friend—you get the point?

You didn't earn those introductions. You were gifted them.

As my friend Jesse Itzler points out, "We are all one introduction away from changing the entire trajectory of our lives." You can make those introductions happen.

The right *who* brings forth the right *results*. And *those people* bring along other *whos*.

If you are in this phase of business, you have three potential groups of who's at your disposal.

1. People you know (including clients)
2. AICs (Ambassadors, Influencers, Connectors)
3. Shoulder industries

Let's dive into each one.

GROUP ONE: PEOPLE YOU KNOW

If you have clients or customers, you are ahead of the game, particularly if these individuals have influence. In her book *Creating Superfans*, my friend Brittany Hodak points out why: "These people believe in you so much they gave you money!"[21]

But contrary to what most would say, this is not the only place to start.

Let me tell you a story about a young man named Jeff. He had an idea (sort of a crazy one) and started a business, knowing full well he was competing against big-time industry players. What did he do first? He made a list of three hundred people he had relationships with.

One by one, he reached out to all three hundred to share his idea. Some laughed. Others said, "That's interesting. Call me if you make it." And a few said, "Amazing! How can I get involved?"

Jeff's method was not as buttoned up as yours. You won't need a list of three hundred—more like twenty to thirty. But his business was a little bigger than yours, and he wasn't just asking for introductions. He was asking for dollars—millions and millions of dollars.

By the way? Jeff's last name is Bezos. And talking to three hundred people he knew was how Amazon.com got started. You see, Jeff knew what all smart people know: Traditional marketing has constraints. Bottlenecks. You have to consider things like budgets (ad spend), algorithms (digital technology), and customer skepticism. I could go on. All these have their place, but not at the price of overlooking people we already know who could make incredible referral partners.

Like Jeff, you just have to unlock that part of those relationships.

Starting with people you know means you have easy and fast access (so you can get started quickly, even if this is your *first* day in business),

---

21   Brittany Hodak, *Creating Superfans: How to Turn Your Customers into Lifelong Advocates* (Page Two, 2023).

can open up a conversation in a comfortable way (so you're not asking for favors, begging, or nagging), and get introduced to A+ players you *don't* know.

What if you're nervous to approach people about business? Then you're normal.

Some startup gurus would play the tough football coach here and say something like, "If you don't believe in yourself, or your idea, or your service, then why should anybody else? "

Not me. When I got started, I told people they should engrave kitchen knives and give them out as business gifts. No rational human would believe this is a good idea, let alone a multi-multimillion dollar one. That's why my experience and approach isn't one of bravado; it is of incremental confidence. Like Mike Tyson's trainer, Cus D'Amato, once said, "A boy comes to me with a spark of interest, I feed the spark and it becomes a flame. I feed the flame and it becomes a fire. I feed the fire and it becomes a roaring blaze."

To spark your blaze, you're going to pick five to ten people who you know well. Then, you're going to send them a "harmless starter" (more on that in the next chapter).

Of your discussions with those five to ten people, not every conversation is going to go perfectly, but a couple will. And your spark is going to become a flame.

That flame will blaze you to the next group of people.

GROUP TWO: AICS

AIC stands for Ambassadors, Influencers, and Connectors.

- An **Ambassador** is a trusted authority in their industry or community. People follow their advice, so if they endorse *you*, prospects show up to your door, presold.

- An **Influencer** is a person with an influential personality (not an Instagrammer, sorry). These are humans gifted with effortless persuasion. If they know, like, and trust you, they'll talk-talk-and-talk about you.
- A **Connector** is a person who knows everyone, including the nines and tens. They're instinctive connectors who walk into a room and gravitate to the players.

Energize an AIC, and they'll become your best salesperson. They do *not*—I repeat, they do *not*, need to be your customer, nor do they even need to be in your industry. In fact, if you can energize an AIC, they could become your best salesperson regardless of whether they've been a customer or not.

I've seen entire businesses built from a single AIC, and not in the "unknown authors who go on Oprah and become household names overnight" kind of way. We're talking in real, normal life.

For instance, I have an old colleague who had a fifteen-year career in corporate America. He hated every minute of it, so he left that job and started a subscription-upkeep business where he shows up to your house a couple times a year to clean out appliances, check smoke detector batteries, and do all the annoying things around your house you don't want to do.

Cool, right? There was only one big problem.

This fella had *no* money for marketing and no connections to the neighborhoods he wanted to get into. But he did have an outgoing personality. And he had a *single* connection with a home inspector—a man with an influential personality whom others trusted. Overnight, my colleague had the attention of his target customers. He made sales. And two months later, he was hiring his first employee.

It only took a single AIC—someone he barely knew—and suddenly, he was off to the races.

Who knows what he'd be doing had he not reached out to connect and pour into that relationship.

Don't know anyone? Or don't know anyone you're comfortable contacting?

This is not a cold prospecting method. Cold prospecting, after all, is rarely relational, and I have no tolerance to pep talk you through mountains of rejections.

Start with people you have easy and fast access to, with whom you can open a conversation in a comfortable way, and with whom you will *not* ask for favors or beg/nag. Don't forget: People you know are connected to A+ players you don't know...yet.

You may be thinking some version of: *But John, what if I'm just getting started? It's my first day as a lawyer, a health coach, or a B2B sales rep, etc., and I'm young, from a small town, new to the area, or [insert another excuse here].*

My response? Great! I have an answer for you too. You'll want to focus your energies and efforts on the third group—**shoulder industries.**

The world's worst business advice is this:

"Just meet people! Go to networking meetings! Get your name out there!" One of my team members refers to this as "father-in-law advice," meaning it's good in theory but terrible in practice. There is no "just getting your name out there." It's got to be with the right people.

And Group Three contains *plenty* of the right people.

GROUP THREE: SHOULDER INDUSTRIES

Shoulder industries. The hidden gold.

Shoulders are noncompetitive industries where your ideal customers/clients spend time, money, or both. They know other professionals who don't do what you do and will happily refer business if they know, like, and trust you. These people often get asked, "Do you know anyone who _____?" It makes them look good to have a solid answer and mediocre if they don't.

For example, if I'm a real estate agent, I get asked about loan officers, appraisers, contractors, roofers, painters, moving companies, house cleaners, etc., which is why savvy agents keep a database of shoulders.

More examples: doctors and dentists, kitchen remodelers and bathroom remodelers, electricians and painters. Those are all obvious, but the gold is in the nonobvious. Take wealth advisors and financial planners. What nonobvious shoulders might they have? How about business consultants or life coaches? After all, they're connected to growth-oriented entrepreneurs and high-paying executives (life coaches ain't cheap).

How about commercial real estate agents and/or developers? They're connected to business titans and family offices, all of whom can afford pricey real estate and have a net worth in the seven, eight, and nine figures.

How about freelancers and self-employment tax specialists and advisors? They're connected to hardworking small-business owners, often with multiple incomes who need tax optimization strategies.

More examples: Medicare specialists (wealthy retirees), debt management coaches (high earners with med school debt), international tax advisors (worldwide income earners), currency exchange agents (expatriates with multiple properties). The list is endless. In fact, using artificial intelligence (and some clever prompts), our college intern found over thirty pages of shoulder industries for just twelve professions. Whew!

Imagine having mutually beneficial relationships with even a small handful of those. Don't you think that's a better investment than Facebook ads? (Hint: The answer is yes.)

Majoring in an Industry

The fastest way to become trusted in an industry is to think like them, speak like them, and understand them.

This is another reason why Clarity Conversations beat the daylights out of asking. Because as you're asking questions of your partner, you're learning their language, their needs, and their world.

What you'll find when you sit down with, say, five CPAs to have

Clarity Conversations is many of them have similar problems—so much so that by your fourth or fifth one, you'll probably ask them questions, get their answers, and then pile on to their answers (or finish their sentences) in a way that makes them pop up from their chairs and say, "Yes, exactly!"

Congratulations. You're becoming untouchable.

This is why, despite me being a fan of having as many Clarity Conversations as possible, there's tremendous power in "majoring" in a certain industry. In understanding how their tribe works. And becoming part of their extended family.

How you pick a shoulder industry to major in is exactly how you picked a major in college: What do you have access to? What fascinates you? And what corner of the world do you wish to serve?

I have many friends in many industries, but there's a special place in my heart for authors, speakers, thought leaders, and coaches... mostly because I try to be one myself. And the way this industry works, in particular how you land on stages, is by connecting with well-loved speakers. I would *never* be where I am today without Joey Coleman, Cameron Herold, Phil M. Jones, and a dozen other people. And of course, DoV...I have always done my best to pay it forward.

People think the author/speaker/knowledge economy is unique, but it's not. Let's look at an example of someone who started from nothing in a completely different, highly localized, industry.

STORY TIME: BRIAN MCRAE AND THE POWER OF REFERRAL INDUSTRIES

Before he was "the great Brian McRae" (as I refer to him), he was simply known as Brian.

Brian was thirty-three years young and just starting a new career.

He had been toiling away in advertising: leaving for work at 6:00 a.m. and arriving back home well after 7:00 p.m. It was affecting his marriage and his children, and no amount of success could make the empty pit in his stomach go away.

So, Brian became a loan officer. The ceiling on his income was gone. He was his own boss and was energized with a new sense of freedom and purpose. Great, but now he had a new problem: a new career, no connections, and no marketing skills.

But he *was* willing to make phone calls—so he did. A lot. In many cases, with no success. That is, until one day, Brian reached out to a connection from his previous job. It was Paul, a guy he'd bought advertising from but hadn't spoken to in years. The conversation went like this:

"I've got good news and bad news. The bad news is, I won't be buying any more advertising from you. The good news is, I started a new career as a lender! [awkward pause] Buuuuut, I'm *not* calling you for a refi."

"Haha. What do you need, Brian?"

"Well, I'm looking to build a referral-based business. And I'm hoping to meet CPAs. Is there anybody you co..."

"Yeah yeah! I've got one of those. Let me make an introduction."

And *that* is how Brian met Bob.

"Hi, Bob. I was talking to Paul. He said you're a great CPA, and I'm a new mortgage broker, looking to build a referral-based business of CPAs. And I was hoping to spend a few minutes learning about your business."

Notice Brian's genuine sense of curiosity. He needed to learn about Bob's business. How could he help him? Remember, Brian's focus was what he could give, not what he could get.

Brian and I share the same philosophy—the philosophy we covered in Chapter 4—that you likely share as well: Don't make asks of people unless there's something in it for them.

Bob and Brian grew their relationship, and Bob became Brian's first champion. Within two years of starting his new role, Brian was the top producer in the office. He was named a top one percenter in *Mortgage Executive* magazine. His boss even put him in charge of others, building a team. Then Brian started training them on his method, proving to everybody in his orbit that the method was reproducible. Within several years, it wasn't just Brian winning. It was everybody together.

This is the power of referral partners in shoulder industries.

"HOW DO I IDENTIFY THESE INDUSTRIES?"

Do you know the type of referrals you want your partners to be giving you? It seems like an obvious question. But if you get this wrong, your list will be out of tune.

Many of you might say, "I am a _____. I want to be referred to people looking for a _____." Great! That's fairly obvious. But you may be in a less obvious situation. For instance, maybe you are recruiting a team. Maybe you are looking for a specific position. Maybe you are looking for a demographic. Maybe you are looking for a psychographic.

The question you have to ask is: "Who will be in a position to refer me to those types of people I'm looking for?" Again, obvious for most, but if your answer is "anybody with a heartbeat," you're wrong, my friend. You need to be specific.

There are three ways to identify shoulder industries:

1. **Be observational.** You're not the only person they do business with. Over the course of a week, who else does your customer "touch"?
2. **Talk to smart people.** A mentor or a good thinker, especially those not in your industry, who might have a completely different way of looking at things.
3. **Use technology.** There are many failings of modern-day technology, including generative AI (artificial intelligence). However, my team and I have found this is one place where AI and savvy web searching, Quora asking, or Reddit lurking can do a world of good.

Consider the following questions as you identify these industries and make connections:

1. Who is your ideal customer? (Affluent families, B2B consultants, property owners, etc.)
2. What are other names/terms for your ideal customer? (Once you know, search "synonyms for," "other terms for," etc.]
3. What additional problems do they face? (Search "topic problems," "problems faced by [insert industry]," etc.)
4. What other problems can occur? (Search "problems caused from/ by [your answer to question three]," etc.)
5. Which professions can solve these problems? (Search "who can help me with [insert problem/solution]," etc.)

Of course my goal is to solve your problem as quickly as possible. So you write a positive review for the book, and give a copy to all your referral partners. LOL! As part of our bonuses, a smart person on my team made a "Shoulder Industry Bot." Yes, this is an AI resource you can chat with that will help uncover new opportunities for you.

And the good news is, you already paid for it by reading this far in the book.

NEW PROBLEM: WHAT DO I SAY?

Now you have identified five to ten people who you know well, you have done business with, or are friendly AICs that might be potential partners. You're in the process of sending them a harmless starter (more on that in Chapter 8). You've identified five to ten shoulder industries, both common and uncommon, where referral partners could exist. You've picked one of the shoulder industries to "major in"—that is, to learn, ask questions, and get curious with someone in a Clarity Conversation. Finally, you've identified three to five people who might be able to introduce you to individuals in that industry.

Great work! But now, you have a new problem: You don't know what to say to spark referral conversations in a non-awkward, non-pushy, non-naggy, non-desperate way. You understand Clarity Conversations, but you don't know how to get from a name-on-a-list to a meeting and a hug.

A good portion of the population would rather be broke than awkward. Jumping into referral conversations with old clients or colleagues carries a perceived risk because, if not done well, we often believe it can harm or alienate the relationship by looking self-serving.

Let's solve that.

In the next chapter, we'll explore exactly how to approach these conversations with confidence and authenticity. You'll learn how to craft messages that open doors without burning bridges, and how to turn casual chats into powerful partnerships.

Remember, the goal isn't just to get referrals—it's to build lasting, mutually beneficial relationships that will fuel your business growth for years to come. Take a deep breath, review your list of potential partners, and get ready to take the next step on your journey to building a thriving, referral-based business.

CHAPTER 8

BREAK THE ICE

The right conversation opener is more important than the right offer. My friend Jeffrey Gitomer, author, international sales trainer, and keynote speaker—shared a perfect example in a blog post, which I'll recap here:

After getting off the plane at LaGuardia, Jeffrey had to use the restroom. Standing at the urinal, he glanced to his left and saw actor Hal Linden, who played Barney Miller on TV. Breaking the unwritten rule of men's room silence, Jeffrey quipped, "The great equalizer of men." Linden howled with laughter.

Jeffrey then asked, "Goin' into the city?" Linden replied, "Yep." "Wanna split a cab?" Jeffrey offered.

"Sure," Linden agreed.

They ended up sharing a ride through Queens, chatting about Archie Bunker and Barney Miller. When they reached the city, Linden even paid the cab fare.[22]

Jeffrey's antennas were up. He had the courage to make the

---

22 Jeffrey Gitomer, "Listen Up! Where Is Your Attention?," *Gitomer* (blog), accessed December 17, 2024, https://www.gitomer.com/listen-up-where-is-your-attention/.

exchange, and he won. It wasn't about winning big, but about having fun and practicing the art of connection. Jeffrey never fails to keep his antennas up and capitalize on opportunities when they occur, and neither should you.

JEFFREY'S BIG 4

- What they do: Jeffrey makes salespeople into sales champions.
- Who they serve: Hungry, fun human beings who are committed to mastering the art of selling, closing, and customer relationships.
- What they *don't* do: Digital marketing or industry/platform-specific strategies.
- Who is *not* a fit: People in need of coddling.

YOU CAN WARM UP ANYONE

You can warm up anyone and break the ice and connect on a H2H (human-to-human) level. Going from not talking to somebody to having a great conversation with somebody merely takes the right words; the medium doesn't matter all that much. It can be phone, face-to-face in-person, video call, text message, social media DM... whatever your comfort zone is.

And the right words aren't necessarily the cleverest words, although they can be. Instead, the right words are the ones that start a meaningful conversation. They eliminate any perceived threat by harmlessly inviting somebody into engagement.

In his book titled *The Book of Survival*, Anthony Greenbank writes, "To live through an impossible situation, you don't need to have the reflexes of a Grand Prix driver, the muscles of a Hercules, the mind of an Einstein. You simply need to know what to do."[23]

Or in this case, what to say.

---

23 Anthony Greenbank, *The Book of Survival: The Original Guide to Staying Alive in the City, the Suburbs and the Wild Lands Beyond* (Hatherleigh Press, 2003); and Douglas A. Wick, "Write Yourself a Swimming Pool—Joe Polish, Dean Graziosi—San Antonio ScaleUp Summit," *Strategic Discipline Blog*, Positioning Systems, July 6, 2017, .

This chapter will teach you to get out there, get talking, and most importantly (like our friend Jeffrey) get harmless.

CASE STUDY: SHOULDER BREAKDOWN

Let's break down how Brian McRae, our friend from the last chapter who switched industries and became a lender, initiated the conversation with his contact (Paul) and got introduced to his first champion (Bob).

By the way, at the time of this writing, Brian tells me: "Bob and I remain friends to this day." When your referral partners become your friends, you know you're doing something right.

Brian started his conversation like this, "Hey Bob. It's Brian McRae. How are you?" It might seem obvious, but he led with an earnest question, one that builds rapport. Phone calls and video calls require this level of rapport to be as effective as possible (duh). There are many frameworks on this. Here's one I like—Family, Occupation, Recreation, Dreams (FORD), for those of us who don't do this naturally:

- "How is your family doing these days? How are your parents/siblings/mutual relationship doing?"
- "Are you still working at [LAST KNOWN JOB]? Any big changes in your career?"
- "How's work going? What's the current environment like?"
- "Are you still into [PREVIOUSLY KNOWN HOBBY]? Any new hobbies or interests?"
- "Have you been able to travel anywhere interesting lately?"
- "Are you still thinking about [OLD DREAM or GOAL]? How's that coming along?"
- "What are some new things/goals you're pursuing?"
- "What are you excited about right now?"

If you haven't talked to an individual for multiple years and you're contacting them for the first time, my biggest tip is this: Think about the conversation ahead of time versus winging it. Don't put the pressure on yourself to think on the spot. Be a professional athlete and visualize the next play or the next pitch before it starts.

STEP ONE: HARMLESS STARTER

Remember, you don't want to be the annoying person on LinkedIn who starts the conversation with: "Hey, that's so cool you're connected to Cameron Herold. Do you think you can introduce me so I can get on his podcast?"

If you begin a long-lost conversation with an ask, you failed. Instead, begin with a harmless starter.

A harmless starter is a memory, an observation, or a gratitude statement. Here's what a good harmless starter can look like in each category:

- Memory: "I was thinking about..." (I was driving by the mall, and I was thinking about the lunch we had at the Mediterranean takeout place and the twenty-five minutes we stood in line!)
- Observation: "I saw that/heard that..." (I saw on Instagram that your kiddo won an award for leadership on the swim team. I guess the apple doesn't fall far from the tree. Nice job, man!)
- Gratitude: "I appreciate so much that..." (I just got off a Zoom call where everybody was talking about the weather. I appreciate so much that when we talk, you always make me feel cared for and listened to. It truly is your superpower.)

There should be emotional power in the harmless starter, like getting a postcard in the mail from someone. Like someone is saying, "I was on vacation, and I thought of *you*."

If you're feeling stuck, try these **Top 10 Harmless Starters**:

1. "I was just thinking about our last conversation and..."
2. "I saw this article and immediately thought of you because..."

3. "Remember that time when we..."
4. "I'm curious, what's your take on..."
5. "I was driving by [place] the other day and it reminded me of..."
6. "I heard/read something interesting recently and I'd love your opinion..."
7. "I've been meaning to reach out and say thank you for..."
8. "How's that [project/goal] you mentioned last time we spoke coming along?"
9. "I came across this [book/podcast/video] that aligns with your interests in..."
10. "I was reflecting on our industry and wondered if you've noticed..."

Remember, the key is to be genuine, show interest, and open the door for a meaningful conversation without any pressure or hidden agenda.

STEP TWO: CASUAL QUESTIONS

For the purpose of harmlessness, it's better to be interested than interesting.

After your starter (in the same text or after a response, whatever feels better) you're going to ask a casual question. Again, this is *not* an ask. It's a lighthearted invitation to engage in conversation.

Examples:

- "How have you been?" or "How are things?" or "What's new?"
- "How's business/work treating you?"
- "How's the family?" or "Been on any adventures recently?"
- "What's one project, thing, etc. you're most excited about right now?"
- "What are you working on? How can I help?" (Tell me more.)

Or my personal favorite I've used for years, again, is, "What am I interrupting?"

Or if it makes sense, tie it into your harmless starter.

"I was driving through Georgia on my way back to see my folks. Thinking about you, man, as I pass your exit. You guys still in the same house? Still loving it here? Or can I convince you to move across the country to be my neighbor?"

You don't need to be clever. You need to be human.

STEP THREE: DOV CONVERSATION

Not every one of these conversations will require you to help or share or introduce somebody. That said, being that a giver always looks to lead with value, if the opportunity presents itself, then take it!

If the conversation moves in the direction of talking about a problem, an obstacle, or even a simple to-do item ("What are you interrupting? I was just searching Italian restaurants for an upcoming date night."), take the opportunity to add value.

Remember, surveillance and solutions. It's what smart people do. The three I use the most in this stage are:

- A share: a book, a piece of content, or a favorite restaurant.
- An introduction: to somebody I know who can help.
- A donation: doesn't have to be a lot of money. At all. Still, if somebody tells me they're working on something philanthropically, I don't tell them, "I'll think about donating." I tell them, "I just donated."

Want an advanced DoV tip? Do the work for them. When sharing something valuable, point out specifically what *was* valuable. Don't just send them a podcast; tell them the minute mark of what was most impactful. Point them to the right chapter of the book. Screenshot and arrow-point the quote in the article. Creating awareness is good, but doing the work for them is ten times more helpful.

Want another advanced DoV tip? (Of course you do, because you're still here reading.) If I'm saying, "How can I refer you business?" I might add, "Who are your ideal customers who you can help the most?"

Now, I won't use this for everybody...only for people with established businesses I know will have a perfect answer to this question.

STEP FOUR: TRANSITION TO BUSINESS

The last part of this formula is the transition to business. This step determines whether it's just a pleasant conversation or an actionable moment.

Most people talk to past clients or old relationships and end conversations with some version of, "If you need anything, reach out!" You've done it, I've done it, we've all done it. Sure, that's polite and takes the pressure off them, but it's *far* too open ended. If they respond with some version of, "Thanks, will do," you're left wondering: *Where do we go from here?*

If you ever ended a date with, "If you want to get dinner again, let me know," guess what? They might never let you know anything. Some people want to be pursued, and the rest of us need to be told what to do. Operationalizing this type of outreach means you might be having a dozen conversations at once, and each convo will happen at its own timing. That's the faith piece of this.

Match their cadence. They might not get back to you right away, and that's okay. I will often text people, in particular if I'm appreciating them or thanking them or gushing over them, with a, "No need to reply, but I wanted you to know I was thinking of you." And wouldn't you know, they always reply. No, it's not a tactic. It's me respecting busy people's time and caring more about being harmless than about getting what I want. That's *more* of the faith part of this.

In every good conversation with a giver, the same thing happens. You'll be given an opening:

- "What about *you*? How can I help *you*?"
- "Thanks for the book recommendation. I'll definitely check it out. What about you, man? What are you working on right now?"
- "Is there anything I can do for *you* right now?"

The answer to this question is *yes*. Do not waste this opportunity. Do not sit there with your foot in your mouth.

Before you start the conversation, know what you need, and ask accordingly if (or when) you're given an opening.

ASK ONE: ASKING FOR SHOULDERS

Look at Brian's verbiage:

"I'm looking to build a referral-based business. And I'm hoping to meet [SHOULDER INDUSTRY]. How would you feel about making an introduction or two on my behalf?"

The key phrase: "referral-based business." Use it often.

ASK TWO: "CAN YOU INTRODUCE ME TO [PERSON]?"

Sometimes we are in a small industry with a finite group of players. Legacy industries, B2B enterprise environments, or any number of situations where a particular partner speaking on our behalf could change our world.

Cameron Herold was this person for me. Even if I ruined Brooks Brothers for him.

If you're looking for a particular referral partner with which to dance, do *not* approach them cold. Get an introduction. Tell your connection, "Thanks for asking. I'm trying to build a referral-based business. Do you have a connection to [PERSON]? Can you introduce me?"

If you don't know anybody who knows the person you want to meet, then keep snowballing up. You're, at most, six degrees away from anybody on the planet.

You may be wondering, *Do I have to be that specific?*

If there's somebody you're trying to meet, yes. Do not rely on their imagination to guess exactly what you need. Even if they know you're trying to meet the person. There is a percentage of people in this world who will never do what you wish them to do unless you ask. So ask.

ASK THREE: INVITE THEM TO A CLARITY CONVERSATION

No surprise here: The Clarity Conversation is the crown jewel of cementing referral partnerships.

Here are some guidelines on successfully inviting people to Clarity Conversations. Note that some of this is review from Chapter 5, but it's important we get this down pat:

- Make it a separate conversation whenever possible. There's relational value in seeing people multiple times in multiple environments versus trying to cram everything into one conversation. It gives the brain time to breathe. This creates memory.
- Get as close to in-person as you can. The relationship is escalating, the environment should be escalating along with it. I know technology is awesome, but you want to get away from electronic friends. That means if you started over a text message, your next step would be a phone call, coffee, lunch, or Zoom call, scheduling a time to visit them at their office. Whatever makes sense.
- Honor the context of the relationship. If you've barely spent five minutes with them, asking them to lunch might be weird.
- Be succinct. It shouldn't take an hour to connect, understand each other, and deliver your Big 4 in a Clarity Conversation. This is why your invite to a Clarity Conversation doesn't have to be big or grandiose. Try, "I'd love to get your thoughts (or counsel) on what I'm trying to do. Can we grab ten to fifteen minutes live?"

When it comes to framing our asks, an attractive piece of the RPT System is there's no blatant asking for referrals. However, if you're breaking into an industry, have no connections, and no capital to waste, you *do* need to ask for shoulder partners.

Remember, "Just get your name out there" is father-in-law advice. You're not asking for business; you're asking for partners. You miss 100 percent of the shots you don't take. And while my business is testimony to "give gifts, build relationships, and blessings will happen..."?

There's a time and place for: "Ask and keep on asking and it will be given to you" (Matthew 7:7).

Ask. Seek. Knock.

CHAPTER 9

PROSPECTING PARTNERS

Sara Hardwick—community relationship strategist and host of the R.I.C.H. RELATIONSHIP SOCIETY—knows very well the importance of specific endorsements in business relationships. Through her connections with Genius Network, she was introduced to Ellen Long, who became a pivotal figure in our referral chain. The two hopped on Zoom and hit it off immediately.

While both investigated the needs of the other, it became obvious Sara was looking for a part-time assistant. "Somebody I can pour into, with a servant heart, an interest in business, and preferably local so we can do coffee dates!" Note: Did you catch the level of clarity?

Ellen introduced Sara to Anna, a member of her college Bible-study network. And wouldn't you know it, Anna just happened to live in the same county as Sara.

The two met for coffee. And Anna was a hit and a half. Before Sara could even pay the bill, Anna presented another introduction—Alexis—who was "the only person she would trust to let her dog out in her own home."

The details Anna provided made Sara's first meeting with Alexis smooth as butter. After all, Alexis showed up presold based on the word-of-mouth from Sara's referral chain.

Alexis, or Lexi as we all know her, was hired quickly. And she has been a butt-kicking contributor since her first week at GIFT·OLOGY.

Whether you're hunting for clients or recruiting for excellence?

The system works when you work the system.

SARA'S BIG 4

- What they do: Sara teaches professionals to systematically stay top of mind, earn word-of-mouth, and transform relationships into referral partnerships.
- Who they serve: Service professionals, small-business owners, and sales leaders earning less than $10 million in revenue.
- What they *don't* do: Transactional reward programs.
- Who is *not* a fit: "Takers"—with a "what can you do for me?" mindset.

FISHERMEN, NOT FISH

The first system every referral-based business must have is the system of prospecting partners. (Again, *partners*. We're chasing fishermen here, not fish). This system will help you control your own destiny— to converse in a way that creates the referrals you want to have, not merely wait and hope they'll be coming in. It does this by taking people who have never referred you (or barely referred you) and getting them into a Clarity Conversation.

But how? We're getting to that.

So far, you've learned: to start with who and that you have access to everyone you need to break the ice and to get out there, get talking, and get harmless. Before we pull it all together and systemize, let's examine the Four Pillars of Breaking into an Industry—regardless of whether or not you just opened up or have been dominating a different vertical for decades. Follow this advice, and you will earn your first partner, first referral, and lasting momentum.

Before we unpack the pillars, make sure to avoid these two big "mental hygiene" mistakes in the Prospecting Partners phase:

- **Mistake #1: Prejudging people.** It's so easy to assume some of the people we know are going to be lackluster referral partners, so we don't approach them. It's even easier to assume some of the people who know us and love us best are going to be home-run partners. Both of those things might be true, or they might not be true. When I started selling Cutco decades ago, I quickly learned the truth: that a prophet is not respected in his own hometown. People take for granted that which is familiar to them. So do you, so do I. Don't prejudge; some will work out, and some won't. If you find yourself in the latter camp now and then, don't sweat it. Just send the next harmless starter.
- **Mistake #2: Being a generalist.** More on this in a second, but it's worth pointing out here. And look, I know it feels counterintuitive to say if you decrease the number of people you serve, you will actually increase your success. But if it isn't the truth!

And now, let's get to those pillars.

PILLAR #1: TREAT CONVERSATIONS LIKE A JOB

You wouldn't lose weight or gain muscle if you only worked out and ate well twice per month, would you? If you want real results, you have to practice with real consistency. For our purposes, that means your conversations are a job, not a hobby. If you treat them like a hobby, they'll cost you money like a hobby. If you treat them like a job, you'll get paid like a job. But if you treat them like a profession, you'll get paid like a professional.

In every business, there are leading metrics and lagging metrics. Leading means something you control, and lagging means an outcome you don't control. In the business of referral partnerships, conversations are leading metrics.

Here's how to get this right:

- Believe that conversations will lead to success.

- Have a daily outreach standard, when you win the day or lose the day. This could be time based (i.e., sixty minutes every other day) or counting outreaches with a deadline (i.e., ten before 10:00 a.m.).
- Remember, it's okay to start small if you're starting a side gig. Even one conversation per day, consistently, can make a big difference.
- Track the days you hit your standard, approaching it like you would your workout or health regimen. Your job is not to miss a day.
- Leverage technology to help you. Apps, for example, can track anything. This is no different.

And finally, be relentless—like the great Brian McRae. Brian, a successful loan officer, once shared with me his philosophy on making calls: "I'll call anyone," he said. "When I first started, I made a commitment to myself. Every day, I'd make at least twenty calls before noon. It didn't matter if I knew the person well or if they were just a name on a list. I'd call."

Brian explained that he treated these calls as his leading metric. "The number of calls I made was entirely in my control. Sure, not every call led to a connection, and not every connection led to business. But I knew if I consistently hit my call targets, the results would follow."

He went on to describe how this approach shaped his success. "Over time, I noticed a pattern. For every one hundred calls I made, I'd typically get about ten good conversations. Out of those ten, maybe two or three would turn into solid leads. And from there, I'd usually close at least one deal."

Brian's story illustrates the power of focusing on leading metrics—the actions you can control—rather than obsessing over lagging metrics like closed deals. By treating conversations as his job and committing to a daily standard, he built a thriving business based on relationships and referrals.

PILLAR #2: BE A SPECIALIST

When business leaders are just entering an industry, they typically make the same mistake: They start out as generalists. They are, therefore, unremarkable. And, in being unremarkable, they are not pursued, referred, or taken seriously in the marketplace.

As much as we all want to admit it, most of what we do is a commodity. That means there are two options: quit or become a specialist.

Specialists get paid more than generalists because they get way more referrals than generalists. Why? Because specialists are far easier to talk about. For example, don't call yourself a plumber. Call yourself a plumber who specializes in industrial and commercial systems, backflow systems (to avoid contamination), water heater systems (including tankless models), and leak detection and repair. See how that feels better?

One of the biggest mistakes you can make in a Clarity Conversation—or in any referral relationship—is to be an "also-ran," a.k.a. "just another option." Nobody refers to the "everybody elses" and the "also-rans."

If your referral partner can't articulate what makes you unique, you're in danger of blending in with everyone else. And in business, blending in is the first step to being overlooked.

To be a referral magnet, it helps to be "extra."

PILLAR #3: ALWAYS BE ADDING

Every deposit into your IRA—your Inventory of Relational Assets (see Chapter 6)—is money. Building your list should be your new atomic habit. From this day forward, you want to make it a weekly habit to increase the number of people in your playbook. That means *next week*, if you haven't gone through all your social media, block off thirty minutes and do that. That means the following week, if you haven't gone through your stack of business cards, block off thirty minutes and do that.

As you meet new people—at your son's little league game, your daughter's cheer competition—remember there are nines and tens everywhere. They walk among us, like ordinary people. Add them.

Why is this important (besides just being a good strategy for connection)? Because adding people breaks your dependency on any one relationship. Even though we don't want relationships to change, things happen. People leave the business. They move. They retire. They pass away.

If you were doing traditional marketing, you wouldn't want to rely entirely on Google traffic or Instagram traffic because as soon as an algorithm changes—which you have no control over—suddenly you don't have anybody visiting your website, which means suddenly you don't have a business. I tell people this all the time: traditional marketing in this day and age is one big pile of building a house on somebody else's property.

But your Relationship Snowball? That plan is growing your equity, not throwing money away on rent. It creates incredible opportunities and sets you up to make really cool choices years down the road—choices that other people on the hamster wheel never get to make. Choices like the year-long waiting list, the ten-times price increase, the new verticals to explore, the hyper-selectivity—they all come about because of the WHOs.

PILLAR #4: MASTER YOUR SHOULDERS

Do you remember in Chapter 7 when we learned about shoulder industries? Those noncompetitive industries where your ideal customers/clients spend time, money, or both? Think doctors and dentists. Painters and electricians. The list goes on for miles.

Identifying relevant shoulders is one thing, but speaking their language is another. How do you get the vocabulary down, quickly? How do you learn the pain points of your shoulders so you can DoV?

Read books they read.

Listen to podcasts they listen to.

Read the reviews of the books they read. Or read their Google reviews.

While driving, get into an out-loud conversation with AI. Ask it to teach you all the nuanced terms and have it grade you on the basis of how you speak—I'm serious! (Go to **RPTsystem.com** for more ideas and tools like this.)

You have to do whatever it takes.

If you don't speak the language, you're an outsider. And people won't trust you.

THE ONE THING

In this stage of business, as you execute the Prospecting Partners System, what's the *one thing* you cannot lose sight of? Here it is. The *one thing* that will mask your deficiencies and catapult you to the next stage: **the Big 4**. Nothing matters more than clarity. So you'd better know these like the back of your hand:

1. What we do.
2. Who we serve.
3. What we *don't* do.
4. Who is *not* a fit.

When you do? You'll see the light bulb go off. You'll get a text message, an email, a phone call, or whatever you requested. The person will name-drop the partner you just mentioned.

You'll hang up the phone. Write a handwritten note (more on that in Chapter 13). The first time, it might feel a little sloppy. You might not feel very confident. But when you master this system, you can start nearly any business, break into any industry, create your first partnership, and earn your first referral—one who shows up prepped, presold, and predisposed to listen.

After that, you'll want to do it again and again.

Are you ready to move on to the next stage? I bet you are!

BUT FIRST ANSWER THESE QUESTIONS

- Do you have a separate playbook where you collect names?
- Do you understand the concept of shoulder industries?
- Have you identified some harmless starters, questions, and transitions you'll be comfortable using?
- Have you thought about a unique or preferred way you could add value to others?
- Do you have time in your schedule where you'll show up and work on relationships?
- Have you "clarified your extra" and figured out your specialization?
- Have you asked for feedback, practiced, and rehearsed your Big 4?

ACTION ITEMS, STEP-BY-STEP

This isn't about perfection. It's about progress. Remember that as you:

1. Identify 5–10 people who you know well, have done business with, or are friendly AICs who might be potential partners. Send them a harmless starter.
2. Identify 5–10 shoulder industries, both common and uncommon, where referral partners could exist.
3. Pick one of the shoulder industries to "major in"—that is, to learn, ask questions, and to get curious with someone in a Clarity Conversation.
4. Identify 3–5 people who might be able to introduce you to individuals in that industry. Send them a harmless starter.
5. Schedule your first Clarity Conversation.
6. Tell us about it at: **CelebrateMyWins.com**—and we might share your Big 4 with others.

PART FOUR

OUTCOME #2

INDUSTRY A-LISTER

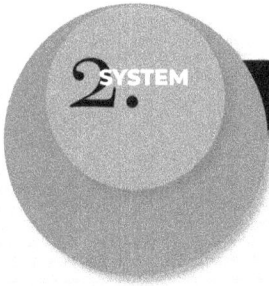

2. SYSTEM

CLEARING RUNWAY
Turn peers into partners, no chasing.

SIMPLIFY | Can, willing, want
(CH.10)

QUALIFY | Greenlight question
(CH.11)

SOLIDIFY | 24-hour FUN
(CH.12, PILLAR 3)

CHAPTER 10

PRIORITIZE YOUR PLAYBOOK

My friend Phil M. Jones made a point once: "John gets himself into rooms he has no business being in because he doesn't wait for an invitation to the table. He sets his own table, and then gets the right people to show up."

Two things: It's not a coincidence that a guy who literally wrote a book called *Exactly What to Say* said it best here, and he's spot on. I'm not all that special. It's all about the power of prioritizing your playbook. The truth is most leaders don't have a clear process to identify the ballers. They rely on advice like, "just ask, follow up, and keep following up," which leads to awkward interactions and desperation with people who might not be all that helpful to begin with. This doesn't build a leader's brand; it sinks it.

Your big break exists, if you have the courage to simplify and qualify. In every industry, there is a group of takers in sheep's clothing. People who, no matter how much you would do for them, won't help you get ahead.

Strong partnerships aren't born from constant nagging. You need a systematic approach to prioritize, qualify, and energize connections. That's how you turn industry contacts into long-term, high-value partners so the best in their circle becomes part of yours! Picking the best relationships in which to invest first is how you turn peers into partners. And fast.

Unfortunately, leaders in this stage often feel stuck, causing them to chase referrals, rather than capturing partners. Two major thoughts that prevent leaders from investing in relationships are: "I have too many to invest in all of them!" and "What if I go all-in on the wrong ones?"

If this is you and you don't solve this dilemma, you'll find yourself in a comfortable plateau. Now, there are worse things than plateaus, surely. But when was the last time you were delightfully surprised by your results in business?

Commit to relationships over marketing, and watch what happens.

By the end of Part Four, you will have learned how to *turn peers into partners without chasing, wasting, or waiting* by following this three-step process:

1. **Simplify.** Answer the question: Which contacts are the best fit? (Chapter 10)
2. **Qualify.** Assess whether they have the ability to support you. (Chapter 11)
3. **Solidify.** Prove you deserve to be taken seriously with a powerful follow-up. (Chapter 12)

After having the right conversation with the right partner, you'll witness firsthand a whole new way to "play the game."

YOUR GAME PLAN: SIMPLIFY. QUALIFY. SOLIDIFY.

In this chapter, we're going to focus on the first step: simplify. We'll explore how to prioritize your potential partners and determine who's worth investing your time and energy into. Remember, not all connections are created equal, and it's crucial to focus on those with the highest potential for mutual benefit.

TREAT DIFFERENT PEOPLE DIFFERENTLY

A great relationship plan treats different people differently. **As I've said before, everybody is equal, but not everyone is equally important for the growth and long-term health of the organization.** So, differentiate, discriminate, and validate (your champions).

Giving special people special treatment isn't rude; it's smart business. Why? Because it's essential for all involved that these key players continue to contribute. Think about that the next time you're worried about "being unfair."

Most leaders have no problem categorizing their prospects using assumptive qualifiers and exotic lead-scoring systems, but once they capture the customer, it becomes "one-size-fits-most" (or all). They use the same communication, same rules, and same rewards. A better approach creates a system that instead favors individuals on two criteria:

1. Exceptional past performance, often an indicator of future performance.
2. High-ceiling potential—not based on gut but based on verbal commitment.

Take the McRae Mortgage Team in St. Louis. Each individual categorizes referral partners on a simple grading system: A/A+ for champions who have referred customer(s) in the past year, B/B+ for potential champions who could refer and have expressed willingness to do so, and so on. We've seen similar systems with our employee-gifting clients. There are people who get the job done and who deserve appreciation. And there are also those who grow the business and who deserve adulation. Which is why they show up, year after year, for their top talent—and why they, like McRae Mortgage, continue to grow.

WHAT MAKES A GOOD INDUSTRY CONTACT?

We learned in Chapter 7 about the power of shoulder industries. Remember, shoulders are noncompetitive industries where your ideal customers/clients spend time, money, or both—a.k.a. other professionals who don't do what you do and will happily refer business if they know, like, and trust you. They often get asked, "Do you know anyone who _____?" It makes them look good to have a solid answer... and mediocre if they don't.

As we think of putting our understanding of shoulder industries to good use, it's time to look at what makes a good industry contact. On the surface, if they touch your target market, they're a potential contact. Sometimes they do a different job for the same group of people. Sometimes people come to them, and they're not a perfect fit, so they refer out. And sometimes, like we'll read about at the end of the chapter, it's a totally random off-the-wall connection—one that gives you an ultimate competitive advantage. No-brainer for you. It also helps to have their contact information, which should be in your CRM or spreadsheet document. (We call ours a Referral Partner Playbook. Go back to Chapter 6 if you missed that.)

CAN-WILLING-WANT

Hopefully you're already thinking of five to ten-plus people who fit that criteria. But that's just the start. Why? Because just because somebody looks good on paper doesn't mean they'll be a great referral partner for you. To be a potential partner, they have to pass the **Can–Willing–Want** test:

- **Can** they? Do they actually have influence? Do people trust them?
- Are they **Willing**? Do they know, like, and trust you enough to refer you?
- Do they **Want** to? Have you proven yourself by demonstrating value enough to become a go-to resource?

These aren't just ideas. I'm going to teach you how to put this tool into action. Over the course of the next few chapters, expect to learn to:

- Identify ten to twenty of your best industry contacts and add them to your Referral Partner Playbook.
- Score these individuals on these three dimensions to find the best eight to twelve to start with.
- Engage these people in conversations (see Chapter 8 if you're feeling awkward about starting the conversation) and then use the Greenlight Question to qualify them.
- Invite those who "pass" into a Clarity Conversation, where you will communicate your niche in the industry with precision and simplicity.
- Solidify the relationship (and your ask) by proving you are to be taken extremely seriously with a powerful follow-up.

Let's begin.

DIMENSION #1: CAN

The first part of **Can–Willing–Want** is, of course, **Can** they, quite literally, lean on their influence to refer you? Do they have a network of your target customers? Do people trust them? When evaluating the **Can**, take care to consider their relative size compared to your business. It's good to be within a rung or two. Leaders at a similar size and status as yourself can grow with you and offer similar value. Versus the asymmetrical dependence of someone much larger or much smaller than you.

DIMENSION #2: WILLING

When we think about whether or not the potential partner is **Willing** to refer you, it's all about probability. Do they know you and can they speak about you from experience? Are they familiar with your industry, do they know what "great" looks like, and can they attest that you're an exceptional resource? The Greenlight Question, revealed in the next chapter, will answer this question with authority.

DIMENSION #3: WANT

Having people who **Want** to refer you comes back to having proven yourself as a go-to resource. One predictor of this would be their past behavior. Have they referred you previously? How long ago? Have they expressed enthusiasm about you, your business, your offering, or helping take you to the next level?

It's easy for people to *say* they want to do something but *actually* doing it is something else altogether. This is why we have the referral runway, which we mentioned in Chapter 5 and will detail again later. The variables at play here in the **Want** stage are pretty cut and dry: If they *could* refer you, they get an average preference. If they *have* referred you, they should move to the top of your list.

(They should also be invited into a Clarity Conversation—*especially* if their referrals were organic, out of the blue, or by accident. Clarity Conversations aren't just about equipping partners to talk about you. They're about relationship acceleration, surveillance of mutual value, and anchoring their memory.)

When you finish assessing your network, you'll likely encounter ambiguity, which is just fine. Our goal in going through this framework is to compare relationships *relative to one another*. You want to figure out who to approach first to get your snowball rolling as quickly as possible.

R.I.C.H. RESOURCE #6

Valuable shoulder industries are waiting to be uncovered, and AI can help you find them. Don't delay on this! Explore our favorite AI tools at **RPTsystem.com**.

STORY TIME: TWO TEENAGERS START A BUSINESS

Consider this: Two college students, nineteen and twenty-one, are both hardworking and entrepreneurial young people who spend their summers sealing concrete—we're talking driveways, patios, and walkways. Their ideal clients? Older homeowners who can't do the heavy labor themselves but need the work done right away. These homeowners are more than willing to pay $800–$1,200 to get the job done quickly and professionally, with no effort on their part.

How could these college students find more clients like that? Go door-to-door? Maybe. Wait for word of their expertise to spread? Sure, but that won't fill up their schedule tomorrow. Instead, they decide to get help from someone who works the front desk at the local athletic club. Why? This front-desk worker handles the early morning shift and knows all the elderly regulars—especially the ones who come in for the 6:30 a.m. water aerobics and stretching classes. When the front-desk worker feeds the students names and numbers, everyone benefits: Problems are solved, clients are happy, and business grows.

Did you catch the shoulder industry? These college students running a concrete-sealing business have a referral partner at the local gym. At first glance, you might think those two businesses seem completely unrelated, but you'd be wrong—very wrong. If two college students can pull this off, there's no excuse for anyone else—except for being too lazy or too afraid to ask.

Look beyond the obvious. Shoulder industries are everywhere.

WHAT'S NEXT?

Now, you have done the following:

1. Identified 10–20 of your best industry contacts and added them to your Referral Partner Playbook.
2. Prioritized them on the dimension of **Can–Willing–Want** to determine the best 8–12 to approach first.

3. Explored potential nonindustry contacts, including hidden gold and random pockets of incredibly influential people.

Great work! But now you have a new problem: You're staring at a bunch of names of people you *think* can help build your business, but you have no idea exactly how they feel about you. More specifically, are they qualified to advocate for you? Or, if they've referred you in the past, was it a referral-by-accident or the beginning of referrals-by-design?

You don't want to ask in an awkward, uncomfortable way. If the goal is to raise your status in the industry, asking the way most people ask isn't going to help.

Fortunately, there is an easy solution.

CHAPTER 11

QUALIFY PARTNERS

Once, when Brian McRae hosted a business networking event, he encountered an incredibly polished and successful real estate agent. Their initial conversation at the event led to a follow-up phone call because this individual expressed interest in getting to know Brian's organization better. This evolved into another phone call and eventually a series of one-on-one meetings.

After several interactions, Brian and his prospect arranged a lunch meeting at one of the area's most upscale restaurants. The gathering included four people: Brian, another member of his team, the real estate professional, and a member of her team. The real estate professional was clearly doing very well, and everything seemed promising.

Finally, during lunch, Brian asked the Greenlight Question (we'll get there, don't worry). The response, though? It was unexpected: "Well, my daughter is in your line of business, and we usually refer her."

In that moment, Brian said he had a realization:

Despite this person being a great individual with seemingly aligned core values, we would at best be a backup position for referrals due to their family connection. The cost of this delayed qualification was significant.

Between phone calls, one-to-one meetings, events, and various conversations, I had invested approximately three hours of time. Add to that the expense of lunch at one of the nicest restaurants in the area, plus the preparation of presentation materials. While I still respect this agent immensely and maintain communication with her, I could have taken a different approach had I known this crucial information earlier. I find it particularly ironic that I actually teach the Greenlight Question concept, yet I failed to follow my own system. Live and learn, then live and learn some more.

See? Brian is still learning. I'm still learning. You are, too, if you're being honest. You're reading this book so we can learn together.

Let's get to more of that and unpack the Greenlight Question.

BRIAN'S BIG 4

- What they do: Brian is a coach who helps relational leaders build, grow, and scale their businesses through offline conversations.
- Who they serve: Small-business owners, commissioned sales professionals, and entrepreneurs.
- What they *don't* do: Brian doesn't do any paid lead advertising, SEO, or anything involving cold traffic.
- Who is *not* a fit: Individuals who obsess over digital marketing methods.

WORK SMARTER, NOT HARDER

I want to tell you about a situation that happens all too often in the business world: There was this up-and-coming entrepreneur, let's call him Alex. Alex had identified a high-profile industry leader—one of our team members, Carissa—who he thought would be the perfect referral partner for his business. Carissa had a vast network, an impeccable reputation, and seemed to align perfectly with Alex's target market.

Excited by the potential, Alex went all out. He sent thoughtful gifts, kept in regular communication, and even offered his services at a discounted rate to get on her radar. For months, Alex invested time, money, and energy into cultivating this relationship, convinced Carissa would become his golden ticket to success.

But here's the kicker: Despite all of Alex's efforts, Carissa never referred a single client his way. It wasn't that she didn't like Alex or his work. The truth was much simpler, yet far more frustrating. She already had a long-standing relationship with someone in Alex's field, a close contact she had known for years.

If only Alex had asked one simple question at the beginning, he could have saved himself months of effort and disappointment. He could have redirected his energy toward partners who were actually in a position to refer business his way.

The lesson here is clear: Don't chase partners who are off-limits. It's crucial to qualify potential partners by making sure you're the preferred person to whom they'd recommend business. Finding this out takes only one question: the Greenlight Question. It's a simple "yes, yes" question, where all possible answers are positive, even if the prospect is unqualified.

If a "perfect person" can't or won't refer you business, that's a good thing because it means you won't waste time, energy, money, or emotional capital trying to make them be someone they can't be. This knowledge frees up your resources for the people who *can* actually become valuable referral partners. Remember, nothing we're doing here is about collecting as many contacts as possible. Instead, it's about cultivating the right relationships that can truly help your business grow.

This chapter will teach you how to eliminate wasted time and resources with one simple question. And by doing so, you can earn industry status without chasing or waiting...and waiting...and waiting. It's about working smarter, not harder, in building your network of referral partners.

QUESTIONS EQUAL POWER

The right discovery questions are insanely powerful. This is true in any type of sales, and it's especially true when it comes to referral partner relationships. Better questions help determine if a potential partner is, as the old saying goes, a prospect or a suspect. They lead to more meaningful conversations and, ultimately, more fruitful partnerships.

Unfortunately, most business leaders are saturated by "empty calorie" questions:

"Nice to meet you. What do you do? Who do you represent?" "What brings you here today?" "Ever attend one of these before?" "How are you?" "How've you been?" "How's business?"

These questions, while polite, rarely lead to actionable insights or deeper connections. They're the small talk of the business world: pleasant, but not particularly nutritious. Better questions, on the other hand, demand specificity—and specificity is actionable. It gives you real information to work with and helps you understand whether this person is truly a good fit as a referral partner.

For example, instead of asking, "How's business?" you might ask, "What's the biggest challenge you're facing in your industry right now?" This gives you insight into their world and might reveal ways you can add value. Instead of "What do you do?" you could ask, "What kind of clients do you most enjoy working with?" This not only tells you about their business but also helps you understand if there's potential alignment between your target markets.

The power of good questions lies in their ability to uncover valuable information, build genuine connections, and guide your relationship-building efforts in the most productive direction. And as we'll see, there's one question in particular that can save you enormous amounts of time and energy in your quest for the right referral partners.

STORY TIME: DAVE TAKES THE PLUNGE

Let me tell you about Dave, a guy who had a solid job as a financial advisor but was stuck in a role that didn't ignite his passion. He had always been drawn to helping seniors navigate the complex world of Medicare, but the thought of leaving a stable career was daunting.

Then one day, he had an epiphany: Why not turn his passion into his profession? Why not do what he truly loved?

So, Dave took the plunge. He shifted gears, leaving financial services behind to focus on Medicare full time. But starting from scratch wasn't easy. He needed a way to build his business without the luxury of a marketing budget. Enter the Greenlight Question, which he learned during a course called "Jumpstart." It was a game changer. By asking the right questions of the right people, Dave organically built a network of referrals with no awkward pitches and no forced conversations—just authentic relationships that naturally led to business growth.

And here's where it gets really interesting: Dave started from zero and quickly grew to average over 120 referrals a year. For six years straight. All without spending a dime on advertising or marketing.

Think about that for a second—120 referrals a year, every year, purely through word-of-mouth. It's a testament to the power of the Greenlight Question and the kind of authentic connections it helps you build. Imagine what that could do for your business.

Now, doesn't that make you want to learn how to do it?

ALL ABOUT THE GREENLIGHT QUESTION

The Greenlight Question is the ultimate referral partner qualifier. It's a transformative question because whenever we're in a business, I always hear this: "I want more referrals. I want relationships. I want to build my business through word-of-mouth through people who know, like, and trust me."

If that's you, too, memorize the Greenlight Question: **"If you had a client/friend or connection/family member who was looking to [CHOICE A] or [CHOICE B], who would you recommend they call first?"**

In this question, Choice A and Choice B are what you offer/what you get paid to do for people. For example: "If you had a friend or family member who was frustrated and looking to switch financial advisors or aggressively start saving for retirement, who would you recommend they call first?"

The obvious goal here is they say: *you!* You're my first choice! I pick you! *I do, I do!*

You're asking this question to see if they like you as much as you're going to like and love on them.

Let's look at a few other examples:

- Tech: "Because you're in tech, I've got to ask: If you had clients or connections who were looking to automate incoming phone calls or reduce their overhead, who would you recommend they call first?"
- Real Estate: "You were always an incredible connector, and I'm looking to build a referral-based business the same way you have. If you had clients, friends, or connections who were looking for a great loan officer or real estate professional, who would you recommend they call first?"
- Recruiting: "I'm always looking to meet [Common Noun] who have [Specific Job, Experience, or Personality]. I come in contact with a lot of professionals, and I like to open doors for nines and tens. If you were looking to add someone like this to your teams, who's the first person that comes to mind?" (Side note: Recruiting is a fantastic use of the Greenlight Question.)

A clear and compelling value proposition is critical when asking this question. This helps differentiate you from others and makes it easier for potential referral partners to think of you when opportunities arise. It directly answers something all of us who have ever invested in referral partners have asked at one time or another: What can I say that sets me apart, or what can I say that gets them thinking about me?

Sometimes when we talk about the Greenlight Question, people say, "But what if they've already referred business to me? Do I still ask?"

If they haven't referred you recently, yes, you should still ask the question. Things might have changed, however, and there might be something you don't know about. If they have referred you recently, don't worry about asking the Greenlight Question. You've already got the greenlight! Take it right to a Clarity Conversation.

But this won't be the norm. Most of the time, your guidance is to ask, ask, ask. And remember, the Greenlight Question is not about putting people on the spot or forcing referrals. It's about opening a conversation, understanding where you stand in their network, and simplifying opportunities for mutually beneficial relationships. It's a tool that, when used correctly, can transform your approach to building a referral-based business.

POSSIBLE RESPONSE #1: "NOT YOU."

I know what you're thinking: What if you ask this question, and they give you a name that's *not* you? This response, while it might seem disappointing at first, is actually incredibly valuable. It tells you immediately this person is not going to be a direct referral partner for you, saving you time and energy you might have wasted trying to cultivate a relationship that wouldn't bear fruit.

That said, if you do get another name, don't stop there. Ask: "What do you like about them?" (*Not* "Why do you like them?")

Why? First, because this question helps you learn the traits that make the other person or business a good fit. Second, if there's a product gap, they might tell you, but it's likely a personal relationship, not a product gap. And finally, you ask because you can use this information. If you're in the recruiting space, you might want to consider this all-star for your team. If you're in the mentorship space, they might be bigger than you, and there's probably something you can learn from them. If you're in a shoulder industry, they could potentially still refer business down the line.

That's why, after I learn about this person, I often ask, "This person sounds amazing! Would you mind introducing me?"

Ultimately, by asking what they like about their preferred contact, you're gaining insight into what qualities are valued in your industry.

This information can help you refine your own approach and value proposition. And even if this person can't be a direct referral partner, they might still be a valuable connection. They could introduce you to their preferred contact, potentially opening up new opportunities for collaboration or learning. Remember, in the world of referrals and networking, sometimes the power is in the second- or third-degree connection.

RESPONSE #2: "I DON'T KNOW."

When you get this response, it's actually a great opportunity. Your two-question reply should be:

"If you wouldn't mind helping me, can I ask what you would be looking for?" Now, they may have an answer to that question, or they may not. Either way, your next question is, "What would it take for me to be that person? What would I need to do to earn that?" If they think about that and have a response, I'd invite them to a Clarity Conversation!

This response is valuable because it opens up a dialogue. You're not just gathering information; you're engaging in a conversation about their needs and expectations. This can help you understand what potential partners in your industry are looking for and how you might need to position yourself to be their go-to referral.

As one person posted in the R.I.C.H. RELATIONSHIP SOCIETY:

> Had a great talk with a general contractor today—went real smooth. Found out what they like in roofers and what drives 'em nuts. Turns out their go-to roofer is leaving the game. Now, we've got lunch set for next week. Goes to show, if you've got the guts to step up and ask, good things happen. Should've been doing this years ago.

Learning the dos and don'ts of a relationship is essential for that relationship to grow. This response gives you the perfect opportunity to do just that.

RESPONSE #3: "YOU, OF COURSE!"

This is the response we're all hoping for, but don't stop there! Follow up with:

"I was hoping you'd say that! Now, is there anything that would keep you from saying that?" This is a solid quality-control question that can yield great responses if you've built trust with the person you're asking. A secondary question people rarely ask but that could be so essential is, "When you talk to that friend, family member, colleague, coworker, whomever, what would you tell them about me?"

Hint: Your clients are not always good at referring people. That's why, in this conversation, you're coaching them on how to refer you (without actually doing the coaching)!

I'm not going to lie to you. The first time I did this, it was really awkward—not for them, but for me! For many of us, it's hard to sit there and listen to why we're so great. However, there's a reason for this question. As they respond, we have the opportunity to learn two things: why customers think we're great (which means ten times more than why we think we're great), and if we need to clarify or adjust anything about the language they use when they talk about us.

Ultimately, Response #3 is the response you want, but it's how you handle it that really matters. By asking these follow-up questions, you're not only confirming their willingness to refer you, but you're also gathering valuable information about how they perceive your value. This can help you refine your messaging and ensure when they *do* refer you, they're highlighting your most impactful qualities.

As a bonus, occasionally you'll have a customer who says something genius! For instance, a tradesman named Michael went to a house to fix their new dining room table. He had just moved from the other side of the state where he'd done everything from restoring antique elevators and automobiles and all this crazy stuff.

When the customer asked how he could refer him business, Michael called himself a "jack-of-all-trades, surface artist, and master crafts-man in the finishing industry." While this was technically accurate, it wasn't helpful for ordinary people who pay money for things. When

Michael asked the customer, "How would you describe me?" the reply was, "You're my furniture restoration expert!"

Michael's gut reaction was, *But I do so much more than that!*

Which, of course, was true. But when the customer—who happened to be a referral trainer—explained that the easier you are to talk about, the more people will talk about you, Michael got that right away. Shortly thereafter, he launched a business web page where he, no doubt, referred to himself as an expert in furniture restoration. Now, of course, when he talks to customers, we all know he has the opportunity to explain that he does way more than that. And if you go to his web page, you'll see pictures of all his amazing work and will likely think, *Oh, this guy is a unicorn! How quickly can I get on his schedule?*

As of this writing, Michael dominates his area. Nothing but five-star reviews. This is a situation where if Michael had started with traditional marketing, he would have blown thousands of dollars on Google ads (because their representatives called him every week once he launched his site) to *maybe* look at data (Michael is not tech savvy) and *maybe* come to the conclusion about what he should be calling himself. Instead, he focused on building a referral-based business. Got the answer in five minutes. And ran with it.

If you're feeling uncomfortable with the question, I've heard that before. You're not alone. Many people are uncomfortable with scripts because they think the script doesn't sound like them or it's disingenuous. If you're one of those people, you have the option to change it... and ruin it. The other option is to change your own thinking. Here are three ways to do that:

- Practice it out loud. Oftentimes discomfort is a function of memory and as memory improves, so does comfort.
- Post in our community with your specific challenge. Who knows? You might be anticipating a problem that doesn't exist. Go to **RPTsystem.com** for access.
- Practice thoughtful preparation. I've never seen this fail, friends.

Plan out what you're going to say and hear in advance of your conversation with a specific person, and watch the magic happen.

At the end of the day, every Greenlight Question takes you someplace exciting because it's a yes/yes! If you're wondering when you should start asking this magical question, the answer is: sooner than you're comfortable with.

STORY TIME: DAWN'S GREENLIGHT SUCCESS

My friend Dawn Baumgartner, founder, coach, and servant leader—knows very well the value of *one question* as not just a recruiting tool, but a relationship-building technique that creates value regardless of the immediate outcome.

First, you should know Dawn has been deeply involved with this content for years, integrating it across multiple industries. She continually says one of the most powerful tools she's implemented is the Greenlight Question, which she recently used in her own business when recruiting for an integrator/operations manager position. Dawn can tell you better than I can:

> I started by posting the Greenlight Question on Facebook, asking, "If you had a friend or family member looking for an operations or productions position, who's the first person that comes to mind?" This approach opened doors to meaningful conversations and allowed people to tag potential candidates. But I didn't stop there. I took this question into every business environment I encountered.
>
> Recently, I had lunch with another coach named Tina and used the same approach. I asked her, "**If you knew somebody looking to hire nines and tens for operations or productions, who's the first person that comes to mind?**"

When people responded with, "Well, they would never leave their current position," I embraced that response. It actually indicates they're committed and love what they do—exactly the kind of person I want to connect with.

In a referral-based business, which is where much of this work focused, the highest compliment is being in a deep, trusted relationship with someone. When I hear someone is a "ten" in their current position, I don't want to disrupt that. Instead, I want to understand what makes them exceptional and build a relationship for the future.

The key is to remove all pressure and focus on building genuine connections. In the referral world, it's about creating a network of excellence where everyone wins—whether they join your team immediately, become a valuable connection, or simply appreciate being recognized for their expertise.

Bingo, Dawn.
Bingo.

DAWN'S BIG 4

- What they do: Dawn coaches leaders to get "unstuck" by taking them through a process that defines their values, roles, barriers, and systems.
- Who they serve: Small- to midsize-business owners, entrepreneurial stay-at-home moms, who are committed to where they want to be... even if they're unsure where that is.
- What they *don't* do: HR, recruiting, or counseling.
- Who is *not* a fit: Anyone who has a fixed mindset, dislikes accountability, or isn't sure if they're ready to take action.

PRACTICE MAKES PERMANENT

Do you remember our buddy Dave who soared to new heights with the Greenlight Question? That didn't happen by accident. He practiced and practiced. Why? Because if you've got a commitment to building a relationship-based business, you've also got to be committed to working at it. And in this case, working at it means getting really good at asking the Greenlight Question. Practicing helps overcome the initial awkwardness and builds confidence in delivering the question smoothly.

Don't overthink this: If you have ten minutes in the car, practice it ten times. Say it to yourself in the shower. Build that muscle so when it's time to say it to a real person sitting across from you, you can do so with the Four Cs: a firm **commitment** to building relationships, the hard-won **courage** to ask, an honest curiosity in your **conversation**, and a budding **confidence** that grows with practice.

What else grows with practice? Learning how to clear the referral runway. We'll learn more about that in the next chapter.

CHAPTER 12

CLEARING RUNWAY

Consistency counts when it comes to pursuing liftoff.

My friend Jesse Itzler—Emmy Award–winning artist, *New York Times* bestselling author, part owner of the Atlanta Hawks, ultramarathon runner, and serial entrepreneur—knows this well. When he was twenty-two, he had no formal business training and had to figure out networking and marketing intuitively. He developed a simple but powerful strategy: writing about ten handwritten letters every day.

Every. Single. Day.

Even while he was sleeping on friends' couches, moving from place to place, he maintained this practice religiously. If he saw someone had given an interesting interview, he'd write them a letter. If someone helped him with something, they'd get a letter. It was Jesse's entire marketing campaign.

This consistency meant he was planting about three thousand seeds annually. Clearly, it worked. Not coincidentally, the guy who co-founded Marquis Jet knows a thing or two about the way to get relational liftoff. But even with all his success—just check out his Big 4 box below if you need more on that—Jesse's not done. I'll let him take it from here:

Even as I've gotten older, I've maintained this practice, though now I send about three texts, DMs, or letters daily—that's still a thousand touchpoints a year. I always make these one-way communications. For example, if I know someone loves jumping rope, I'll send them a relevant video with a simple note like "Hey, thought you might like this." There's never an ask attached.

Today, with phones, I do a lot of video messages. I'll spend three minutes a day reaching out to three different people, maintaining those connections. I still include handwritten letters because they break through the clutter. The key is that these seeds you plant don't necessarily pop up overnight— sometimes it takes years for them to bear fruit, but when they do, just one connection can change the entire course of your journey.

Indeed, it can.

JESSE'S BIG 4 (OR 1)

- What they do: At this point in his life, Jesse just want to spend time with his family and ride his bike. He's good with all the rest.

WHAT THE RUNWAY SYSTEM DOES

The second system every referral-based business must have is the system of clearing runway—giving people a tryout and encouraging them to achieve liftoff. At the end of the day, this system will conserve your resources, allowing you to pour into key partners who will refer you consistent business versus sucking up to people who *can't* or *won't* help you.

How? Simple. You get industry colleagues to reveal their cards by asking the Greenlight Question. Then, you can evaluate their responses and invite the best into Clarity Conversations. It's time to talk about what comes next. So far in this Part Four, you've learned to prioritize your playbook (because not all partnerships are created equal) and qualify partners by eliminating waste with one simple question. Here, we're going to put it all together, including step-by-step action items and how to investigate your infrastructure before getting started.

But first, we need to examine the Five Pillars of Being an A-Lister, regardless of whether you've been using traditional marketing or not, getting referrals or not, or winning or not. Follow these strategies, and you will turn peers into partners without chasing, wasting, or waiting.

PILLAR #1: ALWAYS BE CONTRIBUTING

Contribution isn't a *sometimes* thing. It's an *all-the-time* thing. Building R.I.C.H. relationships means getting "being helpful at a low personal cost" into your DNA. It is rooted in the concept of reciprocity—something that's deeply ingrained in human nature. When one person gives another person a gift or does them a solid, the recipient feels motivated to reward the giver with a positive response of their own.

Researchers claim reciprocity traces back to our earliest ancestors. Our need for survival literally depended on sharing goods and services with each other in a network of obligation. Some of the most compelling research like this around reciprocity comes from *Influence* by Robert Cialdini. Although it was first published in 1984, it's absolutely timeless, and I'd consider it a must-read for you, your team, or anyone else who wants to level up GIFT·OLOGY style.

Think about supermarkets that hand out free food samples. Don't you feel more motivated to buy that product? What about department stores, where clerks give out free samples of cosmetics? This works in practice, not just as a thought exercise. For example, one particular nonprofit discovered that donations doubled from 18 percent to 36 percent when they included a simple gift in the envelope: a set of self-addressed labels. (Note: Word got out, and now everybody does it, which is awesome.)

But it's not so awesome if you're only giving to get, which I've sometimes referred to as "bait-and-switch gifting." Consider this scenario: Someone offers you a "free home-energy audit." The idea is that a technician will come to your home for free and point out inefficiencies that will save you money. However, at the end of the audit, the representative quickly pivots to a hard sell, urging you to purchase energy-efficient windows. He recommends seventeen new windows at $600 each, which...spoiler alert...are available from the company he works for. Suddenly, the person doing your "free audit" wants you to spend more than $10,000. This is a manipulative type of gifting that is contrived, controlling, and transactional. To be crystal clear, that's the opposite of what we're talking about here.

Your contributions must always come without strings attached. I know I sound like I'm stuck on repeat about this, but it's important because "no strings attached" is how we win. It feels harder and riskier at first, but once you buy into it heart, mind, and soul, it turns out to be ten times more fun and more effective.

Think of your local power company offering you that same "free home-energy audit." This time, though, they get to the end and leave you with a few free LED bulbs and recommendations for items like efficient showerheads or insulation. Wouldn't that leave a better impression?

We have agency clients who gift their VIPs a $300 carving set, and some recipients don't take the time to thank them—which is totally okay. Our clients don't hate them or hound them about it. It's the exact opposite of a hard sell. Again, the idea is that if you love on people and pour into them first, they're more likely to want to reciprocate later. After all, it's in our DNA.

What's interesting is this "no strings attached" approach freaks some people out. They might say, "Wait, I haven't done anything for you. Why are you doing this for me?"

When you reply and say, "I want to acknowledge you for your time" or "Just because of the relationship," it almost short-circuits them because they're used to being manipulated. In that moment, you—as a giver—have just gained an incredible advantage.

PILLAR #2: THANKING PEOPLE FOR THEIR TIME

One of the most powerful things I do after meeting with somebody, whether they're a potential mentor, advocate, or business leader, is send them a small gift and thank them for their time, even after the Clarity Conversation. We call this small, follow-up gift the "24-Hour FUN (Follow-Up Now)!" The urgency, here, is that if it doesn't happen within twenty-four hours it's likely to not happen at all. This might feel a bit counterintuitive, as many people only send a gift after a deal gets done or after a referral is made. But remember, a person's time is their greatest asset. And even if it was just a thirty-minute coffee chat, this strategy is why I (and you) won't have to push things and say, "Hey, I'd love your referrals" or "Hey, I'd love to do business with you."

If you're in the market for one of these gifts, a book is the perfect, thoughtful, low-cost option. Because there's no expectation of return, you're not going to spend an amount of money you could regret if the person never gets off the runway, so something around a twenty-dollar price tag is perfect. You can either include a note with the book or write in the pages.

To help make your choice, ask yourself:

- What book did I recently finish that is worthy of sharing with others?
- What book has *most* made an impact on me or my career?
- What can I write in it to make it meaningful? (Always include a note.)

One partner of mine would always write in the middle of the book, inviting the person for a hangout once they made it to a certain section of the book. "Congratulations on finishing! Let's get together and have one of these Clarity Conversations." I don't necessarily recommend this, but I kinda liked the extra qualifier...and this guy was a big deal.

Whether you pick a book or choose something else, an "acknowledgment of time" gift with no strings attached will get you reactions that are priceless. It will get your people face-melting with happiness.

Why? Because most people have never been recognized or appreciated in that way, ever. Maybe that's why, when I reach out to partners I've given this type of gift to a whopping five years ago and ask to get together when I visit their town, they drop what they're doing and come engage with me. Which, at the end of the day, is all we want—to remain top of mind and to have the key people in our network prioritize our needs ahead of somebody else's.

PILLAR #3: FAST FOLLOW-UP

After a Clarity Conversation and thanking them for their time, your work isn't done. To transition onto the runway and get them into the air, you need to do the following:

- **Send a gratitude communication, echoing the sentiment from the meeting.** This can be a text message, which is fine, or a video message, which is even more powerful because they can see your face. This is often an enthusiastic thank-you (and may even include a little humor from the meeting).
- **Send a recap email, including a timeline of any action steps.** I know you know how to write an email, so let's get to the point: Personally, I like to include a recap of the Clarity Conversation high points and add any information I may have forgotten during the meeting. I also include any action steps. This does *not* have to be a long email and can even be a string of bullets. This email, like everything else, should be purely relational. If you're including some type of "Do This, Get That" loyalty plug, you're doing it wrong.
- **Send your low-cost gift, like we just covered—a book, or something relevant from the conversation.** If you're thinking of sending a book, a shameless plug here: Two books that work well in this scenario are GIFT·OLOGY and, I would presume, this one. Any referral partner who cracks it open and resonates with the content will very likely be a partner who leaves the runway and gets airborne fast. This is one of the draws of the RPT System: The takers self-eliminate.

I hate calling this a "follow-up," so instead, we call it "FUN"—which just so happens to be what it is to get referrals.

I recommend sending your FUN within twenty-four hours of a Clarity Conversation. Why? Because you're still fresh in their memory, and frankly it's impressive that you're following up so quickly. Doing this consistently is an atomic habit.

It's also true that your speed of FUN will impact their speed of reciprocity. For example, a team member of ours had a lakeside Clarity Conversation via a chance, impromptu encounter they had while on a walk. The partner was spending the day at a remote lake before vacationing for a week. Before the partner had even gotten cell phone service back, the book had been ordered, a 3-way introduction had been made, and an email had been sent. Incredible efficiency. Even more incredible? The partner logged on toward the end of his vacation and was clearly impressed. I know because there was a new lead for us on his first day back in the office.

What I'm saying is this: If you want referrals to happen fast, be fast. If you want referring you to be a priority, make helping them a priority! If you get this right, you give people a taste of what it's like to work with you—not just as a partner, but also how you're going to treat the people they send you.

PILLAR #4: COLLECT AND CAPTURE

Take the time to pay attention to what potential partners tell you—and I mean really pay attention. What are their hobbies? What do they do with their free time? What are the topics they talk about that make their eyes light up and their voices rise?

This is important because, as you're going to find out later, what makes a great gift is not the cost of the item but having that personal touch. In fact, having that personal touch will often save you money.

For example, I once was on a podcast, and the host mentioned he and his wife were getting ready to celebrate thirty years of marriage. Their favorite thing in the world? Playing spades with their friends. So,

I found the nicest, coolest cards on the planet—which cost me about thirty dollars—and sent it to them with a personal note saying, "Here's the deal, thanks so much for having me on your podcast." They loved it.

To do this well, your listening process has to be ongoing. We've found that once you secretly declare your intention to appreciate somebody, the details on how just seem to emerge. Now, unfortunately I can't do the collecting for you, so you'll need to start paying attention, capturing everything, and documenting it—especially if it has something to do with their inner circle. If I hear "My wife" or "My kids" in a conversation, I interrupt them with a couple questions: "What's your wife's name? How many kids do you have?" I then write these down by putting the notes in my iPhone (not tech savvy, I know). Still, there's nothing I love more than having not talked to somebody for months, and when we catch up, I can ask, "How's Jennifer?" They're usually shocked and grateful just for the very simple act of one human paying attention to another human. Remember, the goal here isn't to be creepy or stalker-ish. It's about being genuinely interested in people's lives and using that information to build stronger, more meaningful relationships. When you can recall these details in future interactions, it shows you care and you've been listening—and that's how you build lasting connections.

If you're wondering if something is worth writing down or not, I recommend erring on the side of doing it anyway. The more the merrier.

PILLAR #5: KEEP IT SHORT AND SIMPLE

Simplicity is key. Explain everything like they're five and use fewer adjectives. Too many adjectives create bloat, and bloat ruins memory. This goes for both your Clarity Conversation and your Greenlight Question.

Here are the common failings I see:

- **Too many adjectives.** We live in a world of (what intrigue expert

Sam Horn calls) INFObesity. Signal versus noise. Be very direct. Start with a beginner's mind. This is not marketing copy. The goal is not to be clever. Language is one of the most violent things in the world. When you use language, you're either destroying something or creating something. Choose wisely.

- **Too colloquial.** Avoid industry jargon. If they're not a client and not in your industry, they don't know what those words mean. Be plain. Or use simple metaphors. Simon Sinek gave one of the most popular TED Talks in the world called "Start with Why." It was a lovely message, viewed trillions of times. But I'm not as smart as Simon Sinek, and neither are most of your referral partners. For the purposes of Clarity Conversations, do not start with why. Think "this is what we do here" sledgehammer mentality.

- **Too much imagination.** Be specific and direct. People often make the mistake of being too general when they describe their services, which makes it hard for others to understand how to refer them. For example, it took me years to get "describing GIFT·OLOGY" correct. I used to call us a concierge service. Or a fulfillment service. People would come up to me after my keynote messages and would ask how we could work together. I was dumbfounded (and boy, so was Rod!). Then we started calling ourselves a relationship agency. And anybody who touched marketing understood us. Then we started saying, "We send gifts out on your behalf. To build loyalty. So, people do stuff." This allowed us to streamline our services. It made us easier to talk about. Get more referrals and grow our bottom line.

THE ONE THING

In this stage of business, what's the feather press that will mask your deficiencies and catapult you to the next stage? Here it is: **Ask the Greenlight Question.** Ask it live, not over text. Ask "who," not "would." And ask as if every answer were a positive one...because it is.

When you're ready to ask the Greenlight Question properly, you'll reach out to somebody with whom you have an important but casual relationship. You'll tell them you have a question. You'll ask the Greenlight Question. And whatever they say, the relationship will change forever—*for the better*.

You will schedule a Clarity Conversation, meet face-to-face, and learn things and connect in ways you never thought possible. You will see some obvious ways you can contribute at a low personal cost. In fact, you may even have to repress your enthusiasm with how much help you can give them.

You'll deliver your Big 4, without too many adjectives. They'll nod in perfect understanding.

You'll send a 24-Hour FUN book, a handwritten note, and a recap email. Maybe you'll follow them on Instagram, if you're into that sort of thing.

They'll thank you profusely. You'll smile because it doesn't feel like effort. And it won't be long before the first call or text or email comes in.

And then you'll read Part Five, so you know exactly what to do next.

BUT FIRST...ANSWER THESE QUESTIONS

- Have you added industry contacts to your Referral Partner Playbook and prioritized them on the dimension of **Can–Willing–Want**?
- Have you become crystal clear in what you're going to say about yourself when asking the Greenlight Question? Run it by other people.
- Have you practiced asking the Greenlight Question out loud until you feel comfortable?
- Do you feel confident in responding to people after you ask?
- Have you picked a favorite book for your 24-Hour FUNs? How many copies have you stockpiled?
- Have you picked a number one DoV and explored how it can be solutions for other people's problems?

If you're not quite there on any of these points, that's okay. Use this as an opportunity to refine your approach and get everything in order before you start reaching out to potential partners.

Remember, preparation is key. The more thought and effort you put into setting up your system now, the smoother and more effective it will be when you put it into action.

ACTION ITEMS, STEP-BY-STEP

This isn't about perfection. It's about progress. Remember that as you:

1. Identify 8–12 individuals you're connected to who would refer you business, but haven't yet. Engage these people in conversations (see Chapter 8 if you're feeling awkward).
2. Ask 3–5 Greenlight Questions until you get a positive response.
3. Schedule and execute a Clarity Conversation.
4. Collect and capture new information: address, inner circle, socials, etc.
5. Execute your first 24-Hour FUN: book, email, and text.
6. Tell us about it at: **CelebrateMyWins.com**—and we might share your Big 4 with others.

These steps might seem simple, but don't underestimate their power. Each is designed to move you closer to your goal of building a strong network of referral partners. **Start with just one person.** Go through the process, learn from it, refine your approach, and move on to the next.

Remember, this is a process. It takes time and consistency. But if you stick with it, if you continue to demonstrate value and follow these steps, you'll see results.

And before you know it, you'll turn everyday relationships into referral partners who are excited and capable of referring business your way.

Now, get out there and start contributing!

PART FIVE

OUTCOME #3

REFERRAL OVERFLOW

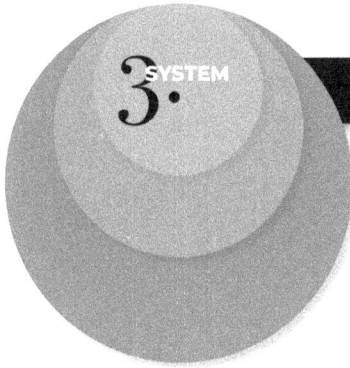

SYSTEM 3.

PERPETUATING GIVERS
Fuel current givers to give more.

GRATIFY | Thank, update, correct
(CH.13)

ELECTRIFY | Strategic gifts
(CH.14)

FORTIFY | Above and beyond
(CH.15)

CHAPTER 13

SURPRISE AND DELIGHT

My friend Jonathan Keyser, founder and thought leader at Keyser, one of the nation's largest commercial real estate firms, purchased a considerable amount of GIFT·OLOGY Artifact Mugs to deepen his referral partnerships. These mugs aren't cheap (though they are awesome), so it was a significant investment.

It's ironic, though, that this story about Jonathan is not about the mugs he gave. It's about one he got—one that doesn't even hold liquid anymore.

I'll let him tell you, in his own words:

> One of my most treasured possessions is my original GIFT·OLOGY mug I received from the team. And it's broken. It actually got slammed in a car door and broke. Even though it no longer holds water, I had it put back together because it means that much to me. The coffee from its last use is still unwashed inside, preserved from when it broke. It's become a special artifact that reminds me of the power of surprise and delight and of the philosophy behind the power of connection.

This perfectly exemplifies what this is all about—putting things in people's homes where they see them frequently, serving as constant reminders of kindness and generosity. It has never been just about making people feel good; it was about staying top of mind through meaningful gestures.

The impact of this approach has been remarkable, from the mugs I gave and more. I regularly receive crying texts and emails from people who receive mugs and other gifts, including knife sets. These aren't just ordinary reactions to gifts: They're profound expressions of appreciation that demonstrate the deep impact of thoughtful giving. In a world of noise, where successful people can have whatever they want, these highly personalized gifts that take time and energy, that can't just be ordered off Amazon but must be crafted with intention, tend to have an outsized impact.

The connection I feel to this philosophy runs deep, and I'm committed to carrying forward this legacy of meaningful giving.

I'm so grateful to be doing this work with and in the company of people like Jonathan. You can have this feeling—and these results—for yourself too. Let's explore how.

JONATHAN'S BIG 4

- What they do: Jonathan runs one of the largest independent commercial real estate advocacy firms in the US, representing tenants and occupiers.
- Who they serve: Jonathan works with tenants, corporations, and end users of commercial real estate.
- What they *don't* do: He does not represent landlords or developers.
- Who is *not* a fit: Retail clients, multifamily projects.

THE BEGINNING OF THE ROAD

Many leaders tend to underestimate the generosity and willingness of their referral partners. This small-mindedness, coupled with busyness, breeds an entitled response from referral recipients: *not enough investigation, not enough appreciation, not enough investment.*

What you want, instead, is to transform your thinking. Getting a referral isn't the end of a process—it's the beginning of one. Adopting a system that covers every milestone, from a 3-way introduction to the close of the sale, energizes your partners and multiplies their efforts.

Word-of-mouth follows the same 80/20 concept as everything else. So invest resources into the people who have already proven themselves. That's what makes the Relationship Snowball so intelligent; this is not "throw enough seeds on the ground and eventually something will sprout." Instead, it's *once a sprout appears, do everything in your power to make it a redwood.*

This is why leaders in this stage often feel stuck. Because you already have too much to do and not enough time to do it, so another referral feels like it only adds to that plate. If you're not able to really focus on your referral program, you might end up replacing referral partners instead of growing them, which can lead to over-reliance on ads, algorithms, and cold outreach, with referrals becoming a supplement to your marketing, not the main driver.

Instead, by treating the giver with just as much urgency as the referral itself, you perpetuate word-of-mouth marketing from your referral sources, causing *less work* over time. Become a disciplined appreciator, then prepare to sit back and be stunned by what your partners are capable of.

I know you're busy, so let's cut to the chase. By the end of Part Five, you will:

Fuel current referral givers to give more, with stronger conviction.

Here's the three-step process for how to get there from where you're at currently.

1. **Gratify.** Habituate thanking, reporting progress, and appreciating givers. (Chapter 13)
2. **Electrify.** Energize givers with powerful, above-and-beyond gratitude gestures. (Chapter 14)
3. **Fortify.** Systematize the process to build a moat around your relationships. (Chapter 15)

At the end of the day, your competition can copy almost anything...
but not your relationships. True partner conviction can't be faked,
bought, or stolen.

Only nurtured. Then envied.

HOW TO UNLOCK LOYALTY THROUGH PEAK MOMENTS

FACT: The brain has limited hard-drive space. We don't remember
experiences in totality. Or accurately. Or fairly. This is true even if
those experiences are remarkable! Say you go on vacation to an exotic,
exciting place. Or you hang out with your kids on the weekend and
feel really connected. Or you lead your team through a hard growth
period. Chances are, you don't remember the specifics of these events
or activities.

They all blend together in the brain.

Monday in the Bahamas feels like Thursday in the Bahamas. One
weekend feels like any other. On a project, team members forget the
steadfastness of your remarkable leadership. There's a flatness to it
all. So, what *does* the brain retain? According to science, it's the highlights and how things end. This is called the peak-end rule.[24] Behavior
engineer Nir Eyal discusses the research behind this concept.[25] In one
study, baseball fans were asked to recall a game they watched. They
tended to remember the best game they had ever seen.[26] In another
study, researchers discovered the order in which people opened presents affected their memories of the holiday. Save the best for last for
better sentiments.[27] (Finally! The debate has been settled!) The same

---

24 Daniel Kahneman et al., "When More Pain Is Preferred to Less: Adding a Better End," *Psychological Science* 4, no. 6 (November 1993): 401–405, https://www.jstor.org/stable/40062570.

25 Nir Eyal, "Peak-End Rule: Why You Make Terrible Life Choices," *Nir and Far* (blog), accessed December 17, 2024, https://www.nirandfar.com/peak-end-rule/.

26 Carey K. Morewedge et al., "The Least Likely of Times: How Remembering the Past Biases Forecasts of the Future," *Psychological Science* 16, no. 8 (August 2005): 626–30, https://doi.org/10.1111/j.1467-9280.2005.01585.x.

27 Amy M. Do et al., "Evaluations of Pleasurable Experiences: The Peak-End Rule," *Psychonomic Bulletin & Review* 15 (February 2008): 96–98, https://doi.org/10.3758/pbr.15.1.96.

goes for how we enjoy our meals. Researchers found people remembered small portions of their favorite dishes as fondly as eating larger portions.[28]

(Aha! So *that's* why the Ruhlin children remember the ninety-second ride at Disney and not the ninety-minute wait in line.)

We can use this information as inspiration to create more peak moments. And sure, some peak moments happen by accident, but they can also be engineered. (For a deeper dive here, read *The Power of Moments* by Chip Heath and Dan Heath.)

For our purposes, strategic gifting is the fastest, least time-intensive, "be-in-fifty-places-at-once" way of doing this. This works because relationships (and your brain) are plastic, not elastic. That means once stretched by a peak moment, they won't shrink. Think of great friends you speak with very rarely—you pick up right where you left off each time they call. Don't you want more professional relationships like that? It doesn't take more time. It takes more peak moments—more highlights, more greatest hits.

In short, relationships activated by strategic gifting remain energized, no matter how much time passes between conversations.

THE POWER OF SURPRISE AND DELIGHT

When people expect something, there's no way to create a peak moment. Peak moments are created when somebody is *not* expecting something. "Surprise and delight" means creating unforgettable moments with your communication and interactions that go *beyond* the expected. It means catching people off guard in the best way possible, leading to deeper emotional connections.

To your referral partners, these moments will feel random. But to you, these moments are planned ("planned randomness," a GIFT·OL-

---

28 Elizabeth Rode et al., "Experienced and Remembered Pleasure for Meals: Duration Neglect but Minimal Peak, End (Recency) or Primacy Effects," *Appetite* 49, no. 1 (July 2007): 18–29, https://doi.org/10.1016/j.appet.2006.09.006.

OGY staple). This is important because when communication is too predictable, it becomes transactional. However, when you reach out with a gesture at an unexpected time, you trigger genuine appreciation because it feels like you're truly paying attention. In a world full of noise, surprise and delight communicates: "I see you, and I appreciate you."

This kind of communication builds trust, loyalty, and active advocacy, because when people feel genuinely delighted, they're inclined to reciprocate with loyalty and engagement.

PLANNED RANDOMNESS

By now, you've probably seen the trend that GIFT·OLOGISTs do things differently. We zig when everybody else zags.

- Most people don't see the value in gifting strategically.
- Most people give gift cards or cheap gifts.
- Most people turn their gifts into promotions by slapping the company logo on everything.
- Most people ask, "What's the least I can do to check this off the to-do list?"

So, when I tell you most companies give one gift a year around the holidays? You guessed it, we're going to go against the grain there as well. Let's talk timing. We take an approach we call "planned randomness," which means from the client's point of view, they're getting an unexpected, amazing gift when they least expect it. It seems totally random. But from *your* side, you'll have strategically planned that delivery schedule well in advance.

This strategy means you're probably going to avoid the times when they're expecting a gift, like on their birthdays, Christmas, and Hanukkah. This is when the noise is highest, everyone else is giving gifts, and your gesture will be more diluted and less impactful.

Planned randomness, on the other hand, means gifting on a

random Tuesday. It means our gifts aren't competing with anything else. They were totally unexpected. And because of that? They mean *far* more.

With this foundational understanding in the books, let's take a look at three key peak moment opportunities you can leverage.

PEAK #1: "THANKS FOR INTRODUCING ME!"

Your first peak moment opportunity is immediately after you get a referral. It *should* look like this: Someone contacts your business, you (or your team) discover the person who told them about you, and you follow up with the referral source.

However, it often looks like this: You are contacted by a new prospect, and if the prospect doesn't mention who referred them, most people don't ask. Even if the prospect *does* mention the referral source, that information is usually not captured—meaning there is also no follow-up. Now, it's possible the referral doesn't remember or doesn't mention how they heard about you. In which case, politely interrogate them to help jog their memory. That's something most businesses don't do, because they either find it uncomfortable or don't think it is important. If your goal is to snowball instead of using the hamster wheel, from this day forward, these two excuses must be unacceptable to you.

"HOW DID YOU HEAR ABOUT US?"

When my wife and I were remodeling our property, I called contractor after contractor. Oftentimes I was doing this during early morning hours, late at night, or in the evenings. And because I'm a referral guy, I was (of course) calling people I was told about from trusted advisors.

I cannot tell you how many times I was not asked by these tradesmen (who make their living off referrals) this key question: "How did you hear about me?" I even told people, "I was referred to you by a friend." Still...nothing. No "Which friend?" No "Oh, wonderful! And who was that?" Nada, nothing.

Except in two cases, and one of those was the individual my wife and I ended up hiring.

Ladies and gentlemen, this must become an atomic habit for everybody in your organization, starting with you. No excuses. No matter where you are, what you're doing, what time it is, or what mood you're in. By consistently asking, "How did you hear about us?" and following up with referral givers, you create a powerful feedback loop that encourages more referrals. This simple habit can dramatically increase your referral business and strengthen your relationships with your referral partners.

PEAK #2: REPORTING POSITIVE PROGRESS

Your second peak moment opportunity is after you interact with the referral and move the plot forward toward possibly doing business together. Whenever there is progress in the relationship, always report back to the referral giver! Progress in this case means:

- Scheduling a call.
- Interacting, talking one-on-one, sending a proposal, etc.
- Eventually doing business together.

Anytime a referral hits a milestone, I want my referral giver to hear about it. This "reporting" of positive progress can be simple text messages. It's more important what you're communicating than how you communicate it. You're really saying: "I take care of every single person you send me," which will make the giver want to send you more.

It also gives you an excuse to be top of mind. Remember, referral givers are not agnostic to your business only. Givers are givers everywhere. Your communication and care for their referrals will absolutely stick out compared to what everybody else does...which is nothing.

Think about the last five referrals you gave somebody for any business.

Did the person you gave the referrals to follow up? How many times? Did they communicate how things were going on the way to a sale or a dead end? Few do this well, but you can be different. Being world class at this looks like embodying the philosophy that no amount of praise, thanking, gifting, or appreciative communication is too good for your referral partners.

PEAK #3: POST-SALE APPRECIATION

Your third peak moment opportunity is after a referral closes. To whatever degree you can in your industry, you need to prepare a surprise-and-delight communication two to three weeks after this milestone. I say "communication" because if your industry prevents you from gifting or caps your spending, you'll have to get creative. Otherwise, you're going to be leaning hard into gifting (more on the details of this in the next chapter). And in Chapter 15, I'll discuss how to go about budgeting for this (note: It's called a war chest).

But for now, understand this:

- It's not going to be costing you money you don't have.
- Referrals are, essentially, "paying for their own marketing."
- Executing post-sale appreciation puts you in a class all by itself.

When you give a gift, unlike when you thank a partner for the referral, you will *not* be mentioning the person—only expressing appreciation. Nothing transactional. This is why strategic gifting is the best, most simple, and arguably the most important system you can add to your business.

BUT WHAT DO YOU GIVE?

At this point, you've bought into the value of peak moments. You understand surprise and delight is the key to electrifying partners and perpetuating givers. Which means you're committing that:

1. For the next ten referrals you get—good or bad, right or wrong fit— send a handwritten note, thanking the giver for the introduction.

2. For the next ten referrals you get—good or bad, right or wrong fit—report positive progress, informing the giver of how you helped their connection.
3. For your next closed referral deal, send a surprise-and-delight gift to the recipient. Do this within four weeks and make no mention of the referral.

Great work! But now you have a new problem: if you're like most leaders, especially men, you're an average (or even below-average) gift giver. You understand the importance of systematic appreciation, but what the heck are you going to buy people to make an impact?

There's no such thing as "it's the thought that counts." And buying what's easy (gift cards and food) might result in the optics of tone deafness, or even worse...moving the relationship backward instead of forward.

We've heard the same things, every month, for the last twenty-plus years:

- "I'm training for a triathlon. No gluten or sweets. Thanks for the brownies."
- "They bought me gift cards to stores my wife hates."
- "My kids have a dairy allergy. Everything went straight into the trash."
- "Alcohol might be a perfect gift for them. But definitely not for me."

Gifting must be done well to be powerful.

Good news, my friends. We have answers.

R.I.C.H. RESOURCE #7

I'll make you a world-class gift giver in under five minutes. Visit **RPTsystem.com** to download my PDF "TOP 10 WORST GIFTS" plus a few of my absolute favorites!

CHAPTER 14

FAST-FORWARD RELATIONSHIPS

The presentation and thoughtfulness behind a gesture can elevate even the simplest of gifts into meaningful moments and take your relationships from transactional to transformational—even if you're in a regulated industry! My friend Matt Evans, who works in finance, knows this very well because he's been both on the giving and receiving ends of this.

Once, when Matt was sick, a referral partner didn't just send over a basic care package or deliver a cup of soup in a plastic bag. This partner sent soup, a special cup, a handwritten note, and so much more. The gift wasn't expensive or fancy, but to Matt, the gesture felt extraordinary thanks to the attention to detail and presentation.

We have a lot to learn from this story, starting with: Incredible friendships don't have to take lots of time. You can move relationships forward through the power of strategic gifting. But as long as leaders tell themselves, "I'm not a good gift giver" or "This isn't important," they'll limit their relational capacity over time and never unlock the full potential of their Return on Relationships (ROR).

We're all familiar with the law of reciprocity. Create peak moments for others (with *no ask*) and givers will do nice things for you in return. This is true on both micro and macro levels.

MATT'S BIG 4

- What they do: As a fiduciary advisor, Matt helps individuals pay off their homes in five to seven years while turning mortgage payments into long-term blessings.
- Who they serve: Business owners and high W-2 earners who wish to align their financial planning with their values and steward their many blessings.
- What they *don't* do: Matt doesn't tell you what you want to hear.
- Who is *not* a fit: People who are not open to being held accountable for the gifts God has entrusted to them.

A REMINDER FOR THE REGULATED

Fast-forwarding relationships through strategic gifting doesn't have to be expensive. And to the nonregulated, I say, "If the regulated industries (some of which can spend no more than one hundred dollars per year) can do it, so can you!"

To do this, you have to play by the rules, which means you have to understand what the rules are first. There's the letter of the law, which is "no bribing people." To that, I think we can all agree: *duh*.

To do this, follow these three rules when giving gifts:

Number 1: NO expectation of anything in return.

Number 2: NO mentions of previous behavior.

Number 3: NO discussion of deals, transactions, or decisions. (That means don't say, or even imply, "You did this for me, so here's this!")

Instead, communicate joy over the other person's character and personal qualities—who they are, why you appreciate them, and, if you got them a cool gift, what the gift says about this person and your rapidly growing friendship. Finally, make sure you investigate how your regulatory body applies the spirit of the law to shoulder industries. Regulatory compliance can get more nuanced in various situations:

- Personal relationships unrelated to business transactions.
- Seasonal gifts with no business expectation.
- Promotional items with company logos.
- Charitable donations made on behalf of clients (especially if client-requested).
- Gifts of educational materials related to the recipient's professional development.
- Group gifts distributed equally among a large team (to dilute individual value).
- Contributions to widely attended events (if invitations are open and nonspecific).
- Nonmonetary items that have no business-related value (like sports tickets, not tied to business dealings).

Make sure you're talking to compliance and other industry professionals and doing your own research. **Regulation can keep you from buying gifts, but it absolutely cannot and should not keep you from appreciating people.** As we've seen a dozen times now, there are tons of low-cost ways to do that. You don't have to be John Ruhlin to be a giver. But if you're going to be a giver, do it like John Ruhlin. A book, with a note, can make a lifelong impact. Or, if you want to give away something more valuable than gold, then consider something like a Legacy Letter workshop.

GIFTING BEST PRACTICES

Personalization matters, friends. A lot more than we think it does.

Think about it: Whether we admit it or not, we project our feelings into the gift-buying process. If we think Apple's cool, we give Apple. If we like Bose headphones, we give Bose. If we love golf, we take everybody golfing. If we love steak dinners, we take everybody out for a steak dinner. But sometimes, your clients don't want another steak dinner. They don't want another night away from their family. They don't want whatever it is *you* want—and they certainly don't want your company name or logo on the gift.

This is a common tactic in some industries—for instance, real estate, where the overarching marketing problem is: "How do I remain top of mind when a need arises?" Numerous experts purport the answer to be something like: "Drown 'em with touches!"

If the GIFT·OLOGY movement could accomplish *one thing* it would be to get companies to stop putting their logo on gifts. All you're doing there is creating advertisements, and advertisements get regifted, given to charity, or thrown away. It's not the thought that counts. It's the thoughtful thought that counts. Every donation center in America has hundreds of items with company logos.

A better path forward is to take yourself out of the equation, put yourself in the other person's shoes, and ask, "How can I create something that would be really meaningful to them?"

SAY THEIR NAME, SAY THEIR NAME

Think of a sports team you like—the specifics don't matter here. You likely have clothing with that team's logo on it, right? What would you rather have next? More clothing with *more* logos? Or something unique with *your* logo—i.e., *your* family name on it?

That's what I thought. To fast-forward relationships with strategic gifting, get those names on there: engrave, monogram, carve, burn, or paint them, but get it done. Why? Because adding their name is the easiest way to double the value of an item. Name is legacy. Leaders make seven-figure donations to get their name on things, and world-class manufacturers will do this for a minimal, marginal cost.

Remember, relying on easy solutions is a sign of "you don't really matter to me." Consider, for a moment, gift baskets. Yuck. Or those horrific Amazon gift notes. Even if you sent one hundred gift notes to one hundred people and typed out each one individually, there's still something wildly lazy and impersonal about those.

With personalization, though, they are *in* the gift—sometimes literally. One thing that's great for families, for instance, is a site called wonderbly.com. They take children's books and let you customize them to include the name and even photo of the recipient's child throughout the book.

Another company we use often is RefreshGlass.com. They create personalized drinkware and home decor made from rescued wine bottles. Anyone can buy glasses from Crate and Barrel, but these glasses have a story, can be engraved, help give back, and can be a conversation piece each time they're used.

Here's more inspiration for personalized gifts:

- Where are they from? Try location-based gifts, like Tactile Craftworks or Homesick Candles.
- Are they foodies? Try Spoonful of Comfort and Last Crumb, both gold standard.

Knowing what matters to somebody, what they'd like, and what they'd use is a sign of connection. By giving a gift in alignment with these details, you're also giving the greatest gift of all in a noisy world: proof that you care and have been paying attention.

PRACTICAL LUXURIES: "I THINK OF YOU EVERYDAY"

Always gift "practical luxuries" that feel personalized. These are items your recipient would love to own but prefer not to pay for, because they already have leftover junk that's getting them by. Note that your gift quality should reflect how you see yourself and your company. For us, that means world-class quality. Our gifts say, "Like our relationship, this gift will last forever."

A lot of times people ask me, "Why are you giving a set of knives or a $2,000 coffee mug as a gift? That seems weird. Why not give a normal, business-oriented gift like an iPad?"

The answer is because iPads won't last forever. And they won't be used every day.

That's the reason why kitchen cutlery, specifically Cutco, is the number one bestselling product in our agency. They're American made and come with a Forever Guarantee, meaning they are often literally the nicest thing in somebody's kitchen. More on this in a moment.

Think about it: If you get something into somebody's hand that's world-class, a bit unusual, and something they'll use every single day, then they will *absolutely* remember you. You become the most top of mind!

Let's do the math together.

- Let's say you buy a world-class gift that'll last fifteen years.
- It's something practical that'll be used 365 days a year.
- That means that person will think of you (consciously or subconsciously) 5,475 times.

And that's just one person. Double that number if their spouse or partner uses the gift, too, and that's 10,950 impressions—probably more, because now the spouse is saying out loud how great you are. Now multiply that by one hundred people, and that's more than one million times people are thinking about you and your business, year-round.

I strongly advise that instead of buying ads on social media, search engines, TV, newspapers, magazines, newsletters, apps, the list goes on...think about the power of weaving something into someone's life and doing it in such a way that provides both utility and luxury.

Sure, you can find a cheaper, generic gift to save some money, but guess what happens? In six days, it gets thrown in a drawer or trash can with all the other cheap junk.

A heart bomb is an extravagant gifting gesture, given to a key relationship, meant to communicate a level of affection *seldom experienced* by the recipient, when they least expect it—a lot of boxes to check, but when you do? Whew. Sit back and watch the magic. To figure out what to send, ask yourself, "What's the *most* I can do to bless this person?" Then, move in that direction. Your spirit, once moved, will find answers for any budget questions that come up. The ironic part is that ROR always pays tenfold.

If someone refers me a deal that nets me $3,000, I'm sending them a gift between $150 and $450. Some may say, "Wow, you're really generous!" Maybe I am, but I'm also smart and incredibly appreciative they're sending me work that helps me and my family. Plus, if they've recommended me to someone before, odds are pretty good they might be inclined to do it again.

There are parameters here, of course. It's appropriate to ask: "So, you do this *every time*? Like, how many gifts is too many gifts? Doesn't that become transactional at some point?"

I've found that sending more than three surprise-and-delight gifts per year begins to feel transactional, but if someone is giving you frequent, premium referrals and deal flow—don't let yourself off the hook. Instead, go bigger! Save 5 percent to 15 percent of each transaction and fund a larger, more impactful, "holy crap" gift. It requires planning, but it's worth it!

Let's look at an example: Say an individual recommends you to ten deals that close, each one is worth $3,000 (profit), and your relationship tithe is 10 percent.

The advice here is not to buy ten $300 gifts. Instead, buy two $300 gifts and one bigger gift, around $2,500—a heart bomb. Have you ever given somebody a gift around the holidays and you feel giddy in anticipation, like you just can't wait for them to open it? It feels like that.

As Brittany Hodak says, "It's been said the opposite of love is not hate but indifference, the opposite of superfandom is not hate but apathy. The 'meh' crowd. Would-be [partners]—or worse, actual [partners]—who just don't care enough to care one way or the other."

Sending gifts, heart bombs, and tracking your giving in your Referral Partner Playbook (see Chapter 6) is the antidote for "meh."

What are your options so you or your team can handle this internally?

THREE BUILD-AS-YOU-GO GIFT SYSTEMS

Low-inertia systems are essential so you can get started. Let's take a look.

1. YOUR OWN CATALOG

Neither Google nor artificial intelligence will get you peak moment gifts. This job is on you, to accumulate over time, in your company "gift catalog."

Have a place with your favorite gift items—segmented, tagged for searchability, and well structured—and invite other team members to contribute to it. That's what we do with our R.I.C.H. RELATIONSHIP SOCIETY members, and it pays off, tenfold.

(Some items in our catalog have become so popular, like Spoonful of Comfort, that our members get their own discount code.)

Other things to consider when adding to a catalog:

- Capture the moment: Take a photo of the item and/or web copy for later reference.
- Document details: Note the shop, market, or location where you found it.
- Connect it to a story: Write a quick note on how the item resonated with you.
- Track pricing: Include a range of costs to help with budgeting later.
- Note availability: Check if it's a one-of-a-kind item or part of a regular collection.

- Add personal meaning: Reflect on why it caught your eye or its sentimental value.
- Research the maker: Learn about the artisan or company behind the product.
- Organize by category: Create categories for ease, specifically delineating by occasion (baby shower, birthday, football season, etc.) or by a room in the home (kitchen, patio, bedroom, etc.).

2. GIFT CLOSET

A "gift closet" is a designated space where you store gifts in advance for various occasions. It allows you to have thoughtful, ready-to-go presents without last-minute shopping stress. Here are other benefits of a gift closet:

- Time-saver: You always have a gift on hand, avoiding rush purchases.
- Fast delivery: Perfect for local recipients when you need a quick, meaningful gesture.
- Cost-efficient: Buy items on sale, in bulk, or when traveling, adding variety at a lower cost.

A gift closet should include stationery and books. I've seen people (like Joe Polish) who keep thousands of books on hand to give on a variety of occasions. At the very least, stockpile your favorite 24-Hour FUN book and any other "gifting special moves" you may have.

For instance, many realtors stockpile their closing gifts—one less thing to think about when you're pushing to close on time. In your gift closet, remember to categorize items by price and/or occasion and keep an inventory system so you know what you have and when you might need to restock.

3. VENDOR PARTNERSHIPS

Vendor partnerships are curated selections of gifts sourced from local companies and artisans who serve as suppliers. The partnership can be local to you or local to your recipient(s). This is especially important for international referral partners, as the cost of shipping (and customs) can often make international gift giving extremely challenging.

Benefits of vendor partnerships include:

- Speedy delivery: Having local vendors ensures quick turnarounds. This is especially important for personalization (like having a local engraver).
- Support for local businesses: Builds strong community ties while offering unique, high-quality items.
- Customization: Local suppliers can often tailor gifts to your specific needs, including handwritten notes, drop-shipping, etc.
- Bulk discount options: Local suppliers may give you the option to save a little money and buy particular products in large quantities at a lower cost per unit—which can help you wow your referral sources even more!

Several best practices:

- Build relationships: Establish strong, ongoing partnerships with trusted local suppliers.
- Diversify inventory: Source a variety of gift options for high-volume referral givers.
- Negotiate exclusives: Secure unique products or special pricing.
- Track inventory: Ensure a steady stock of high-demand items from local suppliers for fast access.

Of course, another option here is to hire an agency, like ours, to do this for you. A good agency will handle selection, logistics, packaging, delivery, and provide heartfelt messaging—for one recipient or one hundred. Visit GiftologyGroup.com if something like that sounds appealing.

But regardless of who's doing the work, referral partners deserve proper appreciation.

WHAT'S NEXT?

Gifting for ROR is wonderful. But for those of us with limited resources (which is most of us), we need to be smart about it. "Just being generous" without discretion is how to become one of Adam Grant's "sucker givers" (from Chapter 2). Giving randomly may feel good, but it's impractical and rarely life-changing. *Trust me, I've done it.*

In the next chapter, we'll tie it all together. How to integrate the best practices of GIFT·OLOGY, alongside intentional communication, to create a mountain range of peak moments.

By integrating gifting into a system, you maximize your Return on Relationships (ROR).

And you ensure your resources go toward connections that energize your business...not just make you feel good.

CHAPTER 15

PERPETUATING GIVERS

Extraordinary gifting requires thinking beyond traditional presents and creating memorable, personalized experiences. Hal Elrod—my dear friend and bestselling author of *The Miracle Morning* and *The Miracle Equation*—knows this. After his second appearance on one of the world's top podcasts (*Impact Theory*, hosted by Tom Bilyeu), Hal was looking for a way to thank Tom.

But how? Tom already had everything a person could conventionally want. Money wasn't buying him anything he didn't have or couldn't get.

Hal strategized and gave Tom something unique: a custom painting featuring Tom and his wife, Lisa, along with their beloved dog. It was seven feet wide and four feet tall, handmade from broken records. Hal had it delivered to Tom's house (with specific instructions to cover it with a blanket), and then he personally flew out to reveal the gift. Hal recalled:

> Tom later admitted how nervous he'd been about my visit, worried that he might be disappointed by whatever I was presenting. Instead, the reveal exceeded all expectations. Though Lisa wasn't home at the time, she sent

me a video text message as soon as she arrived, saying it was one of the greatest gifts they had ever received. She was literally speechless. This wasn't a transactional gesture. Tom wasn't a client. He had simply supported me by featuring me on his show. The gift was purely a thank-you for his support and generosity.

That's the true hallmark of a 3S giver: maximum impact, no expectations.

HAL'S BIG 4

- What they do: Hal helps individuals and organizations wake up to their full potential.
- Who they serve: Individuals, organizations, and businesses who want to help their people show up at their best every day.
- What they *don't* do: Offer a quick fix or "magic pill."
- Who is *not* a fit: Nobody—this message is universally applicable.

DON'T CHASE

The third key to endless word-of-mouth is a system that nurtures and perpetuates existing givers. Don't chase everyone—focus on those already referring you. This system energizes your givers, transforming casual supporters into lifelong advocates by creating peak moments through strategic gifting. These moments make you not just top of mind, but top of heart. No more waiting, hoping, or relying on chance.

So far, you've learned to:

- Surprise and delight: unexpected communication is the key to unlock loyalty. (Chapter 13)
- Fast-forward relationships: how gifting transforms relationships forever. (Chapter 14)

This chapter ties everything together, outlining the Five Pillars of Referral Overflow, no matter how your current partners are performing. Install each of these and you'll inspire your referral givers to contribute more and with greater conviction.

Before we go there, be mindful of these two mental hygiene mistakes to avoid:

- Thinking, *This feels like bribery.* Having a system isn't the same thing as making your relationships transactional. Don't confuse spontaneity with sincerity. If we did the right things only when we felt like doing them, nobody would have any teeth. Remember the DNA shift that builds your Relationship Snowball: going from a 3S giver (sparing, spontaneous, and sporadic) to a 3P giver (planned, percentage, progressive). The path to success is discipline, which means consistently being a giver who embodies the power of "always." The five pillars in this chapter will cover what I recommend you *always* do when giving. So get the thoughts of bribery out of your brain.
- Giving the *wrong* number of gifts. The right number of gifts is two to three per year. If they're giving you more deals than that, add them to your heart bomb budget. That said, the more common problem I see is not over-gifting. It's *under*-gifting. Anybody can send a one-time gift; however, when that's your only approach, you're missing an incredible opportunity that, when done well, looks a lot like compounded reciprocity. When you're consistent and sustain a relationship over time, it tips the scales in your favor so much that I've literally had people reach out to me because they just can't take it anymore!

PILLAR #1: ALWAYS TEACH YOUR BUSINESS

Peak performance coach Todd Herman says, "The greatest opportunity we have, as business owners, is to teach the marketplace how to work with us at a deeper level."[29] I couldn't agree more.

---

29   Todd Herman, personal discussion with Michael Monroe, August 26, 2024.

We must always be teaching our business to our partners. Sure, for you, it's another sales conversation, but when they refer you, their reputation is on the line. Here are examples of how to better teach your business:

TEACH WHEN IN CLARITY CONVERSATIONS

Once leaders get referrals, they assume the person referring them "gets it"—meaning, they assume that person knows how to talk about their business. Moreover, the more Clarity Conversations a leader has, the more they create confusion by falling into two classic "un-clarity" traps: using too much colloquial language (i.e., words only you and your industry understand) and using too much marketing speak (i.e., vague words that would appear on a website).

It's easy to assume that just because someone has sent you a referral, they understand your business inside and out. But here's the reality: Unless you've had a Clarity Conversation, they probably don't. And that can lead to serious miscommunication and missed opportunities. In fact, without a clear understanding, your referral partner might send you the wrong type of clients—or worse, misrepresent what you offer.

Let's say you're a financial planner who specializes in retirement planning, but your referral partner is telling potential clients you're a general financial advisor. Now, instead of getting clients who need your specific expertise, you're getting a mix of people with unrelated needs, leading to frustration on both ends. This isn't just a waste of time; it's a potential reputation risk. The client feels mismatched, you're stuck explaining what you really do, and the referral partner may doubt your ability to deliver on what they thought you offered.

Even if you're already getting referrals, don't assume everything is running smoothly. Sit down with your referral giver and have a Clarity Conversation. This isn't about questioning their competence; it's about ensuring they have the precise information they need to represent your business accurately and effectively.

Even if they appear successful in sending business your way, take the time to clarify. You might discover with a little guidance, they could send you even better referrals—ones who are perfectly aligned with your strengths. *That's* the kind of referral that not only grows your business but also strengthens your relationship with your referral partner.

PILLAR #2: ALWAYS EXPRESS GRATITUDE

"I know I could and should be doing better with this gifting thing, but…"

If you've ever said (or thought) this, save yourself the "but." First and foremost, never miss a thank-you. There is no good excuse. Missing a peak moment increases the odds of breaking a good habit by over 50 percent, and worse, it could be your last chance with that partner.

Here's a conversation I've had more than once:

Question: "How do I operationalize this so it isn't a time suck and I don't forget?"

Answer: "Easy. You need to adopt a system."

Remember, S.Y.S.T.E.M.: "Save Yourself Stress, Time, Energy, and Money."

Every business leader, particularly those leading teams, needs to answer the following: "Given where we are at, what's the best way to systemize this as quickly as possible so we never miss a gratitude peak?"

Let's examine the three main routes—the agency route, the partner route, and the in-house route—including the pros and cons of each.

AGENCY

- Outsourcing your relationship planning to a group of experts.
- **Example:** Annual partnership with the GIFT·OLOGY Group.
- #1 **PRO:** It gets done and gets done well. And scales to infinity.
- #1 **CON:** Cost. Best for people with more money than time, with many recipients.

Many "agencies" nowadays are simply software companies, with a proposition of convenience. Remember the goal is to create peak moments, not check a box off the to-do list.

PARTNER

- Account managers who can supply you with personalized partner gifts.
- **Example:** A professional, year-round Cutco representative.
- **♯1 PRO:** The experience of others. Can be called upon "on the fly."
- **♯1 CON:** Often limited in product selection.

It is helpful to have several gifting partners, particularly for relationships that last five-plus years. Take care to establish your first good partner and go from there.

IN-HOUSE

- An internal employee, who handles all strategy, planning, and logistics.
- **Example:** A full-time "director of customer experience" (or similar title).
- **♯1 PRO:** A high level of flexibility in creating perfectly custom experiences.
- **♯1 CON:** Cost. And when they leave, they often take the expertise with them.

In-house individuals are wonderful, but they absolutely require a certain personality type (which is the first step of our interview process when vetting a new GIFT·OLOGIST).

Make sure this individual(s) isn't just an artist, but a system builder as well. If you're a solopreneur at this point, great! *You* build the habit. *You* create the system and make every piece of it as efficient as possible.

PILLAR #3: ALWAYS PERSONALIZE

Peak moments require personalization. That means making it "one of a kind," even if it's owned (like Cutco) by tens of millions of customers. The moment you add somebody's name on something (again, *not* their logo), you are making it an heirloom. Personalization doesn't have to be limited, however, to engraving, monogramming, carving, burning, or painting. Personalization can also mean curating, tailoring, complementing, or matching.

Often such personalization will involve a spouse or partner. Consider this possible exchange: "Hello. You don't know me. But I am connected to [SPOUSE] through such-and-such. They have been an incredible partner in my business. If it's okay with you, I'd like to buy them a special present (it's a secret)! To do that, I need some help with _____ (the sizing, color, golf club, etc.)."

I've seen this work very well. Once, I received an email from a gentleman who reads our email newsletter and who wanted to buy his gift recipient a really expensive, custom leather belt. To get it right, he introduced himself to the man's wife over Facebook messenger (they'd never met before), and she was more than happy to take a picture of the shoe rack in his closet so he could buy the appropriate color.

Such a move also endears you to your gift getter's partner, which is icing on the cake.

PERSONALIZATION DOESN'T HAVE TO BE EXPENSIVE

When studying gift givers, researchers found that higher prices went with perceived favorable receptions, but when recipients rated those same gifts, price was completely unrelated to enjoyment. In other words, givers often misjudge what recipients want.

Hear me loud and clear: Gifts do not have to be expensive. Yes, you'll hear about amazing gifts that shock and awe. And yes, it might seem like I'm contradicting myself when I tell you to ask, "What's the most I can do?"

But one of our most effective gifts our company has ever produced costs just nine dollars. We've received more referrals from this one nine-dollar item than (in some cases) from the $1,000 gifts we've sent out.

It is...drumroll please...our letterhead. You see, GIFT·OLOGY Group doesn't use your normal letterhead. It's made of solid metal, customized with our logo, weighs about five ounces, and costs three dollars to ship. It's certainly not a colored piece of printer paper with a logo at the top. We send out a lot of handwritten notes, and when somebody gets one that's thoughtful, is personal to them, *and* it comes on nine-dollar letterhead? It's amazing how people respond.

I've had people at some of the biggest companies in the world react to our handwritten notes on steel. This small choice creates a moment, and moments matter more than things.

PILLAR #4: ALWAYS SAVE AND BUDGET

Intelligent givers build a "giving war chest." This is a savings fund by which they can do generous things. Some (like us) save a portion of each sale, like a tithe. Others save a portion of their referral sales only.

Strategy is important here. Regardless, if you're in a low-margin or high-margin business, if you're going to energize and electrify partners with gifts, you shouldn't be spending every dollar. That's sometimes what 3S givers do—they gift on feeling. Maybe they're feeling a little generous during the holidays if they've had a good year, or they put in a line item of $5,000 as a placeholder, or take a partner out for a round of golf, or a nice dinner. But they really don't set a specific budget, because they don't view gifting as part of an ongoing appreciation strategy.

Imagine if that business owner treated the rest of their operations that way?

Spontaneous marketing. Spontaneous customer service. Spontaneous accounting...the IRS would love that, right?

If you're doing this right, the budget for gifting comes out of your margin on the sale. I've heard it referred to as "customers paying for their own marketing." But unlike traditional marketing, which can cost $1.00 to make $1.20, you can set the budget at 5 percent, 10 percent, or 15 percent of net profit—again, like a tithe on the relationship.

This money is set aside purely for betting on relationships. To me, I view a percentage of the dollars I'm investing with gifts as a little like gambling on blackjack—you can't win unless there's money on the table, and if you make enough small bets, some big ones will pay off.

I will use this "relationship building" budget other places as well. For example, say I meet someone at a conference or an event, and we have a connection, they're a good human being, and there's obvious talent there. I might send them a little gift just to acknowledge them. If you're playing business with a fifty-year horizon, you never know where those people are going to be in five years, ten years, or fifteen years. Plus, even if they turn out to be nothing for you from a business perspective, it's just fun to love on people.

I've done this for twenty years, which means I've been around long enough to see some small bets pay off. That's where you get the 100x returns, where you could never, not in your wildest dreams, imagine how important a relationship would be.

By focusing on personalization and consistently budgeting for relationship building, you create a sustainable system for nurturing your most valuable business asset: your relationships. Remember, it's not about the cost of the gift, but the thought and personalization behind it. By setting aside a portion of your profits for this purpose, you ensure you always have the resources to invest in your relationships, even when times are tight.

PILLAR #5: ALWAYS ROMANCE

Romance involves capturing and transferring a feeling. People want to feel loved and cared for, and leaning in like this invites a deeper level of communication and relationship. When Tommy Mello of A1 Garage gave his entire team personalized Cutco knives, for example, he also included a note that said "Contact me anytime" with his phone number. It doesn't get more personal than that.

Tommy's act wasn't done out of the blue; it was strategic, as we've discussed in this book—the product of an origin story. If you think about it, all great superheroes have an origin story: bitten by a radioactive spider, exposed to cosmic space radiation, born as the heir of Asgard (or on a farm in Ohio). Maybe said hero witnessed a tragic family event and developed a fear of bats. Or ate a piece of pizza soaked in green mutagen, then shared it with his half-shelled brothers and the local sewer rat.

Your gifts have an origin story too.

You've seen such tales all over the place: on the back of your favorite craft beer, the wrap-up of the local evening news, written up on the Amazon startup pages. Business leaders obsess over architecting flawless trailer videos and beautifully written "About" pages on their websites. Why? Because origin stories sell. Duh.

Romanticizing a gift with an origin story increases its value exponentially. Here are some questions that'll allow you to write fantastic origin stories with your gifts:

- What inspired you to choose this specific gift?
- Where does this gift come from, and what makes its origin unique?
- What craftsmanship or process went into making this gift?
- How does the gift reflect your relationship with the recipient or the work you do together?
- What special qualities or values does this gift represent?
- What personal connection or story do you have with the place or people behind this gift?
- What feeling or message do you hope this gift will convey to the recipient?

We're all about systemizing, and while it may sound counterintuitive to schedule romance, it's decidedly not. Several R.I.C.H. RELATIONSHIP SOCIETY members swear by this approach:

- Block off thirty to sixty minutes in your calendar.
- Handwrite a love letter to a referral partner.
- Deliver it in person. On its own. Or with a world-class, practical luxury.

Sound extreme? Crazy? Creepy even? Hardly.

One R.I.C.H. RELATIONSHIP SOCIETY member, who regularly practices the habit, shared:

> I usually think about my relationship with the person and let what I write flow from that. It's more work and takes longer this way, but it helps me stay relational and catches me when I start to drift into transactional utility mode...which is unfortunately my natural default!

There is something powerful about occasionally writing your own notes. I know because I write about 10 percent of mine—even though my handwriting would make doctors point and laugh. However, none of that matters. Unlock the power of handwritten gratitude.

WHAT'S NEXT?

When you master this system, you will energize partnerships, build lifelong friendships, and create opportunities that no amount of money could buy. And thanks to your inspirational gifting of world-class, practical luxuries? Your relationships will grow even when you're not around.

BUT FIRST ANSWER THESE QUESTIONS

- How will you accurately trace the source of every referral contact you receive?
- Do you have a system in place where every referral—good or bad, right or wrong—gets acknowledged?
- Do you have stamps, stationery, or thank-you cards stockpiled in an easily accessible area?
- Have you bought in fully to the power of peak moments and the necessity of investing (be it money or time) into your partner relationships? What are your limiting beliefs?
- If applicable, have you had a compliance discussion to ensure what you can do and what you can't do?
- Do you have any favorite world-class, practical luxuries you and your inner circle use every day? What's the best gift you've ever been given?
- Do you have previous referral givers (or partners) who stopped giving? What do you think happened? Is it worth trying to resuscitate those relationships?

ACTION ITEMS, STEP-BY-STEP

This isn't about perfection. It's about progress. Remember that as you:

1. For the next 10 referrals you get—good or bad, right or wrong—send a handwritten note, thanking the giver for the introduction.
2. For the next 10 referrals you get—good or bad, right or wrong—report positive progress, informing the giver of how you helped their connection.
3. Schedule 3 to 5 Clarity Conversations with any current referral givers who never got one. (See Chapters 5 and 12 for more details on how to execute this elegantly.)
4. For your next 2 to 3 closed referral deals, save 5 percent to 15 percent of the net profit in your giving account.
5. For your next closed referral deal, send a surprise-and-delight gift

to the recipient. Do this within four weeks and make no mention of the referral. (Bonus points if it's a frequent giver and you send a heart bomb!)

6. Tell us about it at **CelebrateMyWins.com**, and we might share your Big 4 with others.

PART SIX

OUTCOME #4

GROW BEYOND YOU

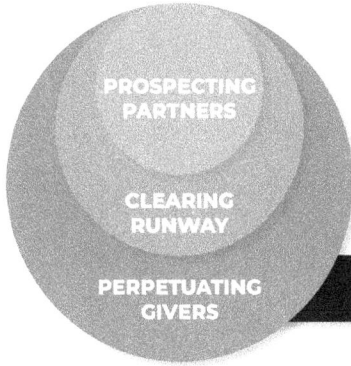

PROSPECTING PARTNERS

CLEARING RUNWAY

PERPETUATING GIVERS

CODIFY | Plug the leaks
(CH.16)

UNIFY TAP | Meetings
(CH.17)

AMPLIFY | Drive the culture
(CH.18)

GROWTH BEYOND YOU
Different protocols for different people

CHAPTER 16

THREE-AT-ONCE

Do you remember my friend Corey Quinn, from Chapter 6? While the CMO at Scorpion, he envisioned expanding into the trillion-dollar franchise industry—a significant departure from his team's established focus on serving legal clients. However, one little problem: no contacts, no connections, and no clear path into the new sector.

Scorpion needed a relational inroad.

The breakthrough introduction came not from Corey, but via an executive team member. This leader had previously worked with the largest and most respected franchise brand in the home services world. His exceptional past work made it easy to reach out and rekindle the relationship.

This connection proved invaluable. Not long after, Corey and team won a small piece of business from this highly respected franchise brand. Scorpion made it their mission to over-deliver on every aspect of that initial engagement. Their outstanding performance not only brought in more business from the franchise and its thousands of independents but, more importantly, it got their snowball rolling in a new industry.

The credibility they gained from working with this visible, well-respected brand was transformative. Other franchise companies took notice. Corey said, "Working with an industry leader spoke volumes about our capabilities and trustworthiness. This single strategic relationship became our catalyst for explosive growth. Within just two years, we successfully closed deals with one hundred other franchise brands." This was one of the initiatives that took Scorpion from $20 million to $150 million.

Imagine one of your team members creating that type of opportunity for your organization.

That doesn't happen by accident. Corey was intentional and systemized—proving that relational leaders get relational results.

THE RELATIONSHIP BOTTLENECK

Let me paint you a picture of what's probably happening in your business right now.

You're crushing it with relationships. Your clients love you. Your network is strong. Referrals are flowing. And that's exactly the problem. Because guess what? Every thank-you note needs your signature. Every follow-up needs your attention. Every new connection needs your presence. You've become so good at relationships that you've built yourself a prison of your own success.

I see this all the time with our agency clients. They come to us saying things like:

- "I know I need to delegate, but nobody can handle relationships like I can."
- "My team just doesn't get the personal touch like I do."
- "The last time I tried to delegate follow-ups, we lost two key relationships."

Sound familiar?

Here's the brutal truth: The very skills that got you here—your natural ability to connect, your perfect timing with follow-ups, your knowing what to say in every moment—are exactly what's holding you back from scaling.

You've become the virtuoso who can't put down their instrument long enough to conduct the orchestra.

Listen up, because this is where the rubber meets road. By the end of Part Six, you'll know exactly how to *run different protocols for different people, all at once and ongoing.*

Here's your roadmap:

- **Codify.** Organize and formalize roles and responsibilities. (Chapter 16)
- **Unify.** Meet consistently to communicate wins and next steps. (Chapter 17)
- **Amplify.** Increase scale by leading people and managing processes. (Chapter 18)

Let's start by reviewing the three systems and how they work together.

THE THREE-SYSTEM SOLUTION

The answer isn't to clone yourself (impossible) or to maintain control over every relationship (unsustainable). It's to build three distinct systems that work together:

1. **Prospecting Partners System (Chapters 7–9)**
   A. Finds and evaluates new potential partners
   B. Creates consistent inflow of relationships
   C. Prevents over-reliance on current connections
2. **Clearing Runway System (Chapters 10–12)**
   A. Tests and nurtures new relationships
   B. Builds trust through consistent touches
   C. Moves someone from potential to actual partner
3. **Perpetuating Givers System (Chapters 13–15)**

A. Energizes current referral sources
B. Improves their conviction when referring
C. Makes them want to give more

Think of it like building a high-performance engine. You need:

- Fuel intake (Prospecting)
- Combustion chamber (Clearing Runway)
- Power delivery (Perpetuating Givers)

Remove any one of these, and the engine sputters. Get all three working together? You've got a machine that runs whether you're in the driver's seat or not.

When this three-system solution runs in our company, we say "JNN" (which I've shared means John NOT Needed!). This means the machine grows beyond the leader of the company. It is something to celebrate.

But here's the catch, and it's a big one: You can't half commit to this. This isn't another "tactic" to add to your marketing mix. This is about transforming how your entire organization thinks about and handles relationships.

Most of them don't think like you. This is where systems bridge the gap.

THE REALITY CHECK

If you're like the rest of us, your relationship systems are either leaky, inconsistent, or both. And trying to juggle three systems at once? That's like trying to pat your head, rub your belly, and recite the alphabet backward—while riding a unicycle.

Here's what more commonly happens:

- New relationships create excitement (and tunnel vision).
- Existing connections get neglected.

- Your team struggles to replicate your "magic."
- Everything bottlenecks back to you.

A young woman approached me after a keynote speech. She was battling this exact problem. In her early thirties, she had built a $3 million consulting practice, great relationships, and steady referrals. But she was working seventy-hour weeks just maintaining connections. Her team was capable, but she didn't trust them with "her" relationships.

"What if they mess them up?" she asked me.

I smiled, having worked through the exact challenge myself.

"They will mess them up. Just like you did when you were learning," I told her. "The question is: Do you want to stay stuck at your current level, or are you ready to build something bigger than yourself?"

I actually saw the light bulb turn on above her head.

Let's get yours shining as well.

STEP BACK, BIT BY BIT

Stop trying to do it all yourself. Seriously. Stop it.

The goal isn't to clone yourself; it's to build systems that amplify what makes you special. Think of it like this: You're a master chef. You've spent years perfecting your recipes. Your regulars love your cooking. But you can't scale a restaurant by doing all the cooking yourself. Instead, you need to:

- Document your recipes (Systems)
- Train your sous chefs (Team)
- Maintain quality control (Management)
- Keep innovating (Leadership)

Your job is shifting from star performer to conductor. You don't need to play every instrument; you need to make sure they all play together.

This means:

- Creating clear processes that others can follow
- Training your team to maintain your standards
- Giving them room to add their own touch
- Celebrating when they get it right
- Correcting (kindly) when they don't

Example: One of our R.I.C.H. RELATIONSHIP SOCIETY members thought nobody could write thank-you notes like she could. She was right—until she wasn't. When her process was finally documented—*they* created a framework and *she* made corrections—her team started writing *better* notes because they understood the objectives.

Building these systems is like setting a flywheel into motion. At first, it takes effort to get it spinning, but each small, consistent action adds to the momentum. Over time, the wheel turns faster, requiring less effort to maintain its speed. The results compound, creating unstoppable progress, and soon, your momentum takes on a life of its own.

Is it easy? Nope. Is it fast? Not even close. Is it worth it? More than you can imagine.

Like a high-performance engine, there's only so many things that can break. In the next couple sections, we'll cover breakdowns, mistakes, and some simple solutions.

PERPETUATION BREAKDOWNS

Let's start with your most valuable relationships: your existing referral givers. You've worked your tail off to earn these relationships, so they deserve your best energy. But I see three killer mistakes people make here:

BREAKDOWN #1: THE PILE-UP PROBLEM

Here's how it happens: You're traveling or someone in your family gets sick, and suddenly you've got:

- Nine thank-you notes to write
- Twelve texts to send (which create more conversations)
- Two to three gifts to arrange
- Multiple follow-ups pending

What happens next? You say those deadly words: "I'll catch up later."

Spoiler alert: Later never comes.

Cameron Herold taught me something brilliant here: "Whenever something consistently isn't getting done, the founder should: (1) kill it; (2) delegate it; (3) outsource it; or (4) hire for it. And 99 percent of the time, the answer is *not* to hire."

BREAKDOWN #2: THE AWOL SYNDROME

Picture this: You just had an amazing conversation with someone's referral. Butterflies in your stomach. Future possibilities dancing in your head. But you're driving, or at the airport, or headed into another meeting, so you don't update the person who made the introduction.

This is the most basic gesture in the whole book—a simple text message saying, "Thank you for that intro, just had a great conversation!" Yet, it's the most often forgotten.

If you've ever had to ask someone, "Did you talk to so-and-so?" or worse, discovered a referral didn't work out only when the referral giver mentioned it later, you know how unprofessional this looks.

BREAKDOWN #3: THE CHEAP THANK-YOU

If somebody gives you a $5,000 net profit deal and you thank them with brownies, well, you're not creating a peak moment. You're broadcasting your cheapness. And for those in regulated industries saying, "I can only spend twenty-five dollars or less," that's just lazy thinking. You're opening the door for your partner to get a better offer from someone more creative.

Here are a few ideas on how to fix these breakdowns.

SMALL DOMINOES, BIG IMPACT

Physicist Lorne Whitehead demonstrated that a domino can topple another 1.5 times its size, creating an exponential chain reaction. Starting with a two-inch domino, by the twenty-ninth, you'd have enough force to knock over the Empire State Building (about 1,454 feet).

For the Pile-Up Problem:

- Create weekly relationship maintenance blocks on your calendar
- Delegate what you can, multitask when you can't—I'll sometimes write notes while on airplanes
- Use a one-page checklist so these notes, text, and gifts don't fall through the cracks
- Assign the right owner to each task (more on this in Chapter 17)

For the AWOL Problem:

- Make it a rule: No conversation ends without an update
- Use voice notes if you're driving or traveling
- Set up a consistent, "one-purpose *only*" communication channel that triggers your team into action
- Have someone on your team monitor and remind you

For the Thank-You Issue:

- Set standard gift levels based on deal size
- Preapprove common gifting scenarios
- Build a "peak moment" protocol

- Always ask: "What's the most I can do?" not "What's the least I can get away with?"

Remember: Your referral givers are agnostic. They're constantly comparing you to every other professional they know. If you're not one of the best and most memorable, you'll soon be among the forgotten.

MISTAKES ON THE RUNWAY

Let's talk about your new partners—those promising relationships that could transform your business. They've had Clarity Conversations. They're showing interest. Now what?

Here are the three deadliest mistakes I see people make:

MISTAKE #1: CORRECTION AVOIDANCE

When someone gives you a "bad referral" (no such thing), it's tempting to just ignore it. Or worse, silently resent them for wasting your time.

Big mistake. Huge.

Here's why: An enthusiasm to refer is a rarer trait than referring correctly. You can teach someone to refer properly, but you can't teach someone to be a giver. Instead of avoiding the conversation, follow this template:

- First, thank them specifically for thinking of you.
- Educate them on ideal fits (without criticizing).
- Then, show them how you helped the referral indirectly.
- Thank them again for being in your corner.

Bonus tip: Your team likely doesn't enjoy correcting others either. When a correction is handled well, celebrate it like a proud parent. Screenshot the text, forward the email—especially if the response from the partner is, "Aha! I get it now!"

This reinforces a culture of precision and accountability.

MISTAKE #2: THE FAVORITES FAILURE

Listen up, because this is crucial: When someone's on your runway, they need to be on your favorites list. That means if they call, you answer. If they text, you reply quickly. If they need something, you make it happen.

Why? Because 80 percent of loyalty is built in the beginning of a relationship. Handle these early interactions with excellence, and you'll build a foundation that can withstand occasional gaps later.

Coming out of a Clarity Conversation, favoritism is the protocol—as long as it's reciprocated. That's the purpose of the runway system. Everyone likes to think of themselves as generous, strategic givers, but it's their actions, not their words, that prove it.

MISTAKE #3: THE CLARITY SHORTCUT

Are you catching yourself thinking, *They're already giving me referrals. Why waste time on a Clarity Conversation?*

If Richard Branson makes time to play chess with new friends, you can make time for proper relationship development. Period. Clarity is power. Don't give up your power.

If you haven't made the time to read Chapter 5 in full, go back and do that now. And if you have? Recall the Big 4 which must be communicated to every partner:

1. What we do.
2. Who we serve.
3. What we *don't* do.
4. Who is *not* a fit.

If you are not having success in this phase, you're likely failing to communicate two (or three, or even all four) of the above.

There's a reason so many of my friends—like Phil M. Jones, Donald Miller, and Michael Bernoff—are so successful.

Because nothing creates change faster than a change in communication.

PUTTING IT ALL TOGETHER

We have to make sure nobody gets left behind. And relationships, while important, are only as urgent as the leader makes them. If each of these systems are running without coordination, check-ins, or checkups—months will go by and processes will be missed.

You do not want to be a leader who talks in theory. "Do as I say, not as I do." Nor should you assume anybody in your orbit is as intuitive as you are at (1) talking about the business, (2) remembering relational details, or (3) enthusiastically visioneering possibilities.

Fortunately, as you'll discover in the next chapter, you can make a massive difference in just one hour per week.

CHAPTER 17

TALK ABOUT PARTNERS

What people say about you in rooms you're not in matters. A lot.

Chad Willardson, my friend and founder of Pacific Capital and Platinum Elevated coaching, knows this. So many of his referrals don't even come from actual clients—they come from people who have observed the impact Chad's making on the entrepreneurs he serves.

Hear it straight from the source:

> These observers are so impressed by what they see that they're willing to put their own reputation on the line to refer us, even though they might not personally qualify for our services. This has taught me that when you're truly making a difference in your clients' lives, you don't have to ask for referrals or introductions—they happen organically because people can't keep you a secret with a good conscience. I've learned that in today's world, where technology and AI are automating so many basic business expectations, you have to go above and beyond with personal impact. It's not just about being top of mind; it's about being an essential part of your client's life. When you achieve that level of impact, your clients and even non-clients become your most powerful advocates, creating a word-of-mouth effect that's one hundred times more powerful than anything you could say about yourself.

Yep. And, as you probably know by now, none of this happens by accident. Or alone.

CHAD'S BIG 4

- What they do: In his financial practice, Chad helps eight- and nine-figure entrepreneurs increase their lifestyle freedom by removing stress, increasing net cash flow, and freeing up time.
- Who they serve: Ambitious, visionary entrepreneurs with at least $10 million to invest and a strong peer network of other entrepreneurs.
- What they *don't* do: Try to be all things to all people. Chad works only with eye-level entrepreneurs.
- Who is *not* a fit: Anyone who is not an entrepreneur (professional athletes, executives, doctors, lawyers, etc.).

IT TAKES A VILLAGE

Anyone who interacts with your referral partners—or manages their information—plays one of three essential roles: Accumulator, Energizer, or Manager.

ACCUMULATORS

Accumulators are the face of the organization. They're the John Ruhlins, Brad Weimerts, and Hal Elrods—the founders and personalities. Most relationships start and reside with them.

Without them, there are no referrals, because there are no referral partners.

The Accumulator's number one priority is having Clarity Conversations to build and deepen those connections.

ENERGIZERS

Energizers are the driving force that keeps agreements moving forward. They overcome obstacles and ensure things get done—no excuses.

Without them, there's no execution, because there are no deadlines.

An Energizer's number one priority is to resurface commitments and drive completion of relational actions, whether it's a heart bomb for a repeat partner or a quick progress text to a referral giver.

MANAGERS

Managers are the chaos controllers. They turn the daily whirlwind of conversations into precision and accuracy. Every call, deal, detail, birthday, and anniversary ends up in the CRM because they leave no stone unturned.

Without them, critical details would slip through the cracks, and triggers would be missed.

The Manager's number one priority is capturing every detail to keep the system running smoothly.

You might have one person for each role, a dynamic duo covering multiple roles, or even one person wearing all three hats. There's no fixed formula. For instance, one Energizer might support several Accumulators, or multiple Managers might handle the details for a highly skilled Accumulator.

Nothing great happens alone.

GREAT PARTNERSHIPS REQUIRE PLANNING

Here's the truth: ROR (Return on Relationship) is not something that just happens. You can't just throw people into your CRM, set up some automated touches, and expect magic.

Talking about partners (TAP) at a regular cadence ensures every seed has an opportunity to sprout. And let me be crystal clear—a TAP meeting is unlike any typical meeting. It stands alone; it's not just another agenda item or add-on. This isn't the place for project updates, sales inquiries, operational discussions, or any other business-as-usual stuff. Instead, TAP meetings are about one thing and one thing only: moving relationships toward their respective end zone.

When you get your accumulators, energizers, and managers in the room together, magic happens. You start seeing quality communication and joyful accountability. You see little victories being celebrated, culture being built, and relationships actually moving forward.

But here's what trips most people up: They try to squeeze partnership discussions into other meetings. It becomes, "Oh, we'll cover that in our weekly sales meeting." Or "We can touch on that during our monthly all-hands."

No. No. No.

Your partnerships deserve their own dedicated time and attention. After all, these are the relationships that can completely transform your business. Would you try to handle your finances by briefly mentioning them at the end of other meetings?

In this chapter, I'm going to teach you exactly how to run these meetings. Not just the agenda (though you'll get that), but how to make them actually work for your business.

TAP MEETINGS: THE GAME-CHANGER

Another meeting sounds about as appealing as a root canal, right? I get it. But TAP meetings aren't just another time suck on your calendar. These are your "Referral Roadmapping Sessions," focused entirely on plotting the path to deeper referral connections. Think of these as your relationship strategy sessions—not just updates or check-ins, but intentional discussions about how to grow and sustain the bonds between your business and referral partners.

Let me break down why these meetings are nonnegotiable:

- **Accountability.** You know what happens when nobody's watching the relationship ball? It drops. Hard. TAP meetings create a space where team members take ownership of their partnerships. No more "Oh yeah, I meant to follow up with them," or "I should probably send them a thank-you gift."

- **Momentum.** Partnerships are like sharks; they need to keep moving forward or they die. These meetings maintain the rhythm needed to keep relationships moving forward. Without them? Your referrals and opportunities stall faster than a teenage driver learning stick shift.
- **Acceleration.** Want to fast-track important connections? This is your chance. By continually revisiting relationships and brainstorming next moves, you can turn potential into action at warp speed.
- **Culture.** We all know what gets recognized gets repeated. Celebrating wins and sharing progress in these meetings fosters a culture where relationships matter. Not just in theory, but in practice.

WHAT A TAP MEETING IS NOT

Let me be crystal clear: A TAP meeting is about referral partnerships. It is *not* a sales meeting. I repeat: not a sales meeting.

Here's how they're different:

Focus

- Sales/Pipeline meetings: "How close are we to closing this deal?"
- TAP meetings: "How can we deepen this relationship?"

Objective

- Sales/Pipeline meetings: Close deals, hit numbers
- TAP meetings: Nurture partnerships, build trust

Participants

- Sales/Pipeline meetings: Sales team, revenue folks
- TAP meetings: Anyone managing referral relationships

Metrics

- Sales/Pipeline meetings: Revenue targets, conversion rates
- TAP meetings: Relationship milestones, partnership growth

Nature of Discussion

- Sales/Pipeline meetings: "What's the status of the Johnson deal?"
- TAP meetings: "How can we show the Johnsons we really value them?"

Wins

- Sales/Pipeline meetings: "We closed the deal!"
- TAP meetings: "They referred us to three new clients!"

Are there similarities? Sure. Might some of the same people be in both meetings? Absolutely. But mix these meetings together, and you'll water down both purposes.

Here's a real example: One of our TAP meetings revealed that a referral partner hadn't sent any leads in months despite a solid history. Through discussion, we learned (from a non–John Ruhlin Accumulator) that the partner's business had shifted focus. Our solution? To have another Clarity Conversation around their new business emphasis.

Another situation: It became obvious that a certain Accumulator (cough, John Ruhlin, cough) hadn't been reporting positive progress to referral partners. In the TAP meeting, we implemented a new system where the account Manager records audio for that Accumulator to pass on. Three sentences became three button presses.

No more excuses.

MAKE THIS UNIQUELY YOUR OWN

Look, I don't care if you call it a TAP meeting. Call it your "Relationship Roundup" or your "Friday Friendship Session"...whatever floats your boat. The name doesn't matter. What matters is that it gets done.

I'm sharing this framework for the first time, and I guarantee some of you (most of whom are smarter than me) will come up with incredible variations. When you do, I want to hear about them. Share them at **CelebrateMyWins.com**. We'll make you look great.

In fact, we've seen some creative adaptations already:

- Organizations where everyone's Referral Partner Playbook is public domain
- Leaders who quiz team members about their playbook relationships
- Teams that use visual boards to track relationship progress
- Weekly gift-planning sessions that look more like creative brainstorms

The main thing is to keep partnerships front and center, which brings me to one of my favorite examples: Pete Williams's meetings with his executive assistant. Now, Pete Williams isn't just any Australian entrepreneur, author, and marketer; he's a founding R.I.C.H. RELATIONSHIP SOCIETY member who's turned TAP meetings into an art form. His weekly sessions with his executive assistants are a master class in simplicity and effectiveness.

Here's his exact agenda (pay attention, because this is brilliant):

1. "Who have I met with this week that we should gift?" Simple question. Massive impact.
2. "What projects are we working on that we could enhance the experience on?" Looking for opportunities to go above and beyond.
3. "What am I doing socially this week that we can have some fun with?" Building relationships isn't just about business.

4. "Who in my work can I Console, Compliment, and Congratulate?" The three Cs that keep relationships warm.

That's it. Four questions. Thirty minutes. Massive results.

No complicated spreadsheets. No lengthy PowerPoints. Just focused attention on what matters most: the relationships that drive his business forward.

It works because it's regular (same time every week), it's focused (just relationship building), it's actionable (clear next steps), and it's simple (anyone can do it). The beauty of Pete's system is that it's perfectly tailored to his business and his style. He's not trying to copy someone else's complicated process; he's created something that works for him.

You might need something different. Maybe your meetings need to be daily instead of weekly. Maybe you need more structure or less. The key is finding what works for your team and your relationships.

BE THE ROLE MODEL. ALWAYS.

If you want your team to care about relationships, you need to be the walking, talking example of what that looks like. Nobody, and I mean nobody, carries more weight than you.

Think of it like parenting (and believe me, running a gifting company gives me plenty of experience with this). There are eyes on you all the time. "What you do speaks so loudly, I cannot hear what you say" isn't just a cute quote—it's the brutal truth of leadership.

Here's what this looks like in practice:

The Law of the Lid. Your team's relationship-building potential is capped by your leadership. You can't expect excellence in execution if you're skipping 50 percent of the steps. Want them to be better? You go first.

Know When You Blow It (Because You Will). I once sent a personalized gift to a family that included the ex-wife's name instead of the current wife's. Talk about awkward. But here's what matters: We owned it, fixed it, and I showed the team what accountability looks like.

Trust me, you can't possibly mess this up worse than we have. Don't think. *Do*.

And remember, your team isn't just watching what you do right. They're watching how you handle it when things go wrong. That's often the more important lesson.

DO THIS, GET THAT: IS THIS APPROACH *ALWAYS* BAD?

It's time to tackle the elephant in the room: When you're running these TAP meetings, someone's eventually going to ask, "Should we be doing more than just buying this person gifts?"

The answer? Everyone's favorite consultant response: *It depends*.

Remember back in Chapters 1 and 2, we talked about why "Do This, Get That" programs usually fail? They're usually devised by someone with a transactional mindset, creating discomfort for others and stalling their snowball before it even begins to roll.

But—and this is a big but—once a relationship is solid, predictable, and dependable, it might be time to take the next step. Think about it: Genuine friends can talk about anything, including adding some monetary spice to an already transformational relationship.

You can consider it when the receiving feels cumbersome. Look, your giving might feel cumbersome (trust me, I know), but the receiving should never feel that way for your partner. If they make a light comment like, "I can't take any more of your gifts," it might be time to transition to something more payout based.

I once gave Cameron Herold a briefcase full of money, but this was after he got all the Cutco and mugs and Smithey his house(s) could hold. The timing was right.

And he loved it.

THE PARTNERSHIP EVOLUTION

Partnerships are like any other relationship: They grow, they change, and they evolve. And sometimes, they're ready for the next level. Here's when that can happen:

When the partner brings it up. I prefer handshakes over contracts. Yes, this has led to me being taken advantage of several times. That's fine. I'd rather be occasionally cheated than perpetually suspicious.

Remember this: If you have a contract, you don't have a willing relationship. This might evolve into that over the years, but for now, keep things light and flexible. You don't know yet if the other person is a giver or a taker.

When you're "having a baby" together. Your Relationship Snowball will, no doubt, create new business ventures and opportunities. Don't confuse building a product, doing a deal, "going in together," or sitting on a board as the same thing as "getting a referral." Operating agreements keep relationships clean. In all things, I tell my partners: friends first. And I mean it.

The bottom line as you TAP (Talk About Partners): Always ask "What can I give?" instead of "What can I get?" Focus on making your partners feel valued. This is critical because strong relationships will always take you places marketing (and contracts) can't. Remember, whether you're meeting about it, gifting for it, or structuring it, the relationship comes first. Everything else is just details.

What gets measured gets managed, but what gets celebrated gets repeated. As we move into Chapter 18, we'll talk about how to scale these systems across your organization. But for now, focus on getting your TAP meetings right because talking about partners is where everything starts.

The question isn't whether you should be having these meetings.

The question is: Why haven't you started already?

LEADING WELL

Systemizing connection is powerful. But don't take it from me.

My friend Robert Glazer shared this insight from his time as CEO of Acceleration Partners:

> One of our three core values at Acceleration Partners is "Embrace Relationship." Our industry, partnership marketing, is built on trust, transparency, and genuine connections, and we prioritize building those genuine connections at every level—whether it's with team members, clients, or partners.
>
> Our culture emphasizes psychological safety, respect, active listening, and open communication as the foundation of all interactions. For our team, it means emphasizing the importance of using one-on-one meetings to connect personally. We want our managers getting a sense of how their team members are doing on a personal level, what they care about most, and what their career aspirations are.
>
> AP also has a culture of healthy, consistent feedback—the leadership team regularly seeks out feedback and makes it clear every employee can safely tell us what they really think. In fact, leaders often share how they learn

and improve in response to that feedback. The goal is to make it clear to our people that leadership cares about them personally, which helps build a relational culture.

And if Robert's success is any indication, that pays off by the truckload, especially when it becomes self-sustaining.

ROBERT'S BIG 4

- What they do: Acceleration Partners is a global partnership marketing agency that helps brands grow through relationship-driven, performance-based marketing strategies.
- Who they serve: Mid-market to enterprise-level companies that view partnerships as a strategic growth channel.
- What they *don't* do: AP doesn't compromise their values for short-term results—they focus on sustainable growth.
- Who is *not* a fit: Companies that prioritize transactional relationships over relational ones and brands that are unwilling to invest time in building trust and mutual success.

Robert finds that strong and effective leadership sets the stage for success throughout the organization. You need to set your team up for success. Your RPT System depends on it.

WHY THREE SYSTEMS AT ONCE

Here's the thing about running all three systems—Perpetuating Givers, Clearing Runway, and Prospecting Partners—simultaneously: It creates an evergreen marketing channel that doesn't depend on any single person (JNN!). Not even you. But before you get too excited about escaping your business, here are two massive mental mistakes I see leaders make in this phase:

- **Delegating too much, too early.** Look, I get it. I'm making some pretty attractive promises here. And I've earned the right to make them because I've lived it, taught it, and watched others succeed with it. But there's a heavy warning that comes with these promises: *you* are the decisive element. The idea that you can get this started and then fall back into your old routine of shaking hands and kissing babies while completely ignoring all the other things you're telling others to do? Recipe for pain. Trust me, I've tried it. It doesn't work. Here's the brutal truth: Your veteran team members are as equally rutted as you are. If you're operating at a six out of ten, they're probably at a two or three. You need to be an eight, nine, or ten to enact real change. And even then, it takes time.

- **Treating it like a tactic instead of an operating system.** Leaders love new ideas. They read a book, attend a conference, take a course, and get fired up about the latest thing. Their teams smile and nod (and cringe, and eye roll) over their leader's enthusiastic flavor-of-the-month. If you're the type of leader who needs constant exposure to new ideas to stay excited, I beg you: Sit with this one for a moment. The Relationship Snowball can change everything for you. But it's not a tactic; it's an operating system. And unlike traditional marketing, you can't just turn it back on if it dies. Partner relationships are like teeth: You don't have to floss them all, just the ones you want to keep. When done right, you're accumulating partners, not replacing them. You're accessing prospects immune to traditional marketing, you're building momentum that compounds over time, and your team is generating opportunities without you.

But remember: This isn't about escaping your business; it's about leading it properly. The goal isn't to disappear. It's to elevate, moving from being the star player to being the coach who builds a championship team. Here are Five Pillars of Relational Leadership:

PILLAR #1: MOMENTUM

There are few things that create momentum faster than a leader with a sense of urgency—momentum is the most powerful force in business. When you have it, you can do no wrong. When it's missing?

Nothing goes right. Here are the key elements that create unstoppable momentum:

VISION

Quick question: Do you have a clear image of where you want your business (and life) to be in a year? Three years? Five? Ten?

Bill Gates said, "Most people overestimate what they can accomplish in a year but underestimate what they can accomplish in ten years." He's right. If you're not crystal clear on where you are, where you're going, and what you do best, then each day is going to feel like a slog through mud.

TIME ALLOCATION

Serial entrepreneur Michael Altshuler nailed it: "The bad news is, time flies. The good news is, you're the pilot."

We have an unstoppable chief of staff, Sharlia, who helps manage my schedule. *And I still mess it up.* Why? Poor discipline. Sloppy routines. Days (even weeks) will pass before I notice I'm flying aimless. It's a lot like mindless eating. Our schedules *love* empty calories.

But momentum hates them.

Ask yourself:

- Am I spending enough time working *on* the business versus *in* it?
- When's the last time I *actually implemented* something new I learned?
- How often do I evaluate and adjust my priorities?

MEETING NEW PEOPLE

One team member accuses me of "swarming people."

"You do this all the time," they say. "Remember when you first met John Lee Dumas, went on his podcast, and bought him a sauna?"

Well, while I prefer not to call it "swarming," maybe they have a point. I believe in fast-forwarding relationships that show potential. Someone like JLD, who's not only a great guy but surrounded by incredible business leaders? Yeah, I'm going all in.

Remember: 80 percent of loyalty is built in the beginning of a relationship. If you're not playing favorites—if you're not "swarming"—you're likely not winning.

PILLAR #2: CULTURE

Culture is what happens when the boss isn't around. That means if your goal is to *not* be around forty-five to fifty hours per week, you'd better become a master at driving the culture you want versus accepting the culture you get.

Here's the most important rule of leadership I've learned (probably from all my mentors): Talk about the organization you want to have, not the one you have. This is easier said than done. For instance, often I see people do what Ben Hardy and Dan Sullivan, authors of *10x Is Easier Than 2x* call "living in the gap"—where leaders endlessly talk about how things *should* be and ruthlessly point out how everyone falls short.

The secret weapon? Stories. Story selling (more on this in Chapter 20) is the key to inspire behavior, calibrate thinking, and get people to want to play at their best possible level. Studies prove that stories are twenty-two times more memorable than facts and figures alone.

Here are the seven types of stories you need in your arsenal:

1. **Foundational Stories:** Share how the organization began, the early days, and the values that shaped it.
2. **Success Stories:** Showcase relational wins (not just home runs) that align with your mission.
3. **Failure Stories:** Share lessons learned from mistakes and how you grew from them.
4. **Innovation Stories:** Celebrate creativity and problem-solving within the team.

5. **Customer Impact Stories:** Tell how your work positively affects clients' lives.
6. **Leadership Vision Stories:** Reinforce what "excellent" looks like when your team nails it.
7. **Employee Growth Stories:** Focus on individual development and internal wins.

There are few things more powerful than a disciplined leader who's also a great storyteller. Your stories shape your culture, and your culture shapes your results.

Here's a great story about stories.

STORY TIME: BUILDING AND MOLDING

When Qualcomm's leadership team noticed a disconnect between their stated values and daily operations, they didn't just write another memo or update their mission statement. Instead, they collected and shared stories of employees living their values.

They launched an initiative called "52 Weeks." For one year, new employees received a weekly email featuring a story about the company's history—milestones, leadership insights, product origins, and even challenges. The stories, chosen to reinforce the future envisioned by leadership, were emotional, visual, and deeply impactful.

Existing employees soon heard about these weekly emails and requested to be included.

One story became legendary: A mid-level manager delayed a major product launch—potentially costing millions—because something didn't feel right about the quality. Instead of getting fired, he became the hero of a story that's still told today. Why? Because it showed everyone that "quality first" wasn't just a slogan on the wall; it was a value worth betting your career on.

Even better? The "52 Weeks" initiative cost the giant semiconductor company *nothing but thoughtfulness*. That's how you mold culture:

not through PowerPoints and policy manuals, but through stories that show what really matters.

PILLAR #3: HIRING FOR FIT

When we hired our first employee over a decade ago, leadership was not my superpower. Thank God for Rod. He's filled in my gaps, especially in hiring. Here's what we've learned:

THE INTERVIEW PROCESS

First, we don't place any ads for hiring. We work 100 percent on referral. Why? Because the best people usually aren't scrolling job boards; they're working somewhere else, probably crushing it.

When it comes to interviewing, we start with a clear job description, and then use personality assessments (not as the deciding factor, but as a filter). For the interview, we won't even get there if someone shows to be a poor fit. And if we do get there, we focus on listening more than talking.

But the real magic happens in the stories we tell during interviews. Yes, stories again. We have three specific ones we always share:

- **Story #1: Values over Revenue.** We tell about the time we engraved the wrong spouse's name on a very expensive personalized gift. It wasn't even our fault; we used the info the client gave us. But we replaced it at our cost *and* sent an apology gift. A potential disaster became a peak moment, and we even got a referral out of it.
- **Story #2: Making the World Better.** Sure, on paper, we sell personalized gifts. But what we really do is fight against technology eating real relationships. We believe real friendships and fellowship are the keys to fighting addiction, depression, and loneliness. When candidates' eyes light up at this bigger mission, we know we might have a fit.

- **Story #3: Our "Only Here" Moments.** We share stories about team members doing unexpected, nice things for each other. The surprise-and-delight culture isn't just for clients—it starts with how we treat each other.

After all, we're a relationship company that deals in gifts. We need people who are going to love that, live that, breathe that.

GIFTING INTERNALLY: NO HYPOCRITES HERE!

When you run a relationship business, your employees scrutinize your actions twice as much as your clients. That old saying, "What you do speaks so loudly I cannot hear what you say" hits differently when you're a gifting company.

Let me show you exactly how we walk our talk at GIFT·OLOGY:

THE NEW HIRE EXPERIENCE

1. Every employee is treated to regular date nights with their spouse or significant other—on the company. This includes the cost of babysitting. Our team knows that success at work starts with connection at home.
2. New interns? They find $300 headphones waiting at their desk on day one. Why? Because I want them to feel appreciated before they even start. I don't want to throw parties for people after they decide to leave.
3. Every employee gets their house or apartment cleaned every other week—on us.

But John, you're thinking, *how can you afford all this?*

Simple: We build it in on the back end as part of compensation. Let's say you're hiring for a position with a $60,000–$75,000 range. You find a great candidate and settle at $70,000. Most organizations would think, *Great, we saved five grand!* But a blessed leader thinks,

Awesome! We've got five grand to spoil, surprise, and delight this person!

We take that $5,000 and set it aside for showing love throughout the year. Sure, tech companies might spend the same on catered lunches and stocked bars, but appreciative gifting hits different.

Our goal? To ruin other bosses forever.

PILLAR #4: COLLECTIVE SKILL

Here's something that might surprise you: We don't use quotas in our organization. Instead, we focus on collective skill development, which I think is more powerful. After all, quotas tell people what to do; skill development inspires them to be better. We drive skill development through daily practices such as role-playing key conversations, facilitating peer feedback sessions, practicing scenario-based learning, and discussing what we're reading and learning.

This multifaceted approach is important because when someone's learning something new, we encourage their progress. But once they know something and do it half measure (or don't do it at all), we call them out.

And yes, that "someone" could be John Ruhlin.

Autonomy is paid for with a passion for never-ending improvement. If you want freedom to make decisions, show me you're constantly working to make better ones. Remember: The goal isn't perfection; it's progress.

When your whole team is focused on getting better together, magic happens.

STORY TIME: GETTING BETTER, ALL THE TIME

One of our newsletter readers, Jeremy, transformed his insurance agency from a transaction factory into a relationship powerhouse. Every Friday, his team has what they call "Better Than Yesterday" sessions.

In one session, someone mentioned how clients always seemed stressed when discussing policy renewals. Instead of just accepting this as "part of the business," they turned it into a weekly skill-building opportunity. The team practiced different ways to make renewal conversations feel more like catching up with a friend than a dreaded annual chore.

As a result, their renewal rates shot up. Their clients even started looking forward to these conversations. I mean...we all have organizational aversions and weaknesses.

What might happen if these weaknesses became strengths?

PILLAR #5: IMAGINATION

Here's a truth bomb: Your organization doesn't have to be perfect. It won't be. Business is about solving problems, and the bumps of a powerful (but imperfect) Relationship Snowball are just one of many challenges you'll face. The good news is you don't need to smooth out these problems alone.

Our team leverages collective imagination in many ways:

- **The "What If" Game.** In some of our brainstorming sessions, every participant will start their ideas with the words "What if we...," even if what follows seems impossible or improbable. Why? Because if your team is focused on constraints, they'll never live in their imagination.
- **The Parking Lot.** We have a dedicated space—digital or physical— where we store ideas that aren't immediately actionable. You'd be amazed how many "parked" ideas turn into breakthroughs later. For example, we talked about upgrading our VIP book shipments for years. The idea of including a small TV screen in the lid of the box kept coming up, but we always defaulted to standard packaging. It lived in the parking lot until the right project came along. When we finally implemented it? Game changer.
- **The Rules of Imagination.** Never squash an idea, especially if

you're the leader (because your words weigh 5,000 pounds). When you're excited, pass it on. Give people freedom to explore (and sometimes fail).

And last, but definitely not least, celebrate extensively when people think big. For example, one of our best testimonials resulted when a team member, Kami, casually asked, "What if we treated this client's family like they were our client?" It seemed obvious after she said it. But it changed everything about how we approached this particular renewal.

Remember: Your business will always take as much as you're willing to give it—calls and texts at all hours, seven days per week. It'll rob from you, your family, and everything you care about...unless you build a team that can imagine and execute solutions without you.

WHAT'S NEXT?

When you master running different protocols for different people, all at once and ongoing, you'll own the most powerful asset in business: a Relationship Snowball.

Think about what this means:

- Your team generating opportunities without you
- Your business growing through relationships, not just transactions
- Your impact expanding beyond your personal capacity
- Your legacy continuing even when you're not there

What will you do with all this abundance?

- Raise your prices because you've got a waiting list?
- Enter that new industry you've been eyeing?
- Create scarcity through a year-long waiting list?
- Partner on those dream projects you've been putting off?
- Finally invest in those new assets you've been considering?

Buckle up, my friend. *It is an exciting time to be you.*

BUT FIRST ANSWER THESE QUESTIONS

Before we wrap up, let's make sure you're ready to implement. Be ruthlessly honest.

- Do you truly understand why you need three different referral systems?
- Can you articulate what you want from each system?
- Have you identified your Accumulators, Energizers, and Managers?
- Is your team aligned with their roles and responsibilities?

ACTION ITEMS, STEP-BY-STEP

This isn't about perfection. It's about progress. Remember to:

1. Identify your strongest system and what makes it work.
2. Tackle your weakest system first.
3. Assign ownership of all your relationships.
4. Get your TAP meetings scheduled.
5. Start celebrating wins—big and small.

Every step forward builds momentum for your Relationship Snowball.

See you out there.

PART SEVEN

UPSKILLING EVERYBODY

CHAPTER 19

TROUBLESHOOTING CHANGE

Donald Miller, author of the exceptional books *Building a Storybrand* and *Building a Storybrand 2.0*, will admit he used to be an extremely driven person who saw relationship building as mere politics—something that got in the way of real work. He believed he had things to accomplish, and there was no reason to build relationships.

Looking back, Donald realizes now that was "an awful view of the world."

He has done a complete 180-degree turn. I'll let him tell you how:

I've implemented specific practices in my organization: weekly staff lunches, weekly all-staff meetings that end with "shout outs" where team members praise each other, and regular leadership team meetings. We've deliberately built social time into our schedule because I've learned teams work better when they know and trust each other.

I've come to see work as a delivery mechanism for creating relationships. In fact, I believe it's one of the primary reasons work exists. I've found that if you spend 50 percent of your time building deeper relationships with people and 50 percent getting stuff done, you'll accomplish more than if you spend 100 percent of your time just focusing on tasks. Any business is like an engine—if one piece isn't connected to the rest, the whole engine fails. While relationship building might feel inefficient, it's essential for everything to work well together.

I agree wholeheartedly.

DONALD'S BIG 4

- What they do: Donald helps people come up with the words they should use to talk about what they do.
- Who they serve: Small- to midsize-business owners.
- What they *don't* do: Donald doesn't do anything else other than help people create sound bites that cause their messages to spread.
- Who is *not* a fit: Donald does not help people answer other questions, such as "What should my product be? What should it cost?"

THE BAD NEWS: CHANGE IS HARD

Whether you're a solopreneur or solo professional changing your own habits or a small-business owner managing the habits and disciplines of employees and adjacent team members, change is hard.

In this chapter, we'll cover the most common roadblocks, challenges, and "yes, buts" that come up when implementing the RPT System. It's designed to help you push through the resistance and actually *do* the work, not just understand it.

Consider this your troubleshooting guide—your reference manual for when things get tough. Because, friends, they will get tough. But with the right mindset and tools, you can push through to the other side. Remember: The path might not be easy, but it's worth it. And you're not walking it alone.

Two "mental hygiene" mistakes when trying to implement new systems and habits:

- **Trying to change everything at once.** It's so easy to get excited about all the possibilities—the Clarity Conversations, the shoulder industries, the gifting strategies—and try to implement them all tomorrow. Don't. That's like trying to transform your health by simultaneously starting a new diet, joining CrossFit, meditating daily, and getting eight hours of sleep...when you currently do none of those things. Real change happens one habit at a time, one conversation at a time, and one relationship at a time.
- **Waiting for perfection.** More on this in a second. But the big word of caution here is not to wait until you've mastered every aspect of the system before taking action. It might feel counterintuitive, but it's been proven again and again: If you decrease your expectations of perfection, you will actually increase your success.

Most people don't show up perfect out of the box; they have to learn as they go. *This* is why most don't reach their full potential, because (again) change is hard. You, however, can be an exception if you:

- **Believe that small changes lead to big results.** In every transformation, there are leading actions (something you control) and lagging outcomes (results you don't control). Don't count outcomes, count actions.
- **Consistency beats intensity when it comes to changing habits.** Have a daily implementation standard, when you win the day or lose the day. This could be time based (thirty minutes of DoVs every day), action based (one Clarity Conversation per week), or goal based (one new habit per month, if you're just getting started). Track the days you hit your standard, and treat it like a workout. Your job isn't to miss any.

And be relentless. For example...

Brian McRae—one of the most successful RPT implementation coaches on planet earth—once shared his early struggles: "I was in loan services for years. I thought I knew how to have conversations. But when I first tried implementing the Clarity Conversation framework? I bombed. Hard."

Brian explained his first attempts felt mechanical and forced. "I had the questions memorized, but they came out like I was reading from a script. It was painful. But I made myself a commitment: I would practice one conversation every single day, no matter what."

"The first week was rough," he continued. "The second week was slightly less rough. By week three, something started to click. I wasn't just saying the words anymore. I was actually listening, really listening, to the answers. That's when everything changed."

He described how this approach shaped his success. "Over time, I noticed a pattern. Every conversation got a little bit easier. Every follow-up became more natural. What started as forced practice became genuine curiosity. And suddenly, I wasn't implementing a system anymore; I was building real relationships."

Brian's story illustrates the power of focusing on leading actions—the things you can control—rather than obsessing over lagging outcomes like closed deals. By treating change like a daily practice and committing to small, consistent actions, he built a thriving business based on R.I.C.H. relationships and referrals.

THE GOOD NEWS: CHANGE IS POSSIBLE

Change happens when the pain of transition is less than the pain of staying the same. The number one pain of transition is not knowing what to do. If you've read Parts Three, Four, Five, or Six—you have the action steps. You know what to do.

So let's explore some mental hang-ups and how to overcome them.

"I DON'T WANT TO FEEL ICKY."

When business leaders first evaluate the RPT System, some make the emotional mistake of feeling "icky" about using a system, script, or process. This can make them hesitant to take action. This hesitation keeps them from contacting people, building relationships, generating referrals, and creating the momentum they need.

As much as we want to pretend otherwise, systems and strategies are necessary for success. That means there is only one of two options: Stay stuck in the icky feeling or reframe your perspective. Let me assure you: Leaders who reframe get better results than those who resist.

Instead of feeling negative about being strategic with human relationships—which wouldn't bother you if we were talking about products or ideas—reframe it. See yourself as a strategic person who *adds value to others, builds authentic connections, creates win-win relationships, and makes a meaningful difference.*

Every time you interact with someone, give them *that* experience. Your comfort zone will expand. And you'll leave analysis paralysis behind.

Relationship systems take the thought out of the mundane so you can focus on the person in front of you. As long as you're not bribing people or leading with "Do This, Get That" incentives?

You're doing something *for people*, not doing something *to them*.

"THIS IS OVERWHELMING/I DON'T HAVE TIME."

Success isn't about doing more—it's about doing less with precision. The goal is to move out of "hobby mode" and implement a focused process that drives real results. How? By narrowing your focus and executing well with those who matter most.

In business, the sheer number of relationships we're expected to manage can feel overwhelming. Each new connection adds complexity, making it easy to spread yourself too thin and dilute your impact. That's why "shrinking the job" is so powerful.

This approach means focusing on a select few—your top ten relationships. *Yes, just ten.* Pick ten people who truly matter, who can propel your success. By prioritizing these key connections, you can invest the time, energy, and resources needed to nurture them fully. The result? A lighter workload, stronger relationships, and far greater results than if you did nothing.

"HOW LONG DOES THIS TAKE TO WORK?"

Every referral-based business faces the same motivational challenge: the lag between action and results. Stay disciplined in the lag.

Motivation and discipline are like pedals on a bicycle—when one is down, the other one needs to be up. As much as we want instant results, real relationships take time to develop.

To help you build muscle, remember the difference focusing on leading metrics can make. These are the actions you control.

For example, you can control the number of harmless starters and Clarity Conversations you have in a week, the amount of follow-up activity you execute in twenty-four hours, the number of DoVs given to potential partners, and so on. One of the biggest mistakes you can make in adopting the RPT System is to be a "results watcher." If you can't stay disciplined on your leading metrics—and you focus on the gap, not the effort—you're in danger of losing motivation when results take time. You can't take an ROI approach to ROR.

To be a referral magnet, it helps to be process focused.

"WHAT IF REFERRAL GIVERS WANT TO STAY ANONYMOUS?"

Referrals requiring discretion can feel challenging, but they're far from impossible. Clients often value privacy for personal or sensitive reasons:

- Inheritors may not want others to know they've come into money.
- Patients undergoing elective or cosmetic surgeries prefer to keep it private.
- Business owners quietly selling their companies can't risk the news spreading.
- Individuals seeking mental health or addiction recovery services need confidentiality.

So, how do you overcome these "covert referral" challenges?

The biggest mistake is thinking, *A system like RPT won't work for us.* Wrong. Covert referrals can work—you just need to get creative.

One inheritance lawyer, for example, discovered their best referral partner wasn't another lawyer but couples' therapists, who often saw conflicts arise before the inheritance.

Another example: If your main service is too sensitive, develop a less private lead-in. For instance, elective cosmetic surgeries, weight loss, or hormonal treatments might offer a "shoulder service" as a gateway. Imagine an energy consultation or wellness assessment, both of which can be administered online. This softer entry point makes referrals easier, leading naturally to your core offering once trust is built.

What about building a process for anonymous referrals? Make it seamless for partners to refer you without breaking confidentiality. Let's say a partner provides a friend's contact info—maybe you send a VIP gift, like a book, to start the conversation. You can include a personalized video to make it even more dynamic.

If a new prospect asks, "How did you get my contact info?"—put yourself in their shoes. What would you like to hear in that situation? How about: "You were referred to us by a current client, but due to the sensitive nature of our services, we prioritize privacy, yours included should you choose to work with us. Which we hope you do!"

With a little creativity, you can empower partners to share your services while protecting their privacy. These thoughtful methods ensure your reputation spreads without barriers.

"MY MARGINS ARE TOO THIN TO BE GENEROUS."

The RPT System was designed for small businesses, often with tight margins. Unlike GIFT·OLOGY agency clients—who might spend $100,000 on relationships without expecting a single referral—RPT practitioners are only buying gifts *once deals close*. That means the money is already made. And like we discussed in Chapter 15, the gifting spend is calculated as a percentage of net profit.

Can I be candid?

As much as we don't want to admit it, most generosity hang-ups aren't about money.

Find ways to add value and be impactful with less spend. Consider a DoV approach that includes things like public recognition (costs nothing), handwritten notes (can mean everything), introductions that create opportunity, and small gifts that communicate "I see you."

One of the biggest mistakes you can make in generosity is to be a "dollar-sign thinker." Start at a level that's comfortable for you. And move toward becoming a 3P giver: planned, percentage, progressive, *not* sparing, spontaneous, and sporadic.

"I DON'T KNOW WHAT TO BUY PEOPLE."

Fast-forwarding relationships is not about the item. It's about being thoughtful.

GIFT·OLOGY encourages seven ingredients of thoughtfulness. We talk about these, ad nauseam, in our books, podcasts, newsletters, and more. You don't need all of them in every gift. But more is better.

- **Choose the best-in-class:** Quality that lasts forever. Never cut corners on quality. Choose items built to last. Focus on craftsmanship.
- **Pick the practical:** Something they'll use three to five times per week. Avoid cute but useless items. Think daily routines and habits. Consider their lifestyle.
- **Look for luxury:** What they want but won't buy themselves. Look for "unnecessary necessities." Focus on upgrades to everyday items. Think premium versions of basics.
- **Prioritize the personalized:** Make it uniquely theirs. Add engraving when possible. Include monograms or custom details. Create one-of-a-kind elements.
- **Integrate their inner circle:** Benefits their key relationships. Think about spouse and family. Consider the team and colleagues. Include their support system.
- **Continue the theme:** Part of an ongoing story. Build sequential gifting plans. Create themed experiences. Develop lasting impressions.
- **Include a handwritten note:** The essential final touch. Sharing words of affirmation covers multiple love languages, doubling the chances of creating a peak moment.

Start small if you're just beginning. *But start.* Some of the most successful gifters I know, like Anita Toth and Vicki Reid, gift simple items that hit just two or three of these elements. They've become role models in the R.I.C.H. RELATIONSHIP SOCIETY, amplifying their impact far beyond the immediate recipients.

"I'M AN INTROVERT, AND RELATIONSHIPS DON'T COME EASY."

When introverts start implementing the RPT System, some try to act like extroverts. They exhaust themselves, don't sustain their efforts, don't maintain consistency, and don't generate the momentum they need. Instead, consider this:

Most relationship building can be done in an introverted way.

Which means there is only one of two options: burn out trying to be someone else or leverage your introverted strengths.

Honest introverts get better results than fake extroverts because honest introverts follow the John Ruhlin playbook (recall: I'm an introvert). Spend more time with people one-on-one, be strategic about stages and small group settings, lean on thoughtful written communication, and prioritize quality over quantity in digital interactions.

Energy is a finite resource. If you don't commit to build relationships while honoring your introverted nature?

You're in danger of burning out and turning your snowball into a puddle.

"THIS WON'T WORK IN MY INDUSTRY, CULTURE, ETC."

I have friends who are masters of word-of-mouth, referrals, and relationship building, spanning nearly every industry and continent. Some of them likely felt the way you do.

Here's the liberating reality: Relationships work everywhere.

Yes, the excuses are comforting in the moment. The excuse is undeniable as you list all the reasons your industry is different, your culture is unique, making you feel like you're off the hook for taking action. But you're not. Once that fleeting comfort passes, reality remains.

The truth is, there's nothing unique about your limitations. Your career path doesn't suddenly make you exempt from relationship principles. It doesn't change human nature, it doesn't eliminate connection needs—it doesn't fundamentally change how people do business.

There are many ways to adapt to the world around you.

Take Hiroshi Mikitani, CEO of Rakuten, an online seller you'd get if you combined Amazon, PayPal, and Expedia. He faced intense resistance when he introduced English as the official language in his Japanese company. This was a groundbreaking shift for a company deeply embedded in Japanese business traditions, where English is not commonly used for day-to-day communication.

R.I.C.H. RESOURCE #11

How do you assess a shoulder industry's relationships without being self-serving? Use the Trusted Advisor Process. Download it now at **RPTsystem.com**.

But Mikitani knew that bridging the communication gap would lead to better collaboration (a.k.a. relationships!) and a more globalized company. By making a bold decision—one that was unpopular at the time—he built connections across cultural lines and turned discomfort into a competitive advantage.

What options do you have for adaptation? What bold decision are you willing to make?

"THEY ALREADY HAVE A GUY."

When business leaders approach shoulder industries, they tend to make the same competitive mistake: giving up at "I already have someone." Most existing partnerships aren't exclusive, which means there is only one of two options: accept rejection and move on or master the Trusted Advisor Process.

This process is Brian McRae's advanced method of assessing relational opportunity.

It involves exploring a potential partner's:

- Context: Understanding current relationships
- Competence: Rating existing partnerships
- Connection: Creating value-based introductions
- Collaboration: Finding win-win opportunities

This process is particularly valuable in industries where multiple professionals are necessary for a transaction—think: real estate, healthcare, legal services, construction, financial services, entertainment, event planning, manufacturing, and knowledge economy workers.

"I KEEP RUNNING OUT OF TIME IN CLARITY CONVERSATIONS."

When business leaders begin implementing Clarity Conversations, many, aiming to be polite, make the same mistake: letting the partner lead the dance.

This can result in you knowing everything about them. And them knowing nothing about you. Which, I think we can agree, isn't a partnership at all.

If you have these problems, consider implementing some of the following:

- Clear, up-front expectations about time.
- "Let's take turns so nothing is missed."
- "With _____ minutes left, let's make sure we cover _____."
- "Before we finish, let's recap the key points."

Nothing is more frustrating than listening to someone talk for thirty minutes, you paying for the coffee, and them adding, "We should do this again sometime!"

If this is happening, apply the steps above and keep at it—you'll get there.

"I AM GETTING THE WRONG TYPE OF REFERRALS."

Every referral-based business, including ours, faces quality-control challenges. So if this is you, it doesn't automatically mean you're doing something wrong.

The real danger isn't that you're getting "bad" referrals (no such thing). The danger is your volume of bad referrals discourages you from executing the necessary systems.

Ask yourself:

- Are you reporting positive progress? (Chapter 13)
- Are you gently correcting? (Chapter 16)

- Have you investigated the optimal Big 4? (Basically this entire book)

I don't know how many ways I can say it.

You absolutely must be able to articulate your business's super-power(s). Keep refining your Big 4 until you master it. Here it is, one last time, for everybody in the back:

1. What we do.
2. Who we serve.
3. What we *don't* do.
4. Who is *not* a fit.

With practice and experience, you'll transform from scripted to memorable: using stories, examples, and clear language, and making it easy for partners to remember and repeat.

In the same way you want to be world-class in your service, be world-class in referral clarity.

"IT FEELS INAUTHENTIC IF I DON'T DO IT ALL MYSELF."

When business leaders start off-loading, they tend to make the same authenticity mistake: confusing control with quality.

Relationships are important, but rarely urgent. Which means if you have this mindset, it's almost guaranteed you will end up *doing nothing with this book.*

Sorry if that's harsh. But I've been witnessing this pattern for twenty years.

Which means there is only one of two options: burn out doing everything yourself, or master strategic delegation. People who delegate get better results than people who don't because delegators have more capacity than soloists and are better at focusing on what matters.

They create delegation systems that focus on:

- Starting small with one simple task
- Choosing low-risk activities first
- Defining and training thoroughly on your standards
- Maintaining vision while releasing control

If you're a solopreneur, with no team, go back and read Chapter 6—specifically the part about team, technology, and triggers.

If you have a team, and wish to incorporate them more deeply, go back and read Part Six—Chapters 16, 17, and 18.

I have twenty years of experience grappling with this limiting belief. *So trust me on this.* Your snowball will grow only as much as your ability to build habits and infrastructure.

Without those, you'll remain small forever.

TO STATE THE OBVIOUS

When evaluating the success of the RPT System, some leaders forget the most fundamental truth: You *must* have a great product or service.

Fundamental to generating a lot of people talking is to have something worth talking about.

If improving your customer experience is a current focus point, I recommend *Creating Superfans* by Brittany Hodak. It's one of the few books I keep on my desk, next to *GIFT·OLOGY*.

She will teach you to build a business like Walt Disney recommended: "Whatever you do, do it well. Do it so well that when people see you do it, they will want to come back and see you do it again, and they will want to bring others and show them how well you do what you do."

Understand the world we live in today.

If someone goes to your restaurant every day and you consistently exceed their expectations, they'll likely bring (or tell) two or three people. But if they got food poisoning from your restaurant, they'll tell ten—*and that's before the nasty Google review.*

This right here highlights why product-only isn't enough. Loyalty comes from *being extra*. That's why we're gifting our referral partners, sending handwritten notes, practicing DoVs, and having Clarity Conversations—all far more time-consuming than simply asking, nagging, or bragging.

And also way more memorable.

It's why relationships can take you places marketing can't.™

CHAPTER 20

YOUR STANDARDS MATTER

Hal Elrod—I've mentioned him before, the genius behind *The Miracle Morning*—had always been a big fan of Aubrey Marcus, the founder of Onnit. Aubrey is the owner of the eight-figure supplement company, host of the *Aubrey Marcus Podcast*, and author of *Own the Day, Own Your Life*. Though Aubrey wasn't a client and didn't know who Hal was, one day Hal decided to send him an engraved set of Cutco knives with all his quotes on them, shipping it directly to his corporate headquarters.

Was it because Hal wanted something in return?

No. Not at all. Hal appreciated Aubrey's work on a personal level and had found it inspiring for his own journey. I'll let Hal take it from here:

> Shortly after sending the gift, I was diagnosed with cancer and spent the next eight months in the hospital, followed by three years of chemotherapy. The gift completely slipped my mind during this challenging period.

Then, my friend Brad Weimert, who is also close to John Ruhlin, texted me to listen to Aubrey's podcast, specifically at the sixteen-minute mark. In that segment, Aubrey was discussing how people connect with influential figures, and he shared my gift story (without using my name), saying, "I had someone send me a gorgeous set of high-quality kitchen cutlery and on every knife they had engraved one of my quotes from my book." He added, "Talk about over and above...if that guy ever wanted my time, you better believe I would give it to him."

After hearing this, I reached out to Aubrey through his website's contact form, explaining that I was the one who had sent the cutlery and apologizing for the delayed follow-up, sharing my cancer journey. Instead of asking to be on his podcast, I invited him to be a guest on mine. He accepted, and this led to him later inviting me onto his show. He even had me back a second time when my next book was released. None of this would have happened if I hadn't followed the principle of giving a gift of appreciation before Aubrey had ever done anything for me.

Hal doesn't do anything halfway. His standards are above and beyond.

Which is why his business results are also above and beyond.

WHAT ARE YOUR STANDARDS?

All the referral systems in the world won't matter if you don't hold yourself (and your team) to high standards. Again, *standards*. We're chasing excellence here, not mediocrity.

Leaders let their standards lapse, not because they're lazy. But because they're busy.

The irony of this, of course, is that raising your personal standards is a path to *less* busyness.

Avoid these two "mental hygiene" mistakes:

- **Confusing activity with excellence.** It's so easy to think because we're doing the work—sending the gifts, having the conversations, making the introductions—that we're operating at a high level. It's even easier to think that because we're getting some results, we must be doing things right. But volume of activity doesn't equal quality of execution. It's up to you to constantly manage "what great looks like" for your organization.

- **Letting circumstances dictate standards.** Don't let external factors determine your nonnegotiables. I know. It's counterintuitive that if you raise your standards when things get tough, you will actually increase your results. But this has been proven time and time again.

STORY TIME: EXCELLENCE IS ALWAYS REWARDED

Carissa, our lead GIFT·OLOGIST, once shared a story that perfectly illustrates why standards matter so much in relationship building.

"We had an agency client who wanted to send appreciation gifts to their top one hundred referral partners," she began. "The budget was tight, really tight. Most companies would have just found the cheapest acceptable option and called it a day."

But Carissa's standards wouldn't let her take the easy route. "I kept thinking about what these referral partners meant to our client. Each one had trusted their reputation to make introductions. They deserved more than 'acceptable.'"

Instead of compromising, Carissa got creative. She spent hours researching unique items that would fit the budget while still feeling premium. She worked with suppliers to negotiate better prices for bulk orders. She even found ways to add personal touches that didn't cost extra but made each gift feel special.

"The client actually pushed back at first," she recalled. "They said we were overthinking it. But I insisted this was our standard—we either do it right or we don't do it at all."

The results? The gifting campaign generated more referrals *in the next quarter* than the client had received *in the previous year*. But the real validation came six months later.

"One of the referral partners was at an industry event. He pulled out our gift—he still carried it with him—and showed it to a colleague, saying, 'This is how they treat their partners.' That one moment led to three new relationships."

This story illustrates a fundamental truth: When you raise your standards, the market notices. Excellence isn't just about doing things well. It's about doing them well when there's every excuse not to.

One standard you must never compromise: how you react when somebody says, "Thank you."

THE MOMENT OF PERSUASIVE POWER

Robert Cialdini's research revealed, "There's a moment of persuasive power after people say thank you."[30] If you're executing the RPT System and DoVing like we teach, you're going to be hearing those two words a lot.

The moment of thanks is a critical opportunity to move the relationship forward. Do you know exactly what to do in this moment? Does your team?

Joe Polish's team excels at creating and leveraging these moments. For example, Mike Dudley, who works on the technology side, noticed a new customer's enthusiastic engagement with Genius Network content—tracking video views, logins, and more. He sent the member a simple message:

"I'm impressed with how quickly you're diving into the content. I love your enthusiasm!"

Moments later, that customer sent him a referral.

Many businesses use the "thank you moment" to ask the Greenlight Question. Contractors can ask during a final walk-through. Solar

---

30 Robert Cialdini, "Influence & Negotiation Skills That Get SCARY Results | Chris Voss, BJ Fogg, Dr. Robert Cialdini," Joe Polish, May 24, 2024, YouTube video, 1:13:50, https://www.youtube.com/watch?v=diQi_TaTbes.

installers, when the system is activated. Realtors, after closing. Estate attorneys, when delivering a trust.

Where do your "thank you" moments occur?

Every "thank you" is an opportunity to deepen relationships. For example, inviting them into a Clarity Conversation. If someone thanks you for a DoV, reply, "I'm glad you appreciated it. I really appreciate *you*! Let's connect soon to explore how we can collaborate further."

Remember, the goal is transformation, not transaction. Focus on using their gratitude to naturally open the door to the next step in your relationship.

After "thank you," everyone on your team should be ready to turn gratitude into a deeper connection.

How many times will you hear "thank you" in the next year? The next three years? Five?

What will your personal standard be for how you seize those moments?

STORY SELLING: BE MORE INTERESTING

Another standard: How interesting are you when you talk about *you*? Every word-of-mouth master must excel at the art of storytelling; or story *selling*, as many call it.

One ingredient you can add right now to make your stories more impactful, more memorable, and far more interesting?

Be more specific.

Specificity (noun): precision of your details and descriptions.

Let me give you three examples. GOOD/BETTER/BEST.

GOOD: "We help business owners get mortgages." *(Basic, but at least identifies a target market)*

BETTER: "Business owners often show minimal taxable income, which makes getting a mortgage nearly impossible. We help them get approved anyway." *(Identifies both the problem and solution)*

BEST: "Meet Jared. He manufactures cooling underwear for vasectomy patients—half a million men annually. Despite his success, his tax returns showed minimal income. We helped him get his dream home while he focused on his...more unique superpower." *(Specific, memorable, and slightly humorous)*

Do you see how "story selling" occurs as you get more specific?

Reason #1: Precision demonstrates your expertise.

Reason #2: Details make you more believable.

Reason #3: Interesting tales keep your prospect's attention.

Many savvy but self-conscious storytellers worry that adding detail makes the story too long or turns people off. But when you match the right story with the right prospect, everything clicks. It won't feel like selling, just telling the truth, which, to me, is exactly what sales should be.

Use stories to increase the weight of your explanations.

Stories make you more memorable, and more memorable makes you more everything.

BATCHING: BE MORE EFFICIENT

A final standard, before we move on to the last chapter: efficiency and excellence. At GIFT·OLOGY, we achieve this with batching.

Batching means enjoying the efficiency of doing the same thing, back-to-back, versus doing that thing sporadically. Batching is necessary because to do something well requires focus.

Research consistently shows that multitasking is a myth. Instead of doing multiple tasks at once, our brains rapidly switch between tasks, which actually slows us down and increases the likelihood of mistakes.

Studies from *Psychology Today* reveal "switch tasking" can sap our energy, diminish our focus, and reduce productivity.[31] Additionally, multitasking reduces our capacity for deep learning and memory retention, making us less efficient over time.

---

31   Nancy K. Napier, "The Myth of Multitasking," *Psychology Today*, May 12, 2014, https://www.psychologytoday.com/us/blog/creativity-without-borders/201405/the-myth-of-multitasking.

In short, focusing on one task at a time will save you time, energy, and improve the quality of your work.

Buy in Bulk: Purchase a set of thoughtful gifts in advance to distribute throughout the year instead of buying one gift at a time.

Collect Share-Worthy Content: Collect, bookmark, or save articles, podcasts, or videos of interest and share them weekly—instead of randomly collecting them throughout the day.

Have a "Giveaway" Bookshelf: If you're going to gift books to potential partners, don't order one book at a time, one person at a time. Buy ten books up front and stack them on the shelf.

Write Multiple Endorsements: Block out time to write all professional endorsements and recommendations in one sitting, streamlining the task.

Cheerlead Consistently: Schedule time, weekly, on social media to comment, congratulate, or repost referral partners' content—making it a consistent habit.

Write All Notes at Once: Don't write three handwritten notes at various times of the day; do them all at once.

Denise Pickett is the president of Global Services at American Express. She writes, literally, hundreds of handwritten notes per year—her all-time record in one sitting is 278! When she's watching TV, listening to music, or flying around the world, she's simultaneously writing notes. That is her personal standard.

What standards do you hold?

A BUSINESS WITH FRIENDS

When your standard is R.I.C.H. relationships, success starts to feel like you're making money with friends. It's not about transactions; it's about trust, shared goals, and mutual wins.

Picture Hal Elrod or Ellen Long, two masters of relationship, where every member of their team is actively involved in building the Relationship Snowball.

They don't just manage sales pipelines—they live and breathe surveillance, capturing every nugget in the CRM, like they're mining for gold. They write handwritten notes, send books, schedule time to send personalized videos, and even "swarm" high-value contacts as soon as they enter their orbit.

Imagine you and your team: where every player is empowered to help strengthen the bond with clients. Systems are in place to blow people away, whether through surprise gifts or well-timed gestures, all because the culture says, "We focus on the people, not the business. That's our strategy to get more business."

Running a business with your friends is fun. This would be my ultimate want for you.

And so as we head into the final chapter, remember the wisdom widely attributed to Haim Ginott:

> I have come to the frightening conclusion that I am the decisive element. It is my personal approach that creates the climate. It is my daily mood that makes the weather. I possess tremendous power to make life miserable or joyous. I can be a tool of torture or an instrument of inspiration, I can humiliate or humor, hurt or heal.

You are the decisive element. Expect more from yourself.

CHAPTER 21

EN-R.I.C.H. THE WORLD

I've been in the world of business for some time, and I've seen some things. (Haven't we all?)

I've noticed that when business leaders achieve success, they face the same existential challenge: They realize success without significance is hollow.

Let me tell you about Seline (name changed for privacy).

"I had everything I thought I wanted," she told me. "The business was thriving. Referrals were flowing. I was making more money than I ever imagined. But something was missing."

That's when Seline noticed a trend in her community. Young professionals, despite being "connected" through every possible digital platform, were profoundly lonely. They had plenty of online followers but few real friends.

"It hit me during a Clarity Conversation," she continued. "This young woman opposite me started crying when I asked about her goals. Not because of the question, but because no one had ever really listened to her before."

That moment changed everything. Seline began using her relationship skills not just for business, but for community building. She hosted monthly connection events where phones were checked at the door. She created mastermind groups focused on personal growth through real relationships.

"The business impact has been incredible," she commented with a smile. "But that's not what drives me anymore. It's watching people put down their phones, look each other in the eye, and build real connections. That's what makes this matter."

Today, Seline's community has grown to over five hundred young professionals who regularly meet, support each other, and build genuine relationships. Her business continues to thrive, but now it's a vehicle for something bigger than herself.

WHAT THE WORLD NEEDS NOW

The final message every relational leader must embrace is their role in the larger mission. We're not just chasing success here. We're pursuing significance.

This chapter will encourage you to see the bigger picture—to elevate and expand your impact beyond just business, not just to accumulate. For those of you who have mastered the RPT System, I encourage you to use these skills to make a genuine difference in an increasingly disconnected world.

THE PLAGUE OF RELATIONAL POVERTY

Every era feels like the worst in human history, but something about today feels uniquely alarming.

The data speaks for itself. Recently, we've seen:

- The US hit an all-time low on the World Happiness Report
- Loneliness peaked higher than ever before
- Social connection muscles have atrophied from disuse
- Young people have started feeling more isolated than boomers
- Men became particularly vulnerable to relationship poverty

Gee, how could this have happened?

INFORMATION ADDICTION AND THE INTERNET

The best comedy is based in truth. Bo Burnham's song "Welcome to the Internet" satirically captures the overwhelming chaos of online content, calling it "a little bit of everything all of the time." With 4.88 billion people carrying smartphones (and counting), this constant connection proves a simple truth: The metaverse isn't coming—it's already here.

Another brilliant comedian, Nate Bargatze, once said, "I believe reading is the key to smart."[32] I would agree. However, reading, podcasting, course taking, media obsessing, and, yes, learning can also be a clever procrastination to the real work of building R.I.C.H. relationships.

I have a friend who is an information addict. He has a decently successful business, great family, and an open mind, surfing both sides of the political aisle—listening to Matt Walsh on the Daily Wire and watching John Oliver on Sunday nights. And yet he spends countless dollars on books, courses, and conferences that he doesn't read, finish, or log in to.

He is living proof people would rather latch onto hope than results.

We treat information like a magic bullet. But it's a distraction. It's a lotus flower, keeping us from the place the real work is done: H2H, human-to-human.

We do everything we can to avoid disappointment. And crushing disappointment is what we will feel when we realize the book, the course, the conference, the politician, or the online influencer isn't the sovereign remedy we had hoped.

It's like that scene in *Good Will Hunting*. Matt Damon doesn't pursue his girlfriend because "Why would I? So I can realize she's not

---

32   Nate Bargatze, "Nate Bargatze Stand-Up Monologue—SNL," Saturday Night Live, October 28, 2023, YouTube video, 9:34, https://www.youtube.com/watch?v=ED5RX-fou34.

so smart? That she's boring? You don't get it. Right now, she's perfect, I don't want to ruin that."

We'd rather be hungry and hopeful than satisfied and successful.

It's the reason, let me remind you, that 58 percent of salespeople ask for fewer than one referral per month, while 40 percent rarely ask.

It's the reason we would all agree: "There are no magic bullets." And then we act the opposite.

It's the reason we know what to do, but fail to do it.

The fact is: Real results must be earned. "Hopium" is a drug. And, like a drug, it can keep us from our endless potential. So please.

Put the machines down. Break the addiction from information. And become fiercely enamored with relationships. Stop the chase for success. And relentlessly pursue significance.

When you make that shift? Your eyes will be opened to one amazing fact.

THERE ARE DIAMONDS EVERYWHERE

A man named Ali lived in a small village in Persia. He was a farmer and he owned a small piece of land on which he grew crops and raised animals.

One day, Ali heard about a diamond mine that had been discovered in a nearby province. He became obsessed with the idea of finding diamonds on his own land and he spent all his time and money searching for them.

But after years of failed searching, Ali gave up.

He decided to sell his land and go in search of his own diamond mine. He traveled from province to province, always looking for the next big find. But it never came. Eventually, Ali became poor and miserable as he realized he had given up everything for a dream that never came true.

Meanwhile, back in his old village...

The man who bought Ali's land discovered thousands of glittery rocks in a muddy creek bed. Intrigued, he brought one of these glittery rocks inside and placed it on his mantle.

He didn't think much of it until, one day, he had a visitor in his home. His visitor, viewing the glittery rock, nearly fainted. "My friend. Do you know what this is? It is the largest diamond I have ever seen!"

Turns out these unpolished, dirty rocks were actually diamonds. The property was covered with them. Ali's land turned out to be one of the largest diamond mines in the world.

Ali had a fortune all along, but failed to take advantage of it.

The moral of the story: We often overlook the opportunities right in front of us.

We waste time and energy chasing something we think we need. But in the end, the things we already have are the most valuable.

As it is with diamonds, it is with relationships. The most underutilized asset every business professional has is their network—your current IRA, Inventory of Relational Assets.

People you already know could partner, refer, introduce, and influence others.

But we treat them like muddy rocks instead of precious valuables.

How do we ensure we aren't making the same mistake? How do we start seeing our relationships for the treasures they truly are?

By participating in community.

PARTICIPATE IN COMMUNITY

When business gets tough, nothing is more powerful than community. Specifically those communities where participants can:

- Engage one-on-one with others—ideally face-to-face.
- Learn from others further along in their journey.
- Share values and experiences transparently and vulnerably.
- Offer and receive encouragement, whether celebrating success or navigating challenges.

The right people raise the water table for everyone.

Here's why I believe this is true. We're all in a rut whether we realize it or not.

In *Winning the War in Your Mind*, Craig Groeschel captures it perfectly:

> If you think you're trapped, if you believe there's a lock on the door, you've bought into a lie. And it is the lie, nothing else, that is holding you back. Yet if you identify that lie, then you can remove it. You can replace it with the truth and be free.[33]

Ruts aren't always obvious. For me, the easiest way I stay stuck is by distracting myself with new projects. It's a cycle:

- Take on something new for the dopamine hit.
- Feel overwhelmed by the workload.
- Start something else to feel better.

Sound familiar? It's a defense mechanism. And the antidote isn't another project—it's vitamin C. Vitamin CONNECTION.

Joe Polish explains in *What's in It for Them?*:

> There's a possibility (even probability) that something great will happen when you put yourself into a small group. I would argue there's no way to get there WITHOUT doing this. People spend more time, energy, and money avoiding it. Their vision, their purpose, their highest good never ends up as big as they could have because they think, "Oh, I don't need that group thing."[34]

Isolation breeds stagnation. We can't think our way out of same-

---

33 Craig Groeschel, *Winning the War in Your mind: Change Your Thinking, Change Your Life* (Zondervan Books, 2021).

34 Polish, *What's in It for Them?*

ness—the brain's job is survival, not elevation. Community shakes us out of that safety zone and into growth.

Community solves problems that isolation can't. It gets us out of ruts, aligns us with others who push us higher, and fills the voids that technology can't.

Find your group. Engage fully. And watch your life and business transform.

THE FINAL CALL: BE A R.I.C.H. RELATIONSHIP EVANGELIST

The world needs more R.I.C.H. relationships. We've talked about what that means:

- *R*eciprocal: where both sides win
- *I*nfluential: each shapes the other's thinking
- *C*onnected: shared values, through highs and lows
- *H*umble: more listening, less fixing

Use systematic approaches that create genuine connections (not superficial networks), build lasting communities (not temporary gatherings), and actually change lives (not just business card exchanges).

That's why we're here, after all.

This is not just about business. Don't wait for someone else to solve the problem.

When you embrace this mission, you can create lasting, meaningful, and truly significant impact that builds better businesses, better communities, and a better world. And you'll be so psyched, you will want to spread this message even further.

BUT FIRST ANSWER THESE QUESTIONS

- Have you recognized the larger mission beyond business success?
- Do you understand the critical role relationships play in healing our world?

- Have you identified how you can make a difference in your sphere?
- Have you built systems to support genuine connection?
- What impact will you make as a relationship evangelist?

ACTION ITEMS, STEP-BY-STEP

This isn't about perfection. It's about progress. Remember that as you:

1. Identify the relationship poverty in your immediate sphere of influence:
   A. Your industry
   B. Your community
   C. Your network
   D. Your world
2. Choose *one* area where you could make the biggest impact through relationship building.
3. Commit to a plan that spreads relationship excellence in that area.
4. Build support systems to sustain your relationship mission.
5. Share your mission with others who might join you.
6. Celebrate and document the impact you create.
7. Share your world-changing story at **CelebrateMyWins.com**.

FINAL THOUGHTS: YOU ARE THE DECISIVE ELEMENT

As we close this chapter and this book, remember that you are the decisive element in all your relationships. *Your* standards create the climate. *Your* daily choices make the weather. *You* possess tremendous power to make relationships either transactional or transformational.

The RPT System's effectiveness depends on the effort you put into it. You can have the best systems, strategies, and intentions, but without a commitment to excellence, you'll never unlock your full relationship potential.

Give more than you take. Expect more from yourself than others expect from you. Create systems that support greatness. Build a culture that celebrates execution. And watch as your relationships transform from good to great, from transactional to treasured.

Because, in the end, your impact will never exceed your standards.

Which means you have total control over how massive your Relationship Snowball can grow.

You are the decisive element. *You* set the standard.

So set it high.

Set it so high it scares you a little.

Set it so high others think you're crazy.

Then build the systems to maintain it.

That's how referral legends are born.

That's how relationship empires are built.

That's how business becomes friendship.

That's how you impact the world.

And that's how you create a legacy that lasts.

JOHN IS NEEDED

As we close this book, I want to remind you of something my team started saying years ago: JNN (John Not Needed). At first, I wasn't sure if this was their way of telling me to get out of the way or a rallying cry for our mission.

The truth? It was both. *And that's perfect.*

Because the message of R.I.C.H. relationships is bigger than any one person. It's bigger than business. It's bigger than referrals. It's about healing a world that desperately needs more:

*R*eciprocal relationships where both sides win. *I*nfluential connections that shape better thinking. *C*onnected communities that share values. *H*umble interactions focused on understanding.

These connections are the gems that make life precious. Now more than ever.

I am just one of many messengers. My final ask is that you would join me to make the world a more generous place. For my daughters. For my friends. And for the many leaders who suspect there's a *better way of doing business* but need role models encouraging them to get out of their heads and into their hearts.

This is our time.

Be blessed, my friends.

Be blessed.

Note from John's Team: The "John Not Needed" concept began in 2021, three years before John tragically passed away. And now that his brief time has been cut short, let it be known...while we often delighted in accomplishing things in John's absence, we were wrong.

Human beings like John will ALWAYS be needed.

So, let's be one of them.

TRAGEDY STRIKES. NOW WHAT?

We never thought we'd have to answer, "What is life like without John Ruhlin?" This was the type of thing that always happened to "someone else."

Unfortunately, we're all "someone else" to someone else.

Let's set aside the pain, tears, shock, and agony—those heavy moments when we hold our family and kiss our children goodnight, *something that will never be the same in the Ruhlin house.*

Let's answer the question from the lens of business. Because, understandably, there is no playbook. There's no protocol. All that's left are questions. *More specifically, three questions.*

We've tried to answer them the best way we know how.

Maybe sharing them will help somebody today.

When your founder—who is also your main marketing engine for a valuable, but extremely niche service—passes away unexpectedly... and there is *no possible way* to replace him...what do we do?

The fate of the company relies on the answer to these three questions:

1. "Do we need to exist?"
2. "If so, why?"
3. "If so, HOW?"

Q1. "DO WE NEED TO EXIST?"

If our company disappeared tomorrow, would anybody miss us? John assembled a talented group. We could all go get different (albeit less cool) jobs.

In reflecting on our relationship with GIFT·OLOGY, our clients, and our role in the machine, each of us needed to decide, *Is this a job or a calling?*

Ultimately our answer, top to bottom, is a resounding: YES. GIFT·OLOGY must go on. And?

Q2. "IF SO, WHY?"

Easy answer: John's legacy.

But as Mondays roll in, "the glory of John" fails to inspire anyone's best in this somber new normal.

Nor is glory what John would want. He loved giving gifts but hated the spotlight. He cared more for people than taking credit. *He worked for a cause, not for applause.*

As technology eats the world, a counterculture is emerging: **the power of offline relationships.**

Have you felt it? *Are you living it?*

This movement has many champions. Some are dedicated to saving our youth (YES). Others, like us, begging business leaders to see *there's a better way!*

Ergo: Are we participating uniquely in this relationship-driven mission? *Or are we simply an also-ran?*

We believe we have something meaningful to share. But?

Q3. "IF SO, HOW?"

Several years ago, a mantra started among our team: "**JNN**" = John Not Needed. We often used this initialism to guardrail our ambitious leader.

Turns out these words were providential.

In 2021—in addition to John working on his second book—we began tinkering with an entirely new business vertical: *community and education.*

Not on how to gift better—we've lived in that space since 2017 (which will continue).

Moreso practical education on **ROR**: Return on Relationship.

How to get the MOST out of relationships while paradoxically wanting and expecting nothing in return.

Not philosophy.

Practical conversations, checklists, and gifting catalogs. For people who wake up believing in the power of human connection. But crave better guidance than "Be nice to everyone today."

And while (duh) education and community are certainly not new? We believe, in watching John Ruhlin for nearly two decades, we are uniquely positioned to teach people *how ROR eats ROI for lunch.*

* * *

These are the type of existential answers that create resolve. If there were ever moments of *going-through-the-motions*, they ended the moment we heard the news.

And so: We march on.

We marvel at the support of John's friends, mentors, and industry leaders. *busy* leaders. That any sane person would feel five-shades-of-guilty asking help from.

And yet—here we are. Here *they* are. Lifting us up.

Heck, if you're reading this right now—*it's because of them.*

Which is the ultimate lesson...one that has left every team member in awe.

The reason we need to keep existing...the new engine and energy behind GIFT·OLOGY?

Relationships can take you places that marketing can't. ™

To paraphrase Tim McGraw, imagine living a life so robust that at your funeral, there's standing room only.

We are bruised. Battered. And still experiencing random outbursts of tears that look borderline psychotic to innocent, unknowing onlookers.

But we are resolved.

And so: We march on.

Gift like John.

—The GIFT·OLOGY team

GLOSSARY

Learn more, ask questions, and get useful resources at RPTsystem.com.

24-Hour FUN (Follow-Up Now) (noun)

Definition: A relational process completed within twenty-four hours of a Clarity Conversation to build trust, reinforce connection, and drive action. It includes three steps: sending a gratitude message (text or video), a recap email with key points and next steps, and a thoughtful, low-cost gift. This prompt follow-up keeps you top of mind and signals professionalism, often speeding up reciprocity.

Example: "After their lakeside Clarity Conversation, he sent a humorous thank-you text, a recap email, and a relevant book—all before the partner returned from vacation, resulting in a peak moment."

See also: Clarity Conversation, DoV (Demonstration of Value)

3-Way Introduction (noun)

Definition: A technique used to introduce two people in a way that emphasizes their positive qualities, shared interests, or values. Unlike sharing contact information, a 3-way introduction includes details that build rapport and trust, encouraging both parties to connect meaningfully.

Example: "A well-crafted 3-way video text isn't just about connecting two people; it's about setting the foundation for a potentially valuable relationship."

See also: Relationship Snowball, Referral Partner Transformation (RPT) System

Accumulator (Role) (noun)

Definition: Accumulators are the primary relationship builders in a company, responsible for initiating new connections and establishing trust with potential referral partners. They meet new people, hold Clarity Conversations, and build rapport and reliability with initial contacts.

Example: "As an Accumulator, she focuses on creating quality connections and getting to know key players in the industry."

See also: Energizer (Role), Manager (Role)

AICs (Ambassadors, Influencers, Connectors) (noun)

Definition: A framework for identifying high-value referral partners based on their roles and influence within their networks. Ambassadors are trusted authorities, Influencers have strong persuasive abilities, and Connectors are naturally networked individuals who know everyone. These roles often help spread word-of-mouth referrals and build credibility within target markets.

Example: "By partnering with local AICs, we gained immediate trust and credibility in our community."

See also: Greenlight Question, Industry A-Lister

Atomic Relationship Habits (noun)

Definition: Small, consistent actions that, over time, strengthen relationships and enhance referral partnerships. These habits create a foundation of trust and reliability, leading to long-term, high-quality referrals.

Example: "By practicing atomic relationship habits like ten handwritten notes per week, I've built a network of reliable referral partners."

See also: R.I.C.H. Relationships, Referral Partner Transformation (RPT) System

Big 4 (noun)

Definition: A framework for understanding and clearly communicating the essence of a person or business by focusing on four key aspects: (1) What they do, (2) Who they serve, (3) What they don't do, and (4) Who isn't a fit. The Big 4 ensures alignment and clarity in referral relationships, helping partners confidently identify and refer the right clients.

Example: "Before partnering with the CPA, we went over her Big 4 to ensure her services aligned with our ideal client base."

See also: Clarity Conversation, Clearing Runway System

Can-Willing-Want (adjectives)

Definition: A three-part evaluation framework for assessing the potential of a referral partner. CAN assesses their ability or capacity to refer (influence, network size). WILLING gauges their interest or openness to refer based on your relationship. WANT measures whether they have a track record or personal desire to refer. This framework helps prioritize partners who are most likely to generate meaningful introductions.

Example: "Using the Can-Willing-Want framework, we focused on partners who not only had large networks but were a similar size as us in the marketplace."

See also: Referral Partner Playbook (RPP), AICs (Ambassadors, Influencers, Connectors)

Clarity Conversation (noun)

Definition: A purposeful dialogue aimed at aligning expectations, goals, and abilities between two parties. This conversation seeks to eliminate misunderstandings and bring focus, ensuring both sides have a clear understanding of each other's business needs.

Example: "After having several Clarity Conversations, my partners knew my perfect target customer, and I became much easier to refer."

See also: 3-Way Introduction, R.I.C.H. Relationships, Big 4

Clearing Runway System (noun)

Definition: A system focused on nurturing and preparing potential referral partners for active engagement. The Clearing Runway System ensures relationships are capable of introducing quality leads by aligning expectations through clear, ongoing communication. This approach prevents unqualified referrals and overinvesting in lukewarm partners.

Example: "Through the Clearing Runway System, we equipped our partners well and energized them to make great introductions."

See also: Prospecting Partners System, Perpetuating Givers System

Connection Day (noun)

Definition: A dedicated day for focusing on building, strengthening, or reconnecting with referral partners and key contacts. Connection Days are used to nurture relationships that may lead to referrals, emphasizing consistent engagement.

Example: "I set aside one Friday per month as my Connection Day to make sure I'm having multiple Clarity Conversations and attracting new partners."

See also: Atomic Relationship Habits, Clarity Conversation

Digital Sharecropping (noun)

Definition: The practice of building a brand or reputation on platforms owned by others, where control is limited. This can make businesses vulnerable to platform changes or restrictions that affect their outreach and audience.

Example: "Instead of relying on digital sharecropping, I focused on offline relationships to reduce dependency on social media platforms."

See also: Referral Partner Transformation (RPT) System, Relational Poverty

"Do This, Get That" (adjective)

Definition: Describes a referral approach based on direct incentives for referrals, where one is promised a reward for providing a lead. While common, this approach may attract individuals interested in the incentive rather than genuinely connecting the right clients to a service.

Example: "Switching from a 'Do This, Get That' program to relationship-focused referrals earned us access to higher-quality clients."

See also: Return on Relationship (ROR), Transactional Relationships

DoV (Demonstration of Value) (noun)

Definition: A follow-up interaction designed to deepen the value of a previous engagement, demonstrating attentiveness, usefulness, and building trust. Rather than asking for something, the DoVing (verb) provides value, such as sharing relevant resources, offering assistance, or making an introduction, reinforcing the relationship and increasing goodwill.

Example: "After our meeting, I sent him a DoV with a link to an article I thought he'd appreciate, relevant to his current focus on parenting."

See also: Referral Partner Transformation (RPT) System, Reciprocity Loop, DoV Superpower

DoV Superpower (noun)

Definition: A unique strength or skill one uses to add value (DoV) to relationships in a way that feels natural and genuine. Your DoV superpower is one that comes naturally, doesn't feel like work, and moves the needle with VIP relationships.

Example: "Gifting was his DoV superpower, helping him maintain strong, referral-driven relationships."

See also: Relationship Snowball, Atomic Relationship Habits

Edification (noun)

Definition: The act of highlighting someone's values, skills, or strengths during introductions, which can deepen relationships and increase trust among referral partners.

Example: "Effective edification in a 3-way introduction makes both parties more inclined to connect and collaborate."

See also: 3-Way Introduction, Presold Lead

Energizer (Role) (noun)

Definition: The Energizer is the momentum driver in the team, keeping referral relationships active and moving relationship projects forward. Energizers make sure tasks are completed on time, maintain high energy during interactions, and ensure that relationships don't stall or stagnate.

Example: "As an Energizer, I work hand-in-hand with my founder (the Accumulator) to make sure all our referral partners feel the love."

See also: Accumulator (Role), Manager (Role), DoV (Demonstration of Value)

Fishing for Referrals Versus Building a Fishing Fleet (metaphor)

Definition: Contrasts a short-term, individual-focused approach to referrals (fishing for single referrals) with a long-term, partnership-focused strategy (building a network of referral partners who bring ongoing leads).

Example: "Instead of asking for referrals one at a time, I focused on building a fishing fleet by establishing strong partnerships who could provide."

See also: Referral Partner Transformation (RPT) System, Referral Partner Playbook (RPP)

FORD Framework (Family, Occupation, Recreation, Dreams) (noun)

Definition: A conversational framework to build rapport and connection by discussing four key areas: family, occupation, recreation, and dreams. Useful in referral conversations to establish trust, uncover shared interests, and deepen relationships.

Example: "Using the FORD Framework, she quickly built rapport by learning about his family and career goals."

See also: Clarity Conversation, Harmless Starter

GIFT·OLOGY (noun)

Definition: The art and science of using thoughtful, personalized gifting as a strategy to deepen relationships and build trust. GIFT·OLOGY emphasizes quality over quantity, focusing on meaningful gestures that resonate with the recipient's interests or needs, often leading to stronger professional and personal connections.

Example: "She applied lessons from GIFT·OLOGY by sending a hand-crafted item discussed in their meeting, creating a peak moment that strengthened the partnership."

See also: Perpetuating Givers System, Peak Moment, Heart Bombing

Greenlight Question (noun)

Definition: A powerful qualifying question to assess if a contact is willing and able to refer business. Typically framed as: "If you had a client or friend looking to [your service], who would you recommend they contact first?" This question helps clarify if they're open to recommending you and allows you to gauge their referral potential.

Example: "She asked the Greenlight Question to ensure the contact was able and willing to refer clients to her."

See also: Clarity Conversation, Can-Willing-Want

Harmless Starter (noun)

Definition: An initial conversational approach designed to feel light and non-pressuring, often used to reconnect or break the ice. It typically involves a memory, observation, or gratitude statement to start a dialogue comfortably.

Example: "Her harmless starter—'I was just thinking about our last meeting...'—opened the door to an easy conversation."

See also: FORD Framework, Greenlight Question

Heart Bombing (verb)

Definition: A strategy of showing appreciation or "bombarding" someone with an over-the-top, maximum-effort gesture or gift. Heart bombing fosters goodwill and deepens the relationship in an instant, while building your brand in the marketplace.

Example: "John was known for heart bombing his referral partners with $2,000 coffee mugs."

See also: Perpetuating Givers System, Referral Partner Transformation (RPT) System

Industry A-Lister (noun)

Definition: A highly respected, well-connected individual in a specific industry who can significantly impact one's referral network or credibility. In addition, becoming an industry A-lister is often a goal for leaders looking to establish authority and build market share in their field.

Example: "Building relationships with industry A-listers gave her access to exclusive referrals and top-tier clients."

See also: AICs (Ambassadors, Influencers, Connectors), Greenlight Question

Inventory of Relational Assets (IRA) (noun)

Definition: A personal list or "inventory" of valuable relationships, often categorized by their referral potential, strength of connection, or ability to create new opportunities. Maintaining an IRA helps leaders prioritize and manage key relationships effectively.

Example: "Updating her Inventory of Relational Assets allowed her to focus on high-impact connections each week."

See also: Prospecting Partners System, Can-Willing-Want

Manager (Role) (noun)

Definition: The Manager is the organizer of the referral system, responsible for capturing details, tracking relationship milestones, and ensuring no opportunities fall through the cracks. Managers keep the CRM updated, set reminders for follow-ups, and make sure all interactions are recorded, supporting the efficiency of both Accumulators and Energizers.

Example: "With a Manager handling the details, Accumulators can focus fully on building connections, knowing everything is tracked."

See also: Accumulator (Role), Energizer (Role)

Matthew Effect (noun)

Definition: The principle that those who already have advantages (e.g., strong networks) continue to gain more opportunities, while those without struggle to gain traction. In referrals, it reflects how established networks tend to produce more leads and connections.

Example: "The Matthew Effect was in full force; the more referrals she received, the easier it became to get even more."

See also: Relationship Snowball, Reciprocity Loop

Peak Moment (noun)

Definition: A standout, emotionally charged experience that leaves a lasting impression in a relationship, often creating stronger trust and deeper connection. Peak moments are intentionally crafted to surprise, delight, or resonate deeply, making them memorable milestones and fast-forwarding relationships.

Example: "The thoughtful handwritten note she included with her gift created a peak moment that solidified their referral partnership."

See also: DoV Superpower, Heart Bombing, Perpetuating Givers System

Perpetuating Givers System (noun)

Definition: The Perpetuating Givers System is designed to continuously engage and energize existing referral partners, keeping them energized to refer new business. By delivering ongoing value and maintaining regular touchpoints, this system ensures referral partners remain loyal, convicted, and enthusiastic about sharing referrals over time.

Example: "With the Perpetuating Givers System, our partners felt appreciated and motivated to keep the referrals coming, creating a consistent flow of new business."

See also: Prospecting Partners System, Clearing Runway System

Presold Lead (noun)

Definition: A potential client or customer who has received a positive impression of you or your business before the initial interaction, often arriving ready to listen and ready to buy.

Example: "Thanks to being a presold lead, the new client came in with high expectations and was ready to work with us from day one."

See also: 3-Way Introduction, Edification

Prospecting Partners System (noun)

Definition: A system designed to identify, evaluate, and engage potential referral partners. The Prospecting Partners System moves high-potential contacts through a structured process to assess their suitability and willingness to refer business. This system is the first step in creating a steady pipeline of new referrals, minimizing reliance on current marketing methods.

Example: "Using the Prospecting Partners System, we identified top contacts who could significantly boost our network of referral givers."

See also: Clearing Runway System, Perpetuating Givers System

Reciprocity Loop (noun)

Definition: A cycle where goodwill actions, such as providing referrals or DoVing, lead to ongoing reciprocal gestures, creating a continuous exchange of value within a network.

Example: "We maintained a strong reciprocity loop with our partners, where each referral strengthened our relationship further."

See also: DoV (Demonstration of Value), R.I.C.H. Relationships

Referral Chain (a.k.a. Referral Family Tree) (noun)

Definition: A sequence of referrals where each new contact generates additional referrals, resulting in a cascading network of connections. The "chain" grows as each referred contact potentially refers further, creating exponential relationship growth.

Example: "The referral chain from this one particular partner is six links deep and we only met nine months ago."

See also: Relationship Snowball, 3-Way Introduction

Referral Partner Playbook (RPP) (noun)

Definition: A structured tool, often outside your CRM, used to manage and grow referral relationships by tracking engagement. The playbook organizes key contacts into categories such as "A" and "B" partners and outlines a clear process of communication. It emphasizes tracking interactions, identifying opportunities to provide value, and maintaining a "next step" mentality to ensure steady progress in building referral partnerships.

Example: "Using the RPP, we were able to identify which partners needed follow-up, brainstorm ways to add value, and prioritize next steps to keep the referral momentum alive."

See also: Inventory of Relational Assets (IRA), Can-Willing-Want

Referral Partner Transformation (RPT) System (noun)

Definition: A structured approach designed to cultivate, manage, and optimize referral relationships, moving beyond individual referrals to establish a network of long-term partners who regularly provide high-quality leads. The RPT System emphasizes building R.I.C.H. relationships, where mutual value and trust replace transactional exchanges.

Example: "Implementing the RPT System allowed us to focus on deepening partnerships rather than messing around with cold marketing or ads. The result has been a steady influx of prequalified clients."

See also: Return on Relationship (ROR), Clarity Conversation, Big 4

Relational Poverty (noun)

Definition: A state where individuals lack meaningful social connections, often leading to isolation, loneliness, and a decline in mental and physical health. Relational poverty can undermine personal and professional success, emphasizing the importance of intentional relationship building to maintain well-being and support networks.

Example: "Recognizing the signs of relational poverty, he prioritized deeper, intentional connections over superficial networking."

See also: Digital Sharecropping, R.I.C.H. Relationships

Relationship Snowball (noun)

Definition: A strategy where relationships continuously generate new connections and referrals. Starting with small, meaningful relationships, the "snowball" accumulates as connections introduce others, leading to exponential growth in new opportunities and clients.

Example: "By leveraging the Relationship Snowball, I transformed my client base from a handful of local connections to a nationwide group."

See also: R.I.C.H. Relationships, 3-Way Introduction, Edification

Return on Relationship (ROR) (noun)

Definition: The compounding value gained from investing in meaningful relationships, as opposed to traditional monetary ROI (Return on Investment). ROR creates exponential business results through the long-term building of trust and loyalty with VIPs.

Example: "By focusing on Return on Relationship rather than just

ROI, we have more clients and new business opportunities that were never on our radar."

See also: R.I.C.H. Relationships, Referral Partner Transformation (RPT) System

R.I.C.H. Relationships (noun)

Definition: An acronym describing high-value relationships that are Reciprocal, Influential, Connected, and Humble. These relationships prioritize mutual benefit, shared values, and genuine connection over transactional interactions.

Example: "Building R.I.C.H. relationships has made marketing more fun and improved my quality of life dramatically."

See also: Referral Partner Playbook (RPP), Return on Relationship (ROR)

Shoulder Industries (noun)

Definition: Noncompeting industries where your ideal clients also engage or spend money. Professionals in shoulder industries can be effective referral partners because they serve similar client bases without directly competing.

Example: "For the financial advisor, accountants and tax specialists were ideal shoulder industries for referrals."

See also: Referral Partner Playbook (RPP), Industry A-Lister

Story Selling (noun)

Definition: A communication technique that uses detailed, specific stories to illustrate value, expertise, and reliability. Effective story selling makes a service or product memorable and relatable, building trust through vivid examples that demonstrate expertise and create an emotional connection with the audience.

Example: "She used story selling to explain how she helped a client overcome a tough financial hurdle, making her services more compelling."

See also: Clarity Conversation, 3-Way Introduction

Talk About Partners (TAP) Meetings (noun)

Definition: Structured, recurring discussions focused on evaluating and strategizing referral partnerships. TAP Meetings provide a space to review progress, identify opportunities to add value, and refine next steps for engagement with partners. These meetings ensure alignment, accountability, and momentum in building strong, reciprocal relationships.

Example: "During the TAP Meeting, they identified which partners needed touches and brainstormed new DoVs to deepen connections."

See also: DoV (Demonstration of Value), Referral Partner Playbook (RPP)

Transactional Relationships (noun)

Definition: Relationships based on immediate, often one-time exchanges, rather than long-term value or loyalty. These connections are less productive, more easily compromised, and overall less valuable compared to relationships built on trust and mutual benefit.

Example: "Asking ourselves, 'How can we move from Transactional

Relationships to R.I.C.H. relationships?' has transformed not only our results, but how we feel about getting them."

See also: R.I.C.H. Relationships, "Do This, Get That"

Trusted Advisor Process (noun)

Definition: A method of building trust and authority with clients by consistently providing valuable insights, guidance, and support. The Trusted Advisor Process focuses on positioning oneself as a reliable source of knowledge and assistance, fostering long-term relationships where clients and partners look to you as a go-to expert.

Example: "Following the Trusted Advisor Process, he became the go-to referral partner for his upstream relationships."

See also: Clarity Conversation, Prospecting Partners System

Upstream Relationships (noun)

Definition: Strategic connections with individuals or businesses that engage with your ideal clients before you do, often serving as a natural source of referrals. Building upstream relationships allows you to position yourself as the next logical step in the client's journey. Often these partnerships are one-way, requiring you to build value in more creative ways.

Example: "By cultivating upstream relationships with wedding planners, she consistently received high-quality referrals for her photography business."

See also: Shoulder Industries, Prospecting Partners System

Zone of Genius (noun)

Definition: The unique area where an individual's natural talents, passions, and skills align, allowing them to perform at their highest level of creativity, effectiveness, and fulfillment. Operating within your Zone of Genius means you're working in your sweet spot—where you add the most value and experience the greatest success.

Example: "By focusing exclusively on his Zone of Genius—attending events and accumulating relationships—he was able to dramatically increase his company's referral opportunities."

See also: DoV Superpower, Accumulator (Role), Energizer (Role), Manager (Role)

ABOUT THE AUTHOR

MARCH 16, 1980–AUGUST 4, 2024

JOHN RUHLIN was the world's leading authority in energizing relational loyalty through radical generosity. As the founder and author of *GIFT·OLOGY*, he revolutionized the art of business relationships, showing how intentional, thoughtful giving could fast-forward key relationships and drive growth. Featured in Fox News, *Forbes*, *Fast Company*, and the *New York Times*, John's groundbreaking insights earned him recognition as the number one performer out of 1.5 million sales reps for one of the world's most recognizable brands. As his business grew, John built the GIFT·OLOGY team to bring his strategies to life, creating an agency that empowered individuals and organizations—including UBS, Raymond James, D. R. Horton, Keller Williams, the Chicago Cubs, and Caesars Palace—to turn business challenges into exponential outcomes, using the power of ROR.

While his professional success was groundbreaking, it was rooted in the same values that defined his personal life. To those who knew him, John was a devoted husband to Lindsay and a loving father to their four daughters—Reagan, Blakely, Saylor, and Layton. His faith and family were his greatest accomplishments and the legacy he was most proud of. They were his greatest inspiration, his grounding force, and his daily reminder of what truly mattered. He dedicated this book to them as the heart and soul of his life's work and the foundation of his legacy.

John was more than a business innovator; he was a deeply genuine person who lived an uncommon life of generosity and inspiration. Whether at home or in the boardroom, he had an extraordinary gift for making people feel seen, celebrated, and recognized for who they were and the impact they had on others. While most are remembered for their kindness after they're gone, John had an unmatched ability to ensure people felt valued and appreciated while it still mattered most. He modeled these principles of radical generosity in both big and small ways, leaving a legacy of connection, care, and love that continues to inspire those who knew him.

GIFT·OLOGY

CONTRIBUTING AUTHOR

MICHAEL MONROE is a Christian, strategist, marketer, trainer, and relentless innovator. He has been published in *Success*, *Forbes*, *Fast Company*, *KillerStartups*, and *CEOWorld*. Michael and John's relationship began on June 10, 2000—the day they independently started their Vector/Cutco careers, a remarkable coincidence that brought them together. Mutual connections accelerated their friendship and led to countless conversations and group masterminds. Having been invited into GIFT·OLOGY's inner circle, Michael has a rare perspective on John's business, habits, and methods, making him uniquely suited to contribute to this manuscript. Through John and Rod's faith, friendship, and philosophies, Michael has been beyond blessed.

ACKNOWLEDGMENTS

August 4, 2024, changed my life forever. John's passing was unexpected and tragic, but his life was full and abundant. The Bible teaches that God works in mysterious ways, and I am living in that truth daily. The outpouring of love and support has been beyond comprehension—a true testimony to the power and reach of authentic relationships.

John loved people like no one else, and the world is loving him back by supporting his family and his legacy. I am in awe and not sure how to fully express my appreciation for your kindness and generosity. My sincere hope is that you "Be John" to those in your network and grow your influence. The world needs more Johns. I pray this book serves as your guide.

There are so many to thank for this book, and I feel truly blessed by each of you. I will do my best not to exclude anyone. First and foremost, I want to express my sincere gratitude to Michael Monroe. Simply stated, this book would never have been completed without you. Your effort to see this project through is nothing short of heroic.

I also want to extend heartfelt thanks to the incredible teams at Chapters, Scribe Media, Amber Vilhauer, Joey Coleman, and Berit

Coleman. Your contributions have been invaluable, and I am deeply grateful for your support.

Additionally, I have experienced the support of so many since John's passing. While I'm sure there are names I may have unintentionally left off, here is my heartfelt list of gratitude. My deepest thanks go to: Liz Neuenschwander, Sharlia Maurer, Sara Hardwick, Carissa Barker, Sharon Radcliff, Kami Schiller, Greta Macabuhay, Molly Townsend, Andrea Salamon, Cameron Herold, Jesse Flocken, Brian McRae, Dawn Baumgartner, Lauren Newman, Colin Noonan, John Hall, Jonathan Keyser, Robert Glazer, John Kane, Jim Stitt Jr., Matt Evans, Christee Evans, Rob Robincheck, Brad Johnson, Justin Donald, Donald Miller, Jon Gordon, Dan Curran, Hal Elrod, Mike Dawid, Brent Bumbaugh, A. J. and Rory Vaden, Brad Weimert, Brendon Maxwell, Brittany Hodak, Charles Byrd, Corey Quinn, David Nurse, Jeffrey Gitomer, John Israel, John O'Leary, Jon Vaughan, Jon Vroman, Mike Koenigs, Mike Michalowicz, Mike Sharrow, Pete Vargas, Phil M. Jones, Todd Herman, Tom Searcy, Carajane Moore, Will Guidara, Garett Gunderson, Jason Jaggard, Shep Hyken, Brad Conlon, Tommy Mello, Patrick Dodd, Joe Polish, Brandon Fong, Steve Harward, Chad Willardson, Brendan Loucas, Don Yaeger, Brad Lomenick, Jack Daly, Pace Morby, Charlie Goodwin, Robert Richman, Dennis and Terri Brazer, Dorie Clark, Justin Batt, Aaron Walker, Alex Trevino, Amy Rowell, Ann Sheu, Chuck Flannagan, Bella Verita, Blake Brewer, Carolina Flores, Chris Green, Chris Robinson, Damon Finaldi, Dan Luigs, Dave Streen, Derek Champagne, Evan J. Blumenthal, Gary Baker, Govindh Jayaraman, Ian Altman, James Rushing, Jason Bradshaw, Jayson Gaignard, John Carroll, John Meese, Justin Breen, Kristin Andree, Laurie Hull, Mariana Juliette, Matt Granados, Nick Najjar, Pete Williams, Phoebe Mroczek, Rick Fessler, Ryan Miller, Stu McLaren, Sulemaan Ahmed, Susan Drumm, Thomas R. Winters, Tim Bryson, Trent Booth, Tricia Tamkin, Phillip Stutts, Patrick Bet-David, Anthony Grebmeier, David Altman, Ellen Long, John and Amy Calvert, Erik Vanhorn, Jenna Kutcher, Christopher Ryan, David Peacock, Richard Sapio, Mike Albertson, Daniel Ramsey, P. Scott Leonard, Cody Foster, Rob Dial, Tanya

Starkel, Darius Mirshahzadeh, Adam Stock, Willis Drake, Tyler Merrick, Jamie Sheils, Vincent Fisher, David Childs, Awaken Pathfinders Apprenticeship, Josh Painter, Benjamin B. Richter, Josiah Grimes, Seth Kinzer, Joseph Giovannoli, Tony Carlston, Andrew Smallwood, Michael Farmer, Paul Sjoberg, Michael McCarthy, Benjamin Fisher, Benjamin Patterson, Roy Schlabach, James Schlabach, Joel Marion, Scott Beck, Theresa Coppens, David E. Williams, Chad Johnson, Emily Housley, Michael and Jessica Mogill, John Osborne, Blair Cornell, Rob Jensen, Garrett and Danielle White, Dan Martell, Todd Ehrlich, Drew Gurley, Shannon Buell, Kevin Kwiatkowski, Keith Schoolcraft, Regina Miller, David Laborde, Digger and Amy Earles, Ed Reynolds, Doug Liptak, Heather Robertson, Danny Swancey, Steven Schwarz, Marc Brutten, Grant Brutten, Nik Tarascio, Jonathan Hughes, Chad Washam, Harold Grinspoon, Will Finnerty, Jerad Hutchens, Grady Jett, Andy Jones, Jeremy Wallace, Shawn Dill, Ivan Barratt, Scott Simonsen, Christina Tosi, Ivan Yoder, Matthew Lehman, Joel Gajewski, Kelly Cook, Dale Meador, David Smith Jr., Joe Quattrone, James Orseni, Brandon Turner, Patty and Francisco Dominguez, Elizabeth and Jochi Ramos, Brandon and Aly Calvo, Gary Sjurset, Galen Hair, Jodi Daniels, Garrett Lynch, Curtis Rippee, Kristi Acee, Aaron Stokes, Trevor McAlees, Melissa Palmer, Scott MacGregor, Darron Hacker, Meredith Moore, Brian Roberts, Lance Bauslaugh.

With Deep Gratitude,
Rod Neuenschwander
Co-Founder of GIFT·OLOGY Group

OUR SERVICES

Done for You Gifting Services: Custom-designed gifts that make an impact.

With twenty years of concierge gifting expertise, our proven method strengthens relationships and fosters loyalty.

Personalized, impactful gifts help companies achieve:

- Better marketing—Drive word of mouth and referrals.
- Better sales—Increase the ease of expansion and cross-selling.
- Better management—Enhance recognition and messaging.

Whether onboarding VIP clients or rewarding top employees, we tailor gifts to reflect your values and maximize Return on Relationship (ROR).

In short: Share your list of recipients, and we'll handle the gifts to deliver meaningful relational results.

R.I.C.H. RELATIONSHIP SOCIETY: A community platform offering tools and strategies to nurture lasting professional relationships.

From energizing referral partners to engaging industry leaders, the

R.I.C.H. RELATIONSHIP SOCIETY is where givers come to connect and contribute:

- Valuable insights—Exchange expertise and best practices.
- Growth opportunities—Build partnerships and joint ventures.
- Mutual support—Share encouragement and solve problems.
- Free referral exchange—Unlock new, trusted networks.
- Educational sessions—Attend webinars and live coaching.

Grow your business with community and collaborative education. And experience the full potential of Return on Relationship (ROR).

In short: Sign up for a membership and unlock a hub filled with tools, resources, and meaningful connection.

Speaking & Workshops: Designed to accelerate referral mastery and maximize Return on Relationship (ROR).

Participants leave with practical tools to build trust, strengthen connections, and drive a powerful referral engine.

To learn more, visit: giftologygroup.com

A NOTE FROM ROD NEUENSCHWANDER, CO-FOUNDER OF GIFT·OLOGY GROUP

As the remaining co-founder of GIFT·OLOGY Group, and with the support of our team, we are committed to advancing our mission of relational generosity. Through our gifting agency and community platform, we empower leaders to build meaningful, expectation-free connections that grow businesses to their full potential. By prioritizing transformational relationships over transactional business, we are confident in our lasting impact.

—**Rod Neuenschwander**, co-founder of GIFT·OLOGY

CO-FOUNDER OF GIFT·OLOGY GROUP

ROD NEUENSCHWANDER co-founded GIFT·OLOGY with the late John Ruhlin, author of *GIFT·OLOGY: The Art and Science of Using Gifts to Cut Through the Noise, Increase Referrals, and Strengthen Client Retention*. As the nation's leading relationship agency, GIFT·OLOGY helps clients accelerate growth by leveraging key relationships, with strategies featured in *Forbes*, *Business Insider*, and numerous podcasts.

Rod oversees operations and strategic objectives, continuing John's legacy of teaching that relationships achieve what marketing cannot. He also leads Ruhlin Partners, guiding struggling companies to recover, grow, and achieve over $30 million in founder wealth events.

An advocate for giving back, Rod has served as chair of Malone University's Board of Trustees and is deeply committed to supporting Christian organizations. He and his wife, Liz, along with their three children, enjoy spending time with family and friends and making a generational impact through their time and resources.

GIFT·OLOGY'S LEADING VOICE IN R.I.C.H. RELATIONSHIP SOCIETY

SARA HARDWICK is a rising thought leader in referral-based business strategies and is GIFT·OLOGY's community relationship strategist. She leads GIFT·OLOGY's membership program, R.I.C.H. RELATIONSHIP SOCIETY, teaching service professionals, small-business owners, and sales leaders to systematically stay top of mind, earn word-of-mouth, and transform relationships into referral partnerships.

Sara's journey into relationship mastery began while still in college, when she founded the internet's largest gifting community. This early success showcased her talent for operationalizing generosity, optimizing referral communication, and creating authentic networks. Today Sara empowers professionals to move beyond transactional interactions, fight relational poverty, and build genuine, long-lasting, R.I.C.H. relationships.

Learn more about how Sara can help grow your organization at www.giftologygroup.com/speaking.